FIFTEEN SEASONS

A MEMOIR

TERRY EVERS

ISBN-13: 978-1-945587-82-5
Library of Congress Control Number: 2022918193

Fifteen Seasons, A Memoir
1. Oregon Coast; 2. Fishing; 3. Boating; 4. Family

Book Design: Dancing Moon Press
Cover Design: Dancing Moon Press

Dancing Moon Press
Bend, Oregon USA
Lincoln City, Oregon USA
dancingmoonpress.com

DEDICATION

This memoir is dedicated to my father, Bruce Evers, who took an enormous leap of faith that swept us away from the ordinary and opened the floodgates to the unimaginable. Who knew back then that the trail he was blazing would have a profound impact on both of us for the rest of our lives? This fifteen-season journey would not have been possible either without the trust, support, and sacrifices of my mother, Carolyn, especially in those early years. Thank you to my sister, Jen, my daughters Kelsey and McKenzie, and other family members who listened to many fishing tales over the years and those who read through some of the early versions of this text. A big thanks to Marge. While you never knew about this project, you played a big part in it becoming a reality. My appreciation extends to all of the fishermen who shared their expertise with us and for their friendships that made those times so special. Finally, I owe a world of gratitude to my wife, D'Ann, who remained supportive through all the highs and lows of the dory days as well as urging me to put those adventures in print to share with the world.

CONTENTS

Dory Trolling Gear Diagram

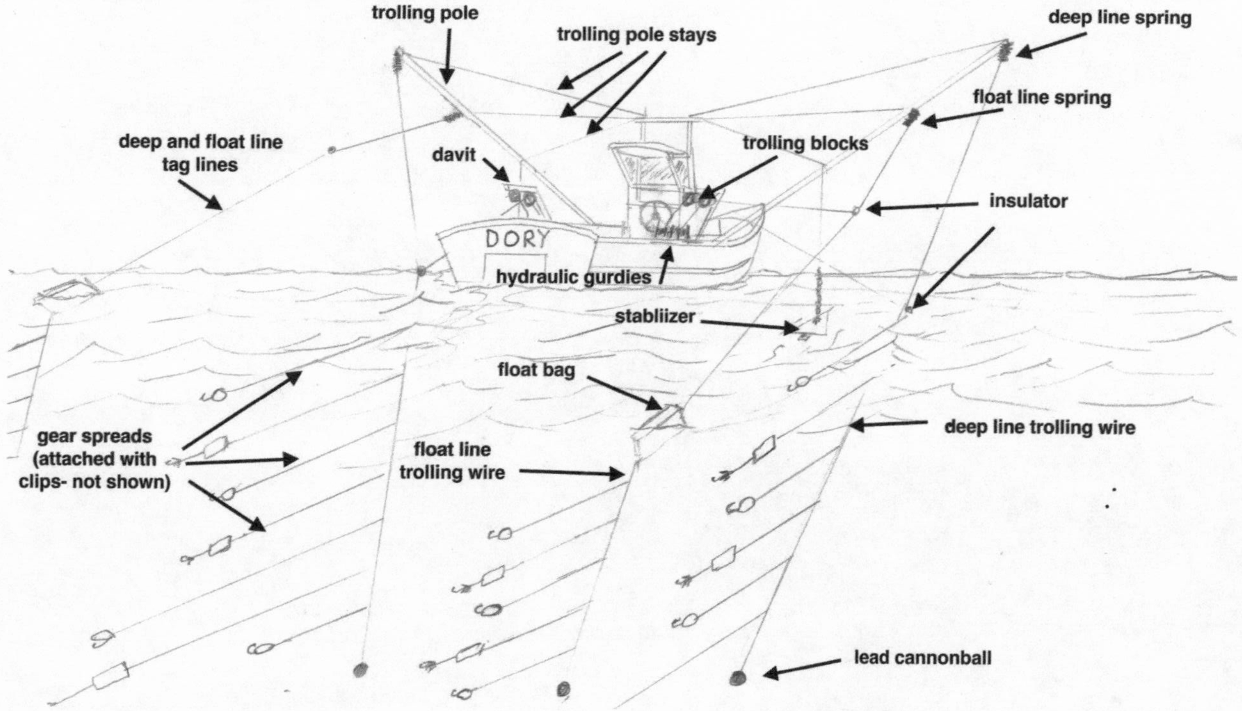

* objects not to scale

FOREWORD

There are some things you just don't prepare for in life, and one of those moments was an emotional meeting with my father to plan for his funeral. My sister Jen, my mother, close friends of my parents, and I had gathered at Mom and Dad's house on an overcast late-January afternoon to do just that. They lived in a nice neighborhood on Salem, Oregon's west side, which was only about a couple miles from the Willamette River. After living on the east side since 1966, they moved there in the early 2000s. In the spring and summer time, the yard of their West Salem home was a landscaping beacon with meticulously pruned plants and a myriad of brightly colored flowers. It was a common sight to see passersby slow down their pace to take in its splendor. On that particular winter day though, the flower beds were barren, dormant, and downcast.

My father, Bruce, was in rapid decline from congestive heart failure, a condition that he had battled for several years. He had been on a daily platter full of meds for quite some time. A few weeks earlier, it was apparent that the crucial diuretic Lasix, a drug that reduces body fluid that was dutifully administered by my mother, was losing its grip. His rockstar cardiologist had gone above and beyond to explore every possible alternative, but even he had run out of options. Dad was placed on hospice, and along with that came the decision to pull him off that lifeline medication. As a result, Dad's cognition and energy levels started to decline. On that January day in his living room, he wasn't running on all cylinders and his thoughts drifted off course at times while expressing his wishes for his impending service. Compounding everything was the hard fall he had taken the previous night, so it was amazing that he was in any type of condition to meet up.

During our rather somber gathering though, Dad managed to weave a tale of our commercial salmon fishing adventures just like he had so many times before. He and I loved to reminisce about our exploits off the Central Oregon Coast in a 22-foot flat bottomed-boat that took place from 1977 to 1991. These tales weren't just merely fishing stories about the one that got away. The conversations that we shared transcended well beyond hook and line and were filled with many awe-inspiring memories and others of pure frustration. They often ran deeper as we talked about the people, their personalities, a culture that was on the brink of change, and the many interactions between father and son that occurred in a space of about 100 square feet on a vast ocean.

Our family had been going through an emotional wringer with Dad's frequent hospitalizations. Mom's physical and emotional exhaustion and the sadness of seeing the rapid deterioration of a once strong and vivacious man were taking their toll. The fishing tale Dad shared that day wasn't epic or spirited like so many in the past. It was something about how good fresh-caught fish was to eat, or something like that. Never-the-less, it was amazing how he still managed to pry open a moment and share a snippet in his foggy state of mind. Sadly, it was the last time he ever launched into those special times that dated almost 39 years prior, and it was the last time we ever talked about them. That night, Dad took another fall and then spent the next five days unconscious. He passed away on the morning of February 5, 2016.

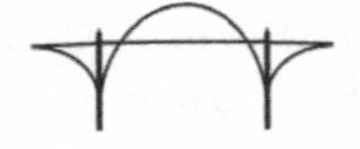

Bruce Evers was born and raised in Bend, Oregon, which lies in Central Oregon and resides just east of the majestic

Cascade Range. Bend used to be a small, sleepy logging town, but now sports a population of over 100,000 and is a prime recreation destination in the Pacific Northwest. Based on the stories he told about his youth, his adventures mirrored those of the boys in the classic film, *Stand by Me*. There were many tales about his explorations that began from his two-story home across from Drake Park and the Deschutes River and led to endless Ponderosa Pines, mounds of lava rock, and miles of desert sagebrush. He took advantage of many of the perks nature offered, including fishing the high lakes along Century Drive for mammoth rainbow trout that frequented the local waters.

A beast on the offensive line for the Bend Lava Bears high school football team, Bruce had aspirations of playing at the collegiate level, but a knee injury put that dream to rest. He attended Southern Oregon College in Ashland, Oregon, and while attending, he married his high-school sweetheart, Carolyn. A year later, I arrived on the scene and we migrated north to Salem after Dad scored his first teaching job. Dad was assigned to teach a rough and tumble 6th grade class in one of the town's most challenging environments. Many of those young learners were hard to handle for most teachers, but from what I have gathered, Dad did an amazing job of keeping them engaged and on a good track. His rather imposing six-foot two-inch broad frame and deep voice probably didn't hurt to quell the most rambunctious of young souls. If that wasn't enough, he also moonlighted as a pizza artist at Shakey's. After four years of that torrid pace and a 1960s teacher salary, he jumped ship to the more financially lucrative education textbook sales business.

While Dad was paving a successful sales career, I was enjoying the perks of our new home in Northeast Salem in a neighborhood called Jan Ree Gardens. It was a fabulous place to grow up, and my childhood was like many of those who grew up in the 1960s and 1970s. My friends and I were always outside when the weather allowed. Riding bikes, playing sports, and building forts were part of the daily routine. Like many mothers of that era, my mom stayed home with my sister Jen and me, and our house became the hub for all the neighborhood kids. She was known as the nicest mother around, and chances were that any child who stopped by would be treated with a popsicle on a hot summer day.

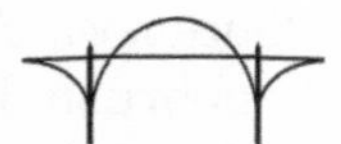

When I was old enough, Dad couldn't wait to take me fishing. My first trip was to Detroit Reservoir, a large body of water an hour east of Salem. Donned with my bulky, blocky, orange life jacket I peered over the side of our battered rental boat as we motored away from the dock. Much to my father's surprise, I suddenly shouted out, "Dad, there are bears crawling on the bottom of the lake!"

"Bears? Hmmm. I don't see any bears, Ter," replied my puzzled father who suppressed a laugh.

"They're crawling everywhere, all under the boat!" I emphatically shouted back.

"No, no, Ter, those are tree stumps. There aren't any bears down there," Dad said trying to de-escalate my fears five minutes into our outing.

"I saw them moving Dad, they're bears!" I said, not letting go of the issue for a second.

"It'll be alright. They won't bother us. Let's go catch some trout," Dad proclaimed assuredly as we motored into the deep water with "bears" disappearing from view. I was excited to catch my first fish, but I was equally amped to knock down one of the bottles of Orange Crush that Dad stashed in the cooler.

We caught our limits by noon, and that outing led to many more memorable trips to more Oregon lakes, rivers, salt water, and even a trek with my Uncle Steve to a remote lake in British Columbia. Like a slow and steady drip, these rich experiences built a strong bond between us and life on the water.

Aside from my growing love of the outdoors, my elementary school years were pure bliss. I embraced everything that K-6 life had to offer. I excelled in most facets of my learning and nearly every day after school I was engaged in some kind of play and even an occasional rock fight with the boys down the street.

As my secondary school years rolled in, life became more complicated. The academic part was no sweat, but my grades in navigating the social intricacies that adolescence dished out were less than stellar. Being an introvert and younger than my peers, the whole social scene hovered above my head. I began to hear more people say I was "quiet." I despised my new label. It was more of just not being in the main vein of the teenage drama talk, and that I embraced the mantra of, "more words doesn't necessarily mean better." Despite the challenges, I managed to hang in there and found ways to fit in on the periphery. There was part of me that liked living on the fringe. Keeping myself occupied wasn't much of a chore as I enjoyed anything to do with basketball, all types of drawing, and spending hours browsing a downtown record store called Rising Sun Records. The location was hard to miss with a giant brick wall mural of Springsteen's Born to Run cover art. It was there that I pieced together the discography and history of dozens of rock artists while flipping through record bins. It was also a time where I began to realize that the vinyl that I took home was entwining intricately with many life experiences.

When Dad invited me to fish with him for the summer prior to my freshman year, I jumped at the chance for another avenue to march to my own beat. Little did I know that it would open a door to otherworldly adventures and forge a unique relationship with my father that would run deeper than I ever imagined.

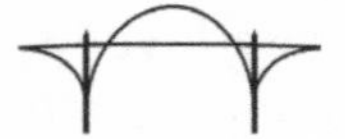

I had heard before that part of the grieving process of losing a loved one is the loss of being able to converse about special memories. The passing of my father hit me like a ton of bricks. I felt the stone-cold reality that there was no one with whom to share those experiences on a deeply personal level. When we talked about certain events, we were always on the same frequency, and each message was received with clarity and complete understanding. The next few years left me yearning to find some type of closure to his passing and to the miraculous fifteen-season chapter in our lives.

One summer day in 2018, I was browsing through our old logbooks, photos, and catch receipts while doing some house cleaning. Upon the urging of my wife, D'Ann, I opened up a laptop, turned my fingers loose on the keyboard, and let those memories fly onto the screen just like Dad said many times over that I ought to do someday.

CHAPTER 1

SEASON 1

IN THE BEGINNING

1977 Setlist

Paul McCartney and Wings "Silly Love Songs"
Heart "Magic Man"
Fleetwood Mac Rumors

Sooner or later, life drops a fork in the road of life. It's mind blowing how each prong can present a completely different life trajectory. As luck would have it back in 1977, I took my first step on one of those prongs with absolutely no regrets. It was springtime and my beloved Portland Trail-blazers were on their run to the first playoff berth after six years of toiling in the cellar. At thirteen years old, I was still clinging on to my hopes and dreams of becoming an NBA all-star, even though I was gravitationally challenged and could only penetrate to the hoop effectively to my right. I had no idea that a few months later, instead of visions of game-winning shots and a future with the Blazers, I would be dreaming of being a highline salmon fisherman at the helm of a dory boat.

Many fishermen come from a family that has been immersed in a long rich history in the industry. The craft is handed down from generation to generation and it is an expected way of life. This definitely was not the case with us. Our legacy had its own crazy path. Sometimes the seeds to something larger are planted much earlier in our lives, often with us not realizing it. Our seeds sprouted on an August morning in 1975. Thick drizzle enveloped Yaquina Bay in Newport, Oregon as my father and I were enjoying some crabbing off a hotel dock during our family vacation. As we pulled our crab rings, several boats heading out in the thick mist for a day of commercial salmon fishing caught my father's eye.

Out of nowhere Dad said, "Those are very seaworthy boats, Ter. They have flat bottoms and are called dories. They take them out in the ocean to catch salmon for a living."

To be honest, the boats looked a bit decrepit to me as they were battle-scarred and didn't have shiny fiberglass cabins like those that were still tied to the docks. A bit less enthusiastic and perhaps with good reason, I replied, "The fishermen must get really wet and cold with no cabin."

One of the fishermen passing by was hunched over at the helm decked out in his wet forest-green rain gear. Water was dripping down from his hood across his face as he half-jokingly shouted, "I don't wanna go!" While I'm sure the drizzly-wet guy would've enjoyed being warm and dry at the coffee shop, he didn't want to be anywhere else. Years later that memory came back to me on a rainy coastal summer day. A strange feeling crawled through my mind as I motored along the bayfront waters. In our own dory I was struck with the realization that I was just like the guy fully donned in soaking-wet rain gear. Some tourist on a dock was likely looking at me with a small amount of envy and some sort of wonder.

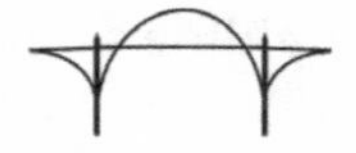

It's fascinating how memories are entwined with the

five senses. A certain song or scent instantly imprints strong emotions in your mind and bam!—the experience is in permanent recall forever. That was certainly the case after going on a charter bottom fishing trip with my father in the spring of 1976. The ocean was an agitated mess, much like in a washing machine while fishing about 13 miles offshore on a windy, drizzly spring day. We successfully avoided seasickness and amassed a cooler full of lingcod and rockfish filets. Before making the two-hour drive back home with our catch, we decided to refuel our chilled souls at a pizza joint along Highway 101 in Newport. It was a typical local 1970s establishment complete with pool tables, groovy dim stained-glass hanging lamps, dark decor, and a jukebox cranking out the greatest hits in the smoky interior. While I was enjoying my Pepsi and slices of Canadian bacon, "Silly Love Songs" by Paul McCartney saturated my eardrums. The blustery day on the salt resonated with me on another level. The rhythm of the waves, the boat's marine radio chatter in the background, the bitter taste of the salty air, the toxic engine exhaust fumes, and lastly McCartney and a few slices of pizza tugged on my heart like nothing had before. I had a taste of something big and alluring, and I wanted more. As I felt this metamorphosis take its grip on the ride home, it left me wondering about my father. *"Did he feel that way, too?"*

Several months later Dad and I embarked on a cold and windy winter steelhead fishing trip along the banks of the Nestucca River. We had nary a bite by noon, and this severely tested the patience of a middle school-age boy. Both of us agreed that enough was enough, and we hiked through the woods and the soggy green farmland pastures back to our muted banana-yellow Plymouth station wagon. Dad put high mileage on his company cars, so every few years he'd drive up with a new pale, block-shaped ride. The shrill, quavering guitar solo of Heart's hit song "Magic Man" penetrated through the static of a coastal radio station when Dad fired up the roaring engine. Unknowingly, those opening high-pitched guitar notes were being registered as a benchmark moment. Since we made a chilled early exit from the river that day, Dad suggested a Plan B.

"Well, rats, we didn't catch any fish today, Ter! Steelhead fishing is like that. Sometimes you don't get a bite for a few trips, but when one hits your gear, all hell breaks loose." He explained. "Let's drive over to the Hebo Inn for a bowl of chili to warm up."

"Is that the place that has hot Dr. Pepper?" I asked as I perked up.

"Yes… it sounds horrible, but if that's what you want, you can order it. But first I want to drive over to Pacific City to look around for a few minutes. It isn't far," he added.

Pacific City is a renowned place on the Oregon Coast where many dory fishermen launch their boats from the beach in a cove protected by Haystack Rock and Cape Kiwanda. He mentioned that he wanted to take a look at some dories that might be for sale. The town was nearly dormant on that winter day. Through the constant fresh spittle from the Pacific adhering to the Plymouth's windshield and the squeaky wiper blades' attempts to fend it off, we noticed a few boats trailered around town. They were tucked away in all sorts of nooks and crannies such as yards and parking lots.

"Are these the same type of boats that we saw last summer in Newport? You remember, the guy in the rain who yelled out that he didn't want to go fishing?" I asked as he got out of the car to inspect a white dory resting on its trailer.

"Yep. Same boats. It's just the guys here launch their boats from the beach and the Newport guys leave the harbor for the ocean," he explained in his teaching voice. "Originally, dories were "double-enders" because both ends of the boat were pointed. They were common on the East Coast and sometimes launched off larger fishing boats. The ones on the West Coast now are usually square-sterned."

"This boat looks pretty small to go out in the ocean to me," I stated as I wasn't inspired by its presence.

"This one is a bit small, but they are surprisingly seaworthy," he reiterated from our conversation the prior summer. "Twenty-two footers are the most common size."

"Are you thinking of buying one?" I asked.

"Oh, I don't know. I have always been intrigued with dories. It's just something I've thought about."

I was taken aback by the interest my father had in these wooden rustic-looking open boats, some of which were smartly painted with dashing trim, big open jaws with teeth painted on the bow sections and had some cool names. Others showed their wear and tear with weathered wood, peeling paint, and faded colors as a testimony for their many tours of duty through the Kiwanda surf. On the ride home that day with the opening guitar licks of "Magic Man" still reverberating in my head, I pondered the notion, *"Is Dad serious about buying one of these boats?"*

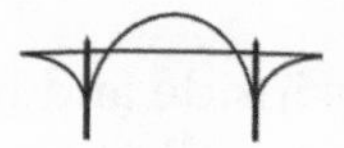

By the time late spring rolled around, the whole boat shopping escapade had slipped off the radar. The Blazers and their run for the NBA title had me and the rest of the state of Oregon in a frenzy. Unbeknownst to me, Dad was in the process of using his business sales skills to make stellar pitches to my mother about the riches that could be earned by a dory fisherman. He raved about how in the prior year, fishermen raked in the bucks. He quite possibly left out the part about how some years can be quite the opposite. Embedded in his oration was the passion he had for his dream to become reality. He must have knocked it out of the park because she gave him the green light to look for a boat. As luck would have it, Dad received a hot tip of a dory for sale in Newport just a few days later. That next weekend Dad invited me to make the trek to the coast with renewed optimism to inspect a dory named *Pisces*.

"A guy named Ray, who was my boy scout leader in

Bend when I was young, heard I was looking for a boat. He knows another guy in town who has a dory for sale. He gave me a call a few days ago and said the *Pisces* could be what I'm looking for," Dad explained cautiously but enthusiastically.

Upon our arrival at the Port of Newport dry dock, we peered through our front windshield at a dory perched on three thick wooden planks supported by a half-dozen rusty 55-gallon barrels. It had a white hull, blue trim, red antifouling paint on its underside, and most notably an interesting telephone booth-like console positioned on its midsection.

"This looks like a cool boat, Dad! I like that telephone booth steering station. At least we could stay a little bit dry when it rains. It looks like it's in good condition." I said in a very clueless, but hopeful tone.

"Well, let's get out and have a look. I want to check out the hull's condition to see if there is any dry rot," Dad said in a very serious tone.

He made the rounds inside and out and from what I could tell, it seemed to pass all of Dad's quality control checks. I didn't hear any disapproving sighs or groans, and I took that as a good sign. As he was making his inspection, I was conducting my own examination. The boat seemed larger than the ones I had previously seen, and I began to picture myself on it at sea as I stood behind the helm and gazed at the bow through the console window. There was an instant connection with the craft. It was sort of like where you meet the one you love and you know right away that you want to spend your life together.

"Whaddya think, Dad? Are you going to buy it?" I flat-out asked.

"It looks like it's in good condition, Ter. It's going to need some sanding and painting for sure. It doesn't come with a trailer either, so I'd have to figure that out. I need to talk to Mom again and then I'll talk to the owner," he explained in a hopeful tone.

Things moved fast. Dad received the official graces from

my mother and got the financing in place to make the big purchase. The next step was the big invite.

"So, I bought the boat, Ter. What do you think about spending your summer fishing with me on the dory? It would be a sacrifice as you wouldn't be able to hang with your friends all summer. I know you've got basketball camp coming up, too, and I don't want you missing that. You could fish now and then, it's really up to you," he presented matter of factly.

It didn't take much convincing. "I want to do this, Dad." I emphatically replied. I knew I'd figure out how to navigate basketball camp, friendships, and all that teenage stuff, but this was the escape from the ordinary that I had hoped for, and I didn't want it to slip by.

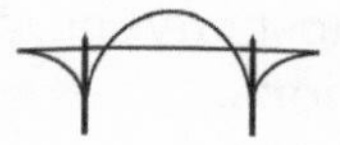

A few weeks later we got down to business on a weekend at the dry dock. This resting place in Newport that was just 20 yards away from the bay was far from dry. It was no more than an extension of a gravel parking lot littered with a chain of mud puddles that created a swath of quagmire. It was both a place where hope and sadness converged. There were old boats, new boats, restored boats, neglected boats, and boat parts scattered about, each with its own tragic or promising story. While most of the world would drive by this place and give it barely any notice, it quickly became a refuge for me. It was a place where I would begin to carve out my own path—an experience that would be more unique than that of most kids my age.

The owners of the *Pisces,* a father-son duo, Rozy and Steve, were from Bend, so there was an instant connection between them and my dad. Rozy and Steve had just purchased a 26-foot Owens fiberglass boat that offered much more comfort than a dory. Steve was an integral part of the Newport bayfront culture. He fished salmon in the summers, worked on larger boats from time to time, and constructed king crab pots. Steve was easy to spot around town, too, as he drove an old faded red VW bug that had a hay bale on its roof rack. He was a tall, strong, and incredibly hard-working guy, yet he was very laid back. He laughed in a mellow way and earnestly gave his approval by saying, "far out!" Steve also introduced us to a hippyish bayfront deli with a cavern-like interior that we quickly embraced named "The Whale's Tale". It touted its poppyseed pancakes and largely organic menu, and it often featured some local folk musicians in the evenings. Over the years, the vibe morphed into a pricier family establishment with a more exquisite menu. It was fascinating to watch my father, who was quite jovial and not the most patient of souls, interact with Steve even though they were so different. Dad had the knack of being able to get along with most anyone, and that was a huge asset in making connections.

Our freshman year began with a laundry list of boat preparation tasks to be ready for the all-species fishing season, which commenced on June 15th. This meant that in the waters off of Newport, fishermen could retain any number of chinook, coho, and pink salmon, which happened to be the common residents. From May 1 to June 15, it was only open for chinooks. Since we were still prepping the boat, getting our feet wet, and I was still in school, we didn't participate in the spring season. One of the first items on the list was to decide whether or not to keep the boat's name. In some nautical circles, renaming a boat is associated with bad luck.

"We should keep the name *Pisces,* Dad, it's cool! Besides, it's Jen's Zodiac sign and I think it has something to do with water," I suggested.

"Steve and Rozy are going to name their new boat, *Pisces II*. Two *Pisces* boats would be confusing out on the water. "I'm thinking of renaming it," Dad announced.

My mind generated an immediate short list of aggressive names like *Fish Slayer and Wave Crusher,* and other similar descriptors that only a teenage boy would gravitate to.

"I want to honor your mother for letting me buy this boat by including her first name. I also want your sister to be part of it, too, with her middle name. I'm thinking of *Carolyn Kay*. What do you think of that?"

"Yeah, that might work," I said, still processing, and realizing there was no way we'd have anything like a cool lightning bolt painted on our hull.

It was a nice name, and a well-deserved tribute to my mother and sister. I totally understood Dad's passion and motivation for the name change. It was just that my thirteen-year-old mind was certain a rad, hard-charging name was a slam dunk. I also knew it was a done deal, and there was no dwelling on it any further. And that was that—the *Pisces* officially became the *Carolyn Kay*.

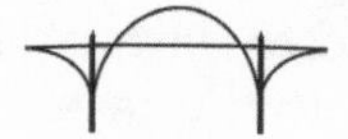

The next step was boat prep. While Dad had never commercial fished, he had owned other wooden boats in his lifetime and knew a thing or two about keeping them in ship shape. I was quickly indoctrinated in the sanding and painting rituals that would become an annual tradition. I got up-close and personal with the boat's entire surface area, including its underside, which acquainted me with coastal muck and a lot of debris finding my eyes and head. My apprenticeship included an introduction to linseed oil, a preservative that we slathered on the inside bare-wood hull in generous quantities. While some people liken its odor to dead fish, it became a feast for my olfactory system and its scent permeated my brain to its deepest recesses. The slightest whiff of it still sends my mind reeling back to those early days.

Despite being immersed in what a lot of people might call dirty work, this new chapter in my life was yanking on my soul. I felt the buzz round the port dock as fishermen were filled with high hopes, and I found an immediate connection with all the commotion. Mixed with sounds of power tools, sea birds, and boat engines, Fleetwood Mac's hit song, "Dreams" was fusing with the dock-side mood. It frequently blasted from the deck speakers of some of the larger boats and was on the short list of tunes played on Newport's AM radio station. Stevie Nicks' mystical vocals nestled perfectly with the ambience of the bayfront's 1970s wavelength. It didn't take long before the whole classic *Rumors* LP followed suit. With doors of adventure opening in every direction, I could hardly wait to get this party started.

After several weekend trips to Newport, the boat was prepped and ready. We had another major detail to take care of though—finding a boat trailer. This was an anomaly since part of the dory culture is all about the ease in which the boats can be trailered to dash off to another port where a big bite was happening. In the case of the Pacific City fleet, a trailer is essential to daily launches in the surf and to trailer up at the day's end. Dad was able to secure an old boat trailer from another acquaintance in Bend. It was a bit of an odd duck as it did not have rollers, which were like large, padded rolling pins that helped the boat roll off the trailer at a launch site. Without rollers, it meant that our dory had to be hoisted at one of the marinas and set in the water. Aside from being annoying, it was stressful. Watching your boat cradled with two six-inch wide straps similar to the material of fire hoses and being suspended over the water was enough to make your stomach cinch in a knot. Fortunately, those nerve-wracking launches never ended in disaster and years later we scored a more dory-friendly trailer.

We had a boat, we had a boat trailer, but we still needed a place to stay. Places of refuge came in many different forms for dory fishermen in the 1970s. The luckiest lived in the area year-round, and probably were among the most rested. There was one group of dorymen who lived in a coastal cottage that was more like a commune. I heard hints of stories of what took place at that residence, and I'm sure one could write a book about that experience. A few dorymen had small cabins covering the bows of their boats and chose to dwell in a claustrophobic form of simplicity and serenity. Most others lodged in the back of their pickups, campers, or trailers in parking lots, someone's property, or RV parks. City ordinances were lax, so there were plenty of free or inexpensive places to creatively set up camp.

Dad found a space under some big coastal pine trees at the Sportsman Trailer Park located near the south end of the Yaquina Bay bridge in a place called South Beach. Our trailer was one of those old warped egg-shaped shells that initially just had an icebox for refrigeration. There was a kick-stand table for dining that folded up into one of the two beds, a propane stove, a scary propane heater, a sink, and a closet. Our domain had a permanent musty smell, and the South Beach water possessed this incredibly repulsive, strong, acrid smell and metallic flavor. No amount of boiling it or trying to disguise it in flavored rice or pancakes could ever mask its vileness. Despite its unpleasantries though, this little bungalow, as we sometimes later called it, was a place of many special conversations. It was a place of refuge from screaming northwest winds, blustery and rainy southerlies, times of frustration and impatience, and moments of euphoria after big catches. Our little shell was the site of fabulous yet simple meals of fresh fish that you have to pay a hefty price for today. It was also headquarters for strategic sessions about where to fish the next day, and self-reflection, especially when either Dad or I was fishing solo.

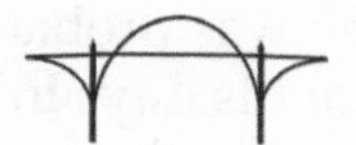

The learning curve in our trolling industry venture was a steep one, certainly for my father who entered it with just a vague idea of how all the equipment and gear came together in the process. I was just along for the ride at the time and was about as clueless as one could be. Dad wasn't shy though, and he used his powers of communication to quickly glean tricks of the trade from a most diverse group of souls about boat rigging and gear selection. The textbook salesman turned part-time fisherman wove his way into discussions with revered old timers who shared a gold mine of wisdom about what to do and what to avoid. This was invaluable information for a couple of greenhorns, but the real sustaining reward was the opportunity to intersect with a culture of fascinating personalities. Through my thirteen-year-old eyes, these acquaintances instantly became larger-than-life characters who carved new pathways in my view of the world. I know Dad had the same feeling as well, and some of these people would continue to reemerge in our conversations up until his very last days.

Despite the little victories in learning how to get the boat prepped and rigged, there was a cloud of stress hovering above us. The reality sank in for me as I tried to fathom a summer filled with daily journeys out on the ocean all by ourselves. I'm sure the stress was ten-fold for my dad as the season was drawing near and he was juggling another job and family life as well.

We ended up mooring our boat in a section of the bay still known as Port Dock 7. In the 1970s, there was an armada of small boats, many of which were dories, that were tied up on the docks near the shoreline. The placement of our boat could not have been primed better for the opportunity to strike up a special friendship that first year. Just across our stern on the new finger of docks away from the shore was a very spiffy 26-foot fiberglass cruiser. The boat was owned by Al, a man who was probably in his 60s at the time, and who Dad knew from his days in Bend. He was also the owner of a big downtown hardware store, and he journeyed to the coast to fish commercially every-so-often, mostly just for fun. Sometimes our conversations with Al were on his boat, as he would invite us over from time to time. Just as often, we would just converse across the water from stern to stern. Either way, Al loved to wax about the fishing industry of yore and always started with the phrase, "Years ago, Bruce..." It was hard to tell if his stories were truly exaggerated or not, but I think at least a few were mildly tweaked. Al's voice would rev up as he progressed deeper into some amusing tale, and this man who usually donned denim-blue overalls and a big grin would launch us all into belly laughs. Even more memorable were the times when we would see him in the evening. Al would pop out on deck to describe in enthusiastic detail his onboard dinner menu, and he would always conclude with his signature "…and pudding for dessert!" With so many unknowns taunting a couple of newbie dorymen, Al's good humor and mentorship were the perfect antidote to take the edge off what would be a very steep learning curve in the weeks to come.

CHAPTER 2

SEASON 1

LET THERE BE LIGHTS!

1977 Setlist

Carly Simon "Nobody Does it Better"
Electric Light Orchestra "Telephone Line"
Pink Floyd "The Dark Side of the Moon"
Santana "She's Not There"

At 4 AM on June 15th, our clangy windup alarm clock rattled our eardrums and jolted us out of our restless night's sleep. Each of us donned our fishing attire, wolfed down a bowl of cereal, and climbed in the car for the drive across the Yaquina Bay bridge toward the docks. Peering out the car's defrosting windows, we could see a flotilla of navigation lights from hard-charging vessels heading out to sea in the early morning hours between the mile-long jetties that offered protection to the harbor.

"Dad, check it out. There are a ton of boats already heading out!" I emphatically informed my father as I scanned the scene below us.

"We're going fishin' today, Ter! I got a feeling we're going to get 'em," Dad responded enthusiastically as he pressed on the gas pedal a little harder to get to the boat sooner.

It was the opening of the coho salmon season, and the fleet was still riding high from the banner year of 1976 when fishermen of all sizes of craft were rolling in the dough. Just like the farming industry, one thing that could be counted on were plenty of highs and lows when it came to yearly harvests. A quick peek at data from the Oregon Department of Fish and Wildlife's website will reveal a mountainous spike in the Oregon Troll Landing Graph for the coho salmon catch in 1976. As expected, there was a tremendous amount of bustling and anticipation on the bayfront, and we were filled with hope and a dose of anxiety. Aside from a brief practice run with Steve just outside the buoy line the week prior to see how the whole operation worked, this was going to be baptism by fire for us.

We pulled into the Port Dock 7 parking lot, gathered our belongings, and ambled down the rickety B finger dock where the boat was moored. It was covered with dew from the overnight moist marine air, and the cowbells on the trolling pole springs clanked like a herd of bovines as we stepped aboard. The 50-horse Evinrude outboard was fired up, filling the surroundings with a toxic but oddly pleasing mix of saline air and a cloud of carbon monoxide. The glow of the depth finder's spinning amber LED bulb inside the steering console along with the green, red, and white navigation lights made the prelaunch even more spellbinding. We switched on the CB radio and the airwaves were filled with tinny adrenaline-fueled voices. Moments later emerging out the chatter was the banter that began to dampen the mood.

"I've never seen so many boats pouring out of the harbor in the dark. It's pitch black out here and it's like a freeway," broadcasted one of the many voices heading out to sea. Suddenly the same voice returned announcing, "This is crazy now! There are several boats heading back in! I'm hearing reports that it's already blowing hard offshore."

The fisherman's traffic and weather report was followed by a cacophony of rough ocean descriptions over several of the popular fishing CB channels. This led to some boats turning around in mid-transit while others needed to experience the sea conditions for themselves to make a decision of what to do. It never occurred to Dad and I that we wouldn't be heading out that morning. Dumbfounded, we looked at one another.

"What do you think we should do, Dad? A bunch of boats are already returning back to the docks. Do you think we should give it a try?" I asked with concern.

"It sounds pretty sloppy out there already, Ter. I think we need to hold tight right now and see if it calms down before trying to head out," he reasoned.

We quickly learned that an important trait a dory fisherman must learn is patience. That was put to the test as we had to wait out two more days of northwest wind. During those three days tied to the dock, there was an upside as we became acquainted with many new people, including a couple of guys from Portland. Upon hearing of the riches earned by fishermen in 1976, they caught fish fever and bought a boat. It wasn't the prettiest boat by any stretch with its hull design resembling a bathtub toy adorned with a very box-like cabin. My father and the duo agreed to run the boats out together as a team when the ocean settled down. A lot of the small boats, especially dories, headed out to the fishing grounds in tandem or in packs for camaraderie, safety, and fish-catching tactics.

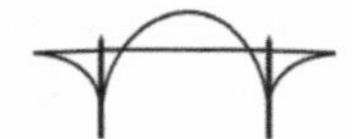

Four days later, another parade of lights illuminated the harbor as we crossed the bridge. In what was becoming a ritual, we both spied the bay below us.

A revved-up Dad exclaimed, "There are a lot of boats headed out and I don't see any headed in. That's a good sign. I didn't feel any wind either back at the trailer. I think we're really going fishin' this time, Ter."

The scuttlebutt on the docks and reports on the CB

radio affirmed that the ocean had settled down and that the opening of the all-species season was on. This was the bread and butter for the day-boat fleet. Anticipation was high for repeats of 100-fish days just like in the previous season. Coho were worth about $1.25 per pound so a hundred of those would yield $500 or more in the early season. Throw in some chinook, which earned $2.75 for the larger ones, and a day boat could earn $1,000 in a single day. Expenses were less than $100 a day, so you can see why tales of catching the Mother Lode were luring new members to the fleet.

They say ignorance is bliss, and that was true in our humble beginnings. Filled to the brim with anticipation and expectation, we fired up the Evinrude outboard. With the navigation lights turned on, CB radio blasting, and bait thawing, we cluelessly pulled away from the dock, unaware it would be like learning to swim in the deep end of the pool. With a hint of sunlight, we ventured between the jetties with our new acquaintances in the lead.

"The bar looks flat, Ter. Keep an eye on their mast light. I don't want to lose them." Dad instructed with urgency.

"I'm trying Dad. There are so many lights out here. It's hard to keep track of them. It's like a city out here. It doesn't seem like we're keeping up with them though," I reported back.

"I'm doing the best that I can," Dad replied as he manned the helm and the throttle.

This was the beginning of a realization that we had an underpowered dory, so keeping up with other boats would be a source of frustration for the whole first season.

It didn't take long before we lost sight of our running partners and quickly realized that we were on our own. It was like being one of the new kids in school on a large playground and having one of your few acquaintances suddenly disappear in a sea of unknown children. Keep in mind that in the 1970s there was no GPS to rely on. Some boats were equipped with a much cruder navigation system called LORAN, or Long Range Navigation, which relied on radio wave signals that were captured and displayed as numbers. Those coordinates could be plotted on a map, much like GPS today, to determine one's location at sea. It was a cumbersome process to capture the signals and many day boats did not have them. We certainly didn't. All we had was our compass and a depth finder, which only measured in feet instead of fathoms. Something else we quickly learned was that reporting your depth in feet wasn't cool. Instead, the measurement of choice by the fleet and navigation charts was definitely fathoms, so we found ourselves having to constantly convert depth units. One piece of crude technology we did have onboard was a transistor radio. There was a radio station beacon just north of the harbor, so you could point the face of the radio at the tower and it would be louder and clearer. Point it in other directions and it would be fainter and scratchier. This was a simple but helpful tool in the fog to determine relative position.

Our first journey to the fishing grounds seemed to go on for eternity. In all actuality, it was more like an hour southwest of the harbor about eight miles offshore. The sky was overcast and there were a few miles of visibility.

"How long do you think we should keep running, Dad? How will we know where to fish?" I asked, as I broke the droning monotony of the outboard motor.

"I see a small group of boats not too far ahead. I think we'll drop our gear there and see how it goes. We're in about 240 feet of water."

A few minutes later we decided it was time to break out of our trance and drop our gear to begin earning our fortune.

"Okay, Ter, I want you to take the wheel and keep the boat pointed southwest. Just watch your compass. I am going to put out the gear," Dad said in a rather tense voice.

The actual gear set up for the salmon trolling is difficult to describe even though it is fairly simple once you see it in action. In short, there are four 1/16-inch diameter stainless steel cable lines weighted by 30-to-50-pound leads or "cannonballs," two of which are deployed midships port and starboard. Two more lines are suspended on rectangular floats 10 to 20 yards behind the boat that, when set, look like two shark fins cruising beyond the boat's wake. Attached with clips to each stainless line are about five to ten short fishing lines with lures or baits called "spreads." A nylon cord is attached to each stainless line to a spring on the boat's outriggers. When a fish hits a spread, the spring attached to the trolling pole often jiggles or dances wildly depending on the species and size of fish and serves as a signal to the fisherman that a fish is on a line. The stainless cables are attached to winches either powered hydraulically or cranked up by hand, which the latter was the case for the *Carolyn Kay* in the early years. Many of the dories that were powered by outboard motors were "handcrankers" because powering a hydraulic pump either required mounting the pump on the outboard itself, or using a Briggs-and-Stratton engine to power the hydraulics. The former was quite burdensome on the outboard, and the latter was like running a noisy lawnmower in the bow section. Therefore, many dory fishermen with outboards sported large biceps. Those whose boats had inboard motors often enjoyed the comforts of hydraulics as the two devices paired well with each other.

When Dad finally got all the gear set, we were poised and ready for an onslaught.

"So, how exactly will we know when we have a fish on?" I wondered as I spied the springs on the poles as they lazily stretched with the rhythm of the light swells.

"Well, I think they'll start wiggling and jumping around pretty good when we get a fish on," Dad replied as best he could with no more experience than me.

"I think I saw something hit the gear. The spring stretched a bit differently than the wave action," I wondered aloud.

"Well, there's only one way to find out for sure. Go ahead, yank up that side and let's see."

Being greenhorns, we had no clue how to read the springs, and for a while, we interpreted every minute movement as a salmon. At that moment we chose our sides of the boat to run gear, with him choosing port because he was a lefty and me choosing starboard as I was a right-hander. My first gear check was slow and tedious. When the examination was over, it revealed no sign of life. The reality was when a fish hit a spread, the spring would jump wildly if a coho salmon were hooked, or more impressively, it would stretch and start pounding in an aggressive fashion if a big chinook was on a line.

"I have a good feeling that we're going to get into some fish soon, Terry," Dad said reassuringly as he could tell that I was getting impatient after an hour of no pandemonium.

As Dad's impatience began to surface, too, we noticed a few springs starting to dance erratically on Dad's side.

"Dad! I think you really have a fish on your side this time. Look at that spring bounce around. I bet it's a big one," I shouted as the spring's cowbells clanked erratically.

"Take the helm, Ter, I'm going to take a look. Keep us going straight." Caught up in the euphoria of the moment, I chose instead to peer over his shoulder. This resulted in the boat gradually making a tight 360-degree turn due to the unequal leverage from pulling gear. While this was happening, I heard a splash over the hum of the engine.

"Hey, Dad! We have a fish on the meat line, too," I said in an amped voice.

This was a short section of cotton line attached to a 5-pound weight tied off to the transom that was dragging a lure. It was all stretched out with a silver yanking on it.

"I'm busy right now. We have two or three fish on this wire," shouted Dad amidst the small frenzy.

In my excited state, I abandoned my post and scrambled to the stern to pull the salmon aboard. This caused the boat to circle in even a tighter circumference. As Dad was in the process of pulling the silvers off his side, I clumsily landed the silver on the deck.

"Check it out! I got the fish, Dad," I triumphantly announced as Dad hoisted two more aboard.

"You need to straighten out the boat right now! We just made a tight circle. Shoot! I hope our gear isn't tangled below the boat," Dad said in a tense and agitated tone.

The ugly truth was that float lines and deep lines had become tangled in an unimaginable mess under the boat due to the tight turn. This was more evident when we were unable to crank up our deep lines any further.

"Aw, damn! We have a big tangle under the boat!"

"Oh man! This is all my fault. I am so sorry, Dad. I just saw that silver on the meat line and thought I should get it aboard before it got away. How are we going to get it all untangled?"

"Well, we're going to find out. I think we're going to have to let out the wire on one side and bring it all up on the other side. Shut down the engine and let's get to work. There are some fish here and I want to get our gear down again soon."

Thus began the hour-long arduous process of untangling the massive bird's nest of stainless-steel cable and monofilament line, which led to a lot of clipping, cutting, and retying. Judging from the way Dad aggressively tossed the tangled hardware on the deck, I knew he was super pissed but was trying his best to keep composed. If there was an upside, it was that we pulled a few more silvers off the gear. A bit chagrined from the experience, we at least had time to reflect on what had worked to catch our little clatter of silvers.

"Those hot-pink wobbler spoons, the ones shaped like an egg with the black spots, seem to be killers. Every single fish we caught was on those. That was so cool when all those fish hit at once! Can you imagine what it would be like in a huge bite?" I remarked as I steered and clipped tangled leaders.

Once our mega-tangle was sorted out, with the remnants of the surgically removed mess tossed up in the bow section of the deck to clean up later, Dad announced, "Alright, Ter, time to dust ourselves off and get back on our feet. Let's get this gear back in the water and find those fish!"

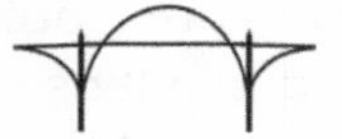

Just as in sport fishing, commercial salmon trollers are quite particular and sometimes secretive about the gear they use and how they rig it. While some metallic spoons like the hot-pink ones we used on our first day had their moments of good fortune, the most popular gear item were hoochies. These squid or cuttlefish-like plastic lures attach to larger metal or plastic flashers, with leaders anywhere from about 16 inches to 36 inches. There are hundreds of color patterns, and every fisherman has their go-to color combo. The common denominator seemed to be green, but of course, some other colors and shades were productive, too. Our first soak of the gear did not include the ones that later would earn thousands of dollars for us. Instead, we had a mish-mash of repugnant color patterns that would make most seasoned troll fishermen wretch, and as you can guess, they were not very effective. Aside from the hoochies and spoons, other fishermen enticed salmon with plugs and sometimes whole herring rigs.

One lingering concern wriggling through our minds throughout our first day was whether the fish we caught were coho or chinook. This was important, as the legal length limit for chinook was 26 inches, whereas for coho it was 16 inches. All the fish we caught were less than 26 inches, so if they were chinook, we would have been in an awkward, embarrassing and law-breaking situation at the fish dock. If a game warden was present, then we would be looking at a big citation.

"So do you think the fish we caught are chinooks or silvers, Dad? How can you tell for sure?"

"I'm pretty sure they're silvers, Terry. Chinooks usually are much larger."

"But what if we get to the fish dock and they are all chinooks? We'll get fined big time."

"Well, take a look in the regulation pamphlet to be sure."

"I dunno, I can't tell the difference from the sketches. What do you think we should do?"

"We're fine. Don't worry about it," Dad said as he tried to ease my anxiety as I envisioned us being fined or arrested upon our first delivery.

As we meandered on our trolling baptismal, we never crossed paths with the bathtub boat we followed out that morning. We radioed them once or twice for an update. They had a few fish and likely didn't know any better than us of their whereabouts. The rest of the day yielded just a few more fish. By early evening, we decided to put the gear in the box and head for the hole. The skies cleared and we could see the coastline well enough to find our way home. With no frame of reference, the ride home seemed as endless as our morning drive. Having brought very little food and just a canteen of water, we were exhausted, dehydrated, and famished. Another lesson learned—bring plenty of provisions! We also started to realize just how underpowered our boat was compared to other dories that zipped by us and planed on the cusps of the gentle swells impressively.

After what seemed like eternity, we finally motored under the grand arches of the Yaquina Bay Bridge. We decided we would sell our dozen fish to the Ocean Fresh fish company that was right next to the Coast Guard station. It turned out my worries of getting taken away in cuffs were for naught. As we opened our fish box, the dock worker announced, "Ah, it looks like you caught a few silvers!" This brought instant relief and netted $72.96 for our maiden voyage. After our delivery, it was off to the gas dock to fuel up, then to put the boat to rest at the moorage. That evening's dinner was spent at an A&W restaurant. We inhaled our burgers and fries and swore that food never tasted so good. Vowing to avoid starvation on our next expedition, we swung by JC Market and loaded up a myriad of provisions.

It seemed like it was just minutes after we zonked out that our windup alarm rang like a fire bell. After figuring out which way was up, we made our way to the docks. Despite our optimism, we were about to find out that the learning curve would continue to be a very steep one. Full of anticipation, we motored out to sea under an overcast sky about three miles offshore. We steered our dory north of the harbor to join a conglomeration of boats on the calm water. Catching a few silvers on the wobbler spoons the day before instilled confidence that we could fill the fishbox if things went our way. Sadly, we made a poor choice of where to fish and we trolled for several frustrating hours before we finally hooked and landed an eight-pound chinook. At least we were able to correctly identify the species this time. This lifted our spirits and brought about a surge of adrenaline to run the gear and coerce a few more. It wasn't meant to be though, and we did not catch a single fish the rest of the day.

Even though we had regrouped after a disappointing second trip, our third trek took our pursuit of patience and persistence to new levels. The ocean was like a mirror-like pond, but heavy fog had crept in like a cat overnight. We decided to go north again because the radio station beacon was north of the bar. We figured it would be an easier task when using the transistor radio to determine our position than trying to do so from the south.

There are different kinds of fog. Sometimes it is dry, meaning that while your vision is obscured, you really don't end up wet and chilled to the bone. The fog on our third venture was different. It was the type that clung to everything including the lenses of our glasses. Adding to our cluelessness, we weren't wearing rain gear. I can't speak for Dad, but for me, it had a lot to do with a foolish teenage mindset that rain gear wasn't cool. Instead, I was decked out in some

1970s bell-bottom jeans and a green down jacket, both of which were soaked to the core. It might have been tolerable if we kept ourselves busy, but without having a single bump on the gear, we became sponges. Our northerly decision was good for safety, but a poor choice for fishing.

"Where are the fish, Ter?" Dad asked to break the monotony.

"They're not here, that's for sure! I'm freezing," I answered back in a subdued tone as my teeth chattered.

"Let's run the gear and make sure it's clean. If we don't get anything going in the next half-hour, then we'll pull the gear and head home. It's going to take some time to find the buoy in this thick muck anyway."

After one final run through our gear, we resigned to a goose-egg catch score and threw in the towel. If we had awards for our fishing days throughout our career, day three would have been deemed "Most Boring and Miserable." Taking it slow and steady, we headed home with our tails between our legs, hoping to lay eyes on the revered whistle buoy.

"Okay, Ter. Judging from the strength of the radio reception, our position, and our depth, we should be close. Keep an eye out for boats," Dad instructed.

A few minutes later I announced, "I see a couple boats heading the same direction."

"That's a good sign. I'm going to shut off the engine. I want you to go up front and listen for the whistle buoy," Dad respectfully ordered.

After I made my way to the boat's bow section, Dad hollered, "Hear anything?"

"Nothing yet. Are you sure we're in the right place?" I answered.

After a few minutes of silently bobbing around in milky air with the engine shut down, we both heard the buoy's low moans.

"I think it's dead ahead. I just can't see it," I called out.

Dad fired up the engine and motored at crawl speed.

Within a minute the imposing navigational aid's silhouette greeted us with a welcoming groan.

"There it is!" I announced along with a fist pump.

Despite the elation we felt with making a safe entry into Yaquina Bay, we still had to deal with the stigma of getting skunked, which means to return without a catch. It was one of the worst feelings of the whole fishing gig. The blow could be softened if you had to come in early, say, for a family reason or a mechanical issue. It was like your peers giving you a pass. Getting skunked on a day with no excuses was a game of mental hopscotch where you felt like you let yourself down. Worse yet, you were left with a fixation that others must think that your fishing skills weren't up to snuff. The sucker punch would come when someone would ask, "How was fishing today?" When you got skunked, you knew this was likely something you would have to answer. All you could do was admit it wasn't your day, learn from those willing to share, and regroup for the next day.

They say ignorance is bliss, and that was a real savior during the next 17 days of fishing. Fishing was poor all over and it was evident that we weren't very good at it either. The most productive day of the bunch after our first day was six silvers, and there were several one to three fish days mixed in. Chinooks were few and far between for us during that stretch, too. Sure, our daily catch averages were lower than average, but many more experienced fishermen were crying the blues at this point, too. One man, who chatted with my dad on the docks on a bright, chilly morning while being blown in by a brisk northwesterly, stood out as the epitome of mid-season frustration. He appeared out of nowhere and was standing near the bow of our boat.

"Good morning, guys," the man announced in a nice but neutral manner. "Did you head out this morning?" he asked.

He was just being cordial as he knew it was too windy to fish.

"Nah, that northwest is already screaming and we heard a few boats on the CB that poked their noses out. They headed back in after getting their butts kicked," replied Dad with a half chuckle in his voice. "Do you have a boat down here?"

"Yeah, I have a double ender on the A Dock. I stayed in, too. It just isn't worth getting your brains beat in for so few fish. It's been a really tough month. I had such high hopes for this season after last year. We plugged the boat several times. I'm really not enjoying this anymore. I miss my wife, too," he said as a small symphony of flags flapped and halyard clips clanged on their masts in the background. After some more chit-chat he paused and lamented, "I think I'm going to sell my boat."

"It's been a tough first year for us, too, but I still feel like the fishing could pick up after this blow. Don't give up yet!" Dad said encouragingly.

"I...don't know. Yeah, I think I'm going to put my boat up for sale today. I hope you guys get into some fish this year, though. Good luck!" he said as he waved goodbye.

"Thanks. Take care!" Dad concluded, not knowing what else to say.

Sure enough, the dejected fisherman followed through because when we strolled by his boat later on that day, there it was, a freshly posted For Sale sign in the cabin window. That was the last we ever saw of the fisherman, and it was a strong dose of the reality of how fortunes could flame out so quickly in the fishing industry.

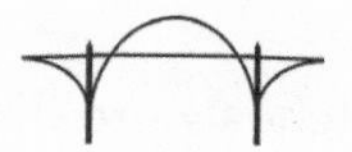

On days when the ocean was too rough to fish, we would either go back home to Salem for a few days or stay in town to take care of business. Even though my roots were starting to take hold on the coast, heading to our real home in "The Valley," which is coastal slang for the Willamette Valley, was always full of rejuvenation. A warm shower and a comfortable bed sure was a welcome reprieve from the trickle of water in the cold, dark, damp, concrete restroom at the Sportsman and my spongy mattress in the trailer. I missed my mother and sister a lot, so I was always excited to return home to see them. Aside from frequent calls home from the germy, chilly payphones, we sometimes went for several days before seeing them. Fortunately, they made the drive to see us and stayed in a motel. This usually meant a nice meal out and a little extra dose of luxury.

When I went home, I usually would connect with some of my friends, which was a good reminder for me that I was still a young guy who needed to stay in touch with my youth. Hanging out with Dad brought many wonderful experiences, but a little bit of space now and then was a good thing, especially for a teenager.

One of the most frustrating aspects while home was attempting to articulate what we did on our boat. Even though Newport was only two hours away, people in my hometown had little to no understanding of what our fishing experience was all about. Most figured we ran a charter boat operation or trawled with nets. When we explained we didn't do either, but still used hooks and lines, we were met with befuddled expressions. Trying to describe our operation was something we struggled with for the rest of our fishing days.

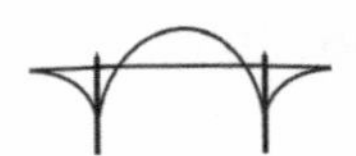

Even though our catches were dismal, our voyages were spiced up now and then with some weird encounters. One of which took place while trolling in thick fog somewhere off of the Yaquina Head lighthouse along the 30-fathom line. It was one of those days where the fog was thick as pea soup on the water's surface, but about 10 to 20 yards above the waterline it was a beautiful sunny day. You could see the sun throwing every trick it had to melt through the dense misty ceiling. We were on a southerly tack and following a rip when out of the blue I heard something odd.

"I swear I hear a dog barking! Listen!" I randomly announced while pulling the gear on my side. I instantly had this mental picture of us just yards away from the perilous surf with all our gear down while a family and their dog joyously played on the beach.

"I hear it too, Ter," Dad said as he was puzzled as I was. "I hope we are not close to shore. Check the depth again, Dad. What does it say?"

"We're at 26 fathoms, so I highly doubt we are hearing anything from the shore."

"Wait, look! It's Henry and his dog is barking at a salmon he just caught!"

Henry's silhouetted boat had just emerged out of the thick featureless curtain off our port bow. He was an upbeat, stout guy with a long red beard. His crewman was a German Shepard that barked uncontrollably when a fish came aboard. It was a huge relief to know we weren't close to shore, and it was uplifting to know there were at least a few silvers in the area.

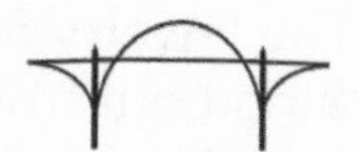

Fishing remained spotty for most of the small-boat fleet until the latter half of July when word spread like wildfire that some boats caught silvers north between Yaquina Head and Cape Foulweather. After a long day of just a half-dozen fish, we were fortunate to run into a doryman named Dick. He was a wild sort who often sported a head full of shoulder length hair, a full bushy brown beard, and mirrored sunglasses. It didn't take him long to get very animated, and he usually left us in stitches describing a fishing tale.

"...So this one silver smacks a hoochie on the surface, jumps out of water and lands on the deck. It's stunned and leaning up against the engine well, and then whoop, it just tips over deader than a doornail!" he said laughingly as he reenacted the scene with all sorts of hand motions.

He talked about his recent success with the school of fish up north and a hot new gear item he was so jazzed about.

"This...is what you need to buy—the T-13!" He proclaimed assertively as he dangled it in front of us in a tantalizing fashion. Then he shifted into his usual dramatics, "Silvers were chomping down on these little guys like no other. I had fish bouncing on every line. It was a crazy place and they were all coming on T-13s!" This all-star fishing lure was a miniature version of the squid-like lures everyone used. It was neon green-yellow and commonly called a "mini-hoochie." Thinking the T-13 could be our golden ticket, it wasn't long before we made a trip to a gear store to pick up a few packages.

There were four main gear stores in town. One catered more to sport fishing, but had some commercial gear and was always open before sunup. Another was the main supplier for commercial fishing boats of all sizes and had everything from soup to nuts, a phrase my mom often used. The third sold everything from gear to boat supplies for any type of craft. The prices were outrageous and many of the locals aptly referred to it as, "The Jewelry Store." There was one gear store, though, that stood out from the rest.

The place was called the Harbor Barber, a little shop on the hill just above the Coast Guard station and gained its namesake from being a barbershop by day with a fishing gear store tucked in the back at night. It might sound a bit sketchy, but that is exactly what it was. It was a great set up with its evening hours. If you were in a pinch after a long day of fishing and ran out of fishing line, you could stop by the Harbor Barber instead of having to wait for the other stores to open the next day. The store owner was a slender man with slicked-back gray hair combed over the side who had a cackling laugh. From what we gathered, he didn't fish much, but he knew a good business plan and had a strong pulse on the hottest gear.

When Dad and I entered the little back room of the gear shop, The Harbor Barber, as we referred to him, was right at our service. "Hello, gentlemen! What can I do for you?" he asked with his best slick but cordial sales-pitch tone.

"We're looking for some T-13 hoochies. Do you have any?" Dad asked.

"Do I have T-13s? Of course! Ha, ha! They're flying off the shelf so you better get some fast. I'd get several packages if I were you. Guys are catching fish hand-over-fist," he answered in his cackling manner. "You probably need some more monofilament line, swivels, beads, and hooks to go with that. I've got them right here." Taking his advice, we bought three packages of the T-13's, and of course, all the accessories and more. "Good fishing," he announced, as we headed on our way out. "We'll see you back soon!" He was right. We made many trips to his gear shop and never left empty-handed. He was a brilliant salesman and the store was around for several years before quietly closing up shop.

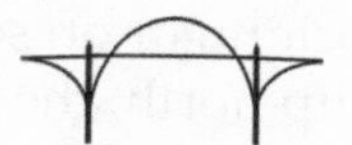

With our gear trays loaded up with a new arsenal of T-13s the next morning, we headed north along with a majority of the fleet. While far from a banner day, we put nine big silvers in the box and most bit the heralded T-13s. When fishing with hoochies, a very popular technique was to place a small chunk of herring on the hook of the rig. The idea was to provide an added scent to attract fish, and it was gospel among most of the small-boat fleet. This was the fishing equivalent dipping french fries in ranch sauce. We also learned that many of the most successful fishermen constantly ran their gear. They continuously checked each line for debris such as seagrass, jellyfish, incidental catch of other species, and kept all bait fresh. This was something that we weren't doing religiously, and it likely was a culprit in our poor catches early on. Unbeknown to us at the time, most of the larger trollers didn't subscribe to the "Chunkie Theory," and many thought it was total rubbish. About nine years later, this gear tactic became a sore spot between my dad and I as I learned a lot of new tricks while working on a larger boat.

We were blessed with glassy-slick ocean conditions on the next two days that definitely saved our season, and possibly our future in the industry.

"The ocean is like a pond, Ter. Let's get underway and head up to where we left off yesterday. I got a good feeling we are going to be throwing silvers over both shoulders today." Dad announced with the boyish grin he would get when he was excited.

Al was heading out in his boat, too, so we teamed up with him for the ride up north. After going through the usual pre-launch motions, we motored out of the marina toward the bay for the next step in the process. The wooden outriggers on our boat were about 22 feet long, which was the length of our dory. While docked, the outriggers were always secured upright, or on some dories that also launched from the surf up north, the poles were stored forward-facing the bow. The ritual for all boats in the trolling industry regardless of size was to pause in the bay and lower the poles to 45 degrees of the port and starboard sides of the boat. Once the poles were in position and secured, boats would then venture out of the bay.

Upon arrival at the fishing grounds, stabilizers or "Flopper Stoppers" were deployed from each pole from the location of the first pole stay. The heavy metallic "Floppers" looked similar to F-15 fighter jets, and once they were deployed a few feet below the surface, they performed their job of minimizing the bobbing and rolling while working on deck. With those in place, it was the moment of truth to send down the gear to see if our predictions would come true.

Clear skies, even with a flat ocean on a summer morning, often meant the wind was going to plaster you later on. The forecast called for calm seas though, and all signs pointed to a comfortable ride. No sooner did we start to set gear, fish started smacking it.

"Dad, I think we have some fish on my deep line. It's jerking all over the place. Look at it!" I yelled as I let it out.

"Let it all the way down, Ter, for now. I want to get our gear in the water. As soon as we get all four lines down, pull your deep line," Dad replied.

"Wow, both float lines are going off. The float bags are even bobbing. Check it out," I remarked as Dad was putting down his deep line.

"We dropped right on a school of silvers. Yep, I got one yanking on my deep night now," Dad added. "Okay, it's set, go get 'em, Ter!"

"Fish!" I said, then handlined it to the boat, gaffed it, and landed it in the kill box. Moments later, "Another fish. It's another silver." The fish flapped wildly in the box before being dispatched. Soon thereafter, another fish was brought aboard.

"Nice job, Ter," Dad applauded. "Okay, after you check your wire, send it back down and I'm going to check my deep. I think I have at least two on. We have some fish on the floats, too, but we might have to check them later. If this day goes as I think it will, your mom is going to be thrilled when I call her tonight."

The action ebbed and flowed that day with a mix of crazy clatters and spells of inaction. The next day was a carbon copy. Our catch both days for silvers was in the mid-twenties, and we got a feel for the first time of the hard work involved when fish were biting. When things got crazy, we found our groove as a team. One person would steer and clean fish so that we would deliver a high-quality product. At the same time the other person would run the gear and pull fish aboard. Then we would switch. It was the first of many times in the years to come where Dad and I functioned like a symphony.

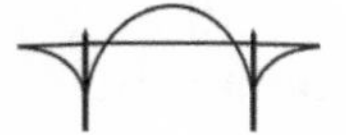

Along with our first dose or real coho action, we had some close encounters of the marine wildlife kind. In an area known as the condos, where some condominiums were nested on the shoreline between Yaquina Head and Cape Foulweather, we spied something suspicious ahead about 20 yards off our port bow. It was hard to distinguish, but we did notice an odd-looking fin flapping back and forth. As we trolled in for closer examination, Dad cried out, "Oh my gosh, Terry! What is that? It looks like the head section of a shark! Look at that big eye. Be careful not to steer too close. The last thing we need is that big fish tangled in our gear."

"You're right, it does look like half of some kind of big fish. What do you think it is?" I asked.

"What an amazing fish, Ter. That big fin just waved on the surface and made that woosh-woosh sound."

"That was cool, Dad, but I don't think it made a sound though," I commented as Dad just grinned, still in the after-glow of the moment. This was the first of many reenactments to come where dad included mysterious sound effects in his description of an episode. I learned over time just to go with it and enjoy how amped up he would get sometimes.

Dad made a radio call to Al, and we learned that we were in the neighborhood of a gigantic sunfish that likely weighed several hundred pounds. Picture a large, gray, laterally, semi-flat fish head with a tail, and you have a mola mola, as they are known in some parts of the world. Our fishing careers would have many more meetings with the bizarre-looking species.

Only a few days later, we had another hair-raising encounter with a different sea creature. Between gear checks, I spotted a huge black shark-like fin standing resolute above the waterline on another flat-calm ocean. Based on the size of the appendage, our minds immediately went into great white mode.

"Dad, do you see that! It's a huge shark fin!" I yelled and pointed. "Right over there, about 25 yards off my side toward shore. I think it's a great white shark!" We cautiously and curiously continued to troll north, half-hoping to get a closer look, and half-fearing a terrifying encounter. Our trajectories continued on a slow convergence, and eventually the behemoth was off of our stern.

"Look at that thing, Ter! It's just resting on the surface. I don't think it's a great white."

"I hope our float bags don't run over it. It looks like they sure could," I remarked.

"Oh crap! Hit the throttle, Ter, now! We don't want to snag it. It could sink us." Following his command, I punched the throttle as the resistance on the gear vibrated the entire boat.

"Alright, I think we cleared it. You can throttle back now, Dad instructed."

Just like the sunfish episode, Dad hailed one of our fishing friends nearby, describing our visitor. The reply yielded that it likely was a basking shark, probably inhaling a banquet of zooplankton. Cetorhinus Maximus was too busy gorging itself to care about our presence and was more of a peaceful sunbather than a man-eating machine.

Our intersections with wildlife didn't stop with the mola mola and basking shark. A chilly morning southwest of Newport along the 30-fathom line in mid-August delivered another adrenaline rush. We were on a northerly troll into some wind waves that were just starting to whitecap. Along with the drone of the outboard motor and crackling of the airwaves from the CB radio, there was a symphony of whoosh sounds from the folding waves. While I was running my gear, Dad said out of the blue, "Bless you!"

Confused, I replied, "Uh...I didn't sneeze, but thank you." The lull in our conversation after my response was suddenly filled with a loud "whoosh" off our stern between the propwash tail and our float bags. It was definitely not a sneeze. The next words spoken by Dad were of a dramatically different tone.

"Oh, crap! It's a killer whale, and it's close to the gear. Terry, get the cable cutters from the console. If that whale gets wrapped in our gear, we're in big trouble. It's really close."

Despite its intrusion in our comfort zone, I was in awe of the power that animal possessed. It aggressively surged through the choppy water on its northeast-bound course, just aft of the starboard deep lines.

Stepping out of my gaze, I followed the captain's orders and rummaged through the console for the cable cutters, all the while keeping a hand on the helm and an eye on the whooshing cetacean. I wasn't paying attention to Dad, who had scrambled up to the storage area in the bow of the boat. When he reappeared by my side, I yelled, "What are you doing with that shotgun? Since when did we have a gun on board? Don't shoot it!"

"No, but if it gets too close, I might try to scare it away!" Dad explained.

"I'm pretty sure that would be against the law, Dad"

Dad wasn't a big gun guy, nor was I. He said it wasn't loaded, but his anxiety was high with horrifying visions of utter destruction.

"It better not get tangled in our gear!" Dad said, nearly hyperventilating.

It was at that moment that I realized the depth at which orcaphobia had a grip on my father. His hands were shaking and his voice was quavering. Being a cocky teenager, I couldn't comprehend the responsibility my dad had to make sure I returned home in one piece. He had made a promise to my mother he would do just that. My thinking was more along the lines of, *"What could go wrong?"*

"Whoa, check it out. Look how it is cruising through the water. That dorsal fin is huge," I shouted.

"Those are amazing animals, Ter. It can keep swimming

away from us though," Dad added as he was putting the gun away. Dad never would have taken a shot. He liked whales, just not on the fringes of our wake.

The ocean traveler from the family *Delphinidae* continued to veer away. We watched in astonishment as it eventually blended into the choppy waters. As our visitor departed, Dad poured a cup of coffee and he spilled most of it on the deck with his hands still shaking.

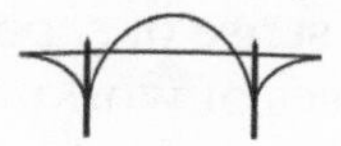

With some improved catches under our belts, we had a new sense of confidence. We definitely weren't highliners, but we were headed in the right direction. The fishing tapered as the season wore on, but as we learned more new strategies, our daily catches became more comparable to our peers. We also started catching some chinooks on a hot plug called the Little Joe 120 and late in the season we landed a 23-pounder.

When mid-August rolled around, I felt the looming presence of school and Dad's school textbook sales occupation summoned him back to reality. From mid-June through mid-August, Dad's job was rather quiet. Teachers were all on summer break, so there weren't audiences of educators to give riveting sales pitches to. When they returned to their classrooms in the latter part of August though, Dad needed to be present with his best game face. During our drives through town, I would glance at a bank's electronic reader board. I never paid it much attention, but one day it produced an ominous and nauseating feeling as it revealed the date, which edged closer to the start of the school year. It seemed like a cruel in-your-face countdown that created a pit in the gut and generated a lot of unpleasant thoughts.

"Ten more days left in the season."

"My first year of high school."

"Registration."

"It'll be nine or ten months before we fish again."

"Ughh...I don't want to go back."

By late August, our season was all but over. We kept the boat in the water through September and managed to fish a couple of Saturdays for chinooks near shore with no success. After Labor Day, some postpartum fishing depression set in. Throughout the summer we had made friends with several dorymen and other small-boat fishermen, and most had thrown in the towel and returned to their "regular" or "winter jobs." It was a weird sense of separation, as they returned to their alternate universes of working in chemistry labs, wiring houses, filling prescriptions, deckhanding on crab boats, driving trucks, and teaching high school biology. Fusing with this sense of finality were the soundscapes of the autumnal pop charts. Carlos Santana's searing guitar solo on the band's version of "She's Not There," Carly Simon's power ballad "Nobody Does it Better," and the melancholy hit "Telephone Line" by the Electric Light Orchestra became the bellwether of the changing season.

Withdrawal symptoms hit harder in the fall and winter. My mind was adrift. Instead of dialing in on mitosis and meiosis in biology and crafting composition skills in my English classes, I swung my course to gear setups and boat designs. Gazing through the rain-splattered school windows while punching keys monotonously in typing class on dark, stormy days, I would envision what the ocean conditions were like in the places I had spent so much time a few months beforehand. The same mental picture surfaced when I spun Pink Floyd's *The Dark Side of the Moon* LP. Its moody tones instantly spurred images of the ocean in the deteriorating fall weather.

To help cure the offseason blues, my father and I spent many an hour strategizing on how we could significantly improve our catch in the 1978 season. We continued to discuss trolling speeds, gear setups, and the best fishing grounds. We wondered where our fishing friends were, what they were doing, and whether we would ever see them again. We even made the two-hour drive to Newport's bay-front. We walked the lonely and often drizzle-soaked docks, and meandered through the quiet gear store to buy some gear just to get a fix until the real season arrived. During those months of longing and planning, my father financed a new 70-horsepower outboard engine. We knew it would save us a lot of time and energy, which we hoped would translate into greater catches. To top that off, he scored a used LORAN, which was about the size of a toaster oven. With our arsenal of new gear, equipment, strategies, and optimism, we couldn't wait to put it all into action.

CHAPTER 3

SEASON 2

SECOND WIND

1978 Setlist

Alan Parsons Project *Pyramid*
Billy Joel *The Stranger*
Jackson Browne *Running on Empty*
Steely Dan *Aja*
Wings *London Town*

Despite the hardships many fishermen encountered in 1977, the Port Dock was bustling in the springtime as skippers and crewmen readied their crafts for a new start. We felt that air of resilience as well and our boat was shipshape by May. The *Carolyn Kay* was once again parked at the B Dock, and everything seemed just right. Al was already telling us about his dinner menu, the Rozeski's were back aboard the *Pisces II,* and we were getting acquainted with other members of the fleet, including Tom. Tom was a free-spirited, hard-working guy who showed up with his dory in 1978 full of worldly experiences. He was a teacher, trapper, and traveler, and was always seeking a venture that was "profitable," a word he often brought up in conversation. His dory, the

Honyok, was parked just a few slips away from us. Although a bit worn, his craft was plenty seaworthy and a good fish catcher. Something that set Tom apart from other dorymen were the incredulous predicaments that befell him during the summer of 1978.

Adding to the rejuvenated spirit, fresh tunes from Billy Joel, Jackson Browne, and Paul McCartney swirled on the airwaves and echoed about everywhere you went. Each of these masterpieces naturally seemed to complement the buzz in the air. I was beginning to realize there was a strong music-ocean connection that would stick with me for the rest of my life.

Amongst all the pre-season bliss, the fish processors threw a wrench into the works by offering a very low price per pound for coho. There was a strong fishermen's association, and the consensus was that there was going to be a strike coastwide. Thus, it meant instead of opening up the season on a very calm ocean on the 15th, we would be "on the beach," a phrase that meant stuck on shore, waiting for the association's reps and processors to agree on a fair price. In what was like a scene from a movie, we found ourselves hovering on the periphery of a parking lot meeting where the fishermen were assembled and listening to the association president, who was standing in a pickup bed, proclaiming there would be no backing down. Dad had joined the association over the winter and we even had a decal on our boat to prove it. The upside for us was that the strike allowed us to work out a few bugs in the operation of the newly installed LORAN, which required some voodoo to get an accurate fix on a location.

On June 17th under a clear sky, a gentle swell, and light winds, our second season commenced. The short-lived strike had come to an end as a fair price had been agreed upon. Absent from our menu was some of the ghastly looking gear that repulsed salmon the year before. In addition to the ever-popular T-13, our new lineup also included hoochies with cool nicknames such as the PC Special, Alligator,

Rainbow, and Cop Car. The tantalizing pink egg wobbler spoons with the black spots from our first year earned a starting spot on our wires as well. For king salmon, we entrusted the Little Joe 120 plug and some other Tomic-brand plugs to carry out their duties down deep.

"Holy cow, Ter! This new engine zips. Feel how the bow comes up on a nice plane. We'll have our gear in the water in no time," Dad remarked over the engine's revving tones. "We've got a perfect ocean today. Are you ready to throw 'em over both shoulders?"

I gave him the thumbs up sign, and soon we were tossing silvers aboard. The first day was a success and we hauled in 24 coho, which netted us $114.00.

We returned to our trailer that evening pretty hyped up with such a promising start, but our fortunes were short-lived. The next dozen days left us either stuck on the beach, fishing snotty oceans, or catching just a handful of fish. Fortunately, the lackluster start changed for the better on June 30th.

While fishing offshore of Beaver Creek, which is a beautiful non-tidally influenced waterway that shallowly bleeds into the sea, we trolled the 30-fathom line in calm seas under a partly cloudy sky. The silvers were biting in spurts and we pulled in 20 for the day. Better yet were the two large chinooks that we boated that each weighed in at 15 pounds after being dressed out. We had started running hoochie-flasher rigs down deep, and it paid off.

The highlight of that day though was our first halibut. The 30-fathom line was not known as the halibut hotspot as the prized flatfish were more commonly found several miles offshore at The Rockpile, The High Spot, and the Heceta Banks. Nevertheless, one of our deep springs started bouncing and stretching, but as it stretched out in chinook-like gyrations, there were some weird vibrations mixed in.

"Dad. Check out my deep spring. Something big is down there!" I shouted.

"It could be a big king but look at how it's vibrating. I'm

wondering if we have a blue shark?" Dad wondered.

"Man, this thing is pumping on the davit hard," I reported.

"Let me know how I can help," Dad said as he kept the boat on a steady course.

When the clip broke the water's surface we noticed the monofilament line was pointed straight down, in contrast to dancing around in every conceivable direction with a coho going berserk or with a chinook sweeping the taut line aggressively at an angle perpendicular to the hull of the boat. Pulling hand over hand I yarded up the line and shouted out, "Dad, it's a halibut!"

"Hold on, Ter. I'll get the shark hook rig and I'll help you out."

"Alright, Dad, here it comes. When it gets to the surface let's both gaff it and haul aboard."

As we were about to plop it on the deck, we both were doing a mental download of the halibut stories that we had heard from other fishermen, which included protocol involving shotguns, harpoons, shark hooks, and ropes. Broken arms and legs and drowned fishermen were horror stories that also went along with tales of large barn doors, as the big ones were sometimes called. It turned out that the flatfish was in the 30-pound range, but it wasn't an old-man-of-the-sea moment. It did generate an explosion of activity when it hit the deck, though.

"Whoa, its tail is going crazy. Hand me the fish bopper!" I hollered.

"Careful, Ter, you don't want it to whack your hand." Dad advised.

I commenced beating its tail madly as I had visions of it shattering every bone in my body. When it was obvious that I was wasting my time, I just bopped it on the head and that pretty much ended the drama on the deck. Even though it was an overreaction on our part, that fish got the adrenaline pumping big time as it helped make for a nice payday. This all took place before there were more restrictive seasons, so any legal-sized halibut could be retained and sold. We still really wanted to use that shark hook for something, so we put it in action for a nice photo op.

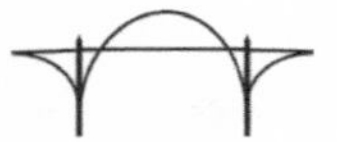

The next 40 days could best be described as scratch fishing, a common industry term that means fishing is at a slow or moderate rate and you're using a lot of ingenuity and effort to catch each one. We scratched like crazy and used every technique possible in our fishing toolkit to get fish on our hooks. Coho catches ranged from just a few fish to about 30 per day. Chinooks were still coming aboard in sparse numbers but up from our first year. We constantly ran the gear, adjusted trolling speeds, made erratic turns, you name it. Gear checking was easier said than done when you were hand-cranking thirty-pound lead weights 150 to 250 feet with resistance up and down all day. Since we were cranking our own sides of the boat, it felt like we would look like hermit crabs by the end of the season. There were many times we'd eye the hydraulic gurdy guys with more than an ounce of envy.

There was a windy day at the dock in early August where I was goofing around and caught some small shiner perch on a rod and reel. Herring was the whole bait of choice for salmon trollers, not shiners, but I saved a few and put them on rock salt for preservation.

"Hey, Dad. I'm going to rig one of these shiners on the meat line tomorrow just for an experiment."

"Oh, okay. Sure you can give it a try..." Dad chuckled. I could tell my dad didn't think there was a snowball's chance in hell that it would be successful, but I was happy he gave me the green light nonetheless.

The next morning I was very anxious to get the deep and float lines set so that I could rig up my grand experiment. I knew the odds were slim of catching a fish as I lowered the line off the stern. With the aid of the foamy, churning prop wash, the shiny, salt-dried baitfish weaved and swirled with a satisfying wounded-like motion. After trolling for about half an hour, I made my way aft to check the extra line and my eyes nearly popped out of their sockets.

"Ohhhh geez! Check it out! The meat line is stretched out. Something's on there," I yelled above the drone of the outboard motor.

"No kidding?" Dad said, a bit bewildered.

"It's tugging like a big fish. Look, it's starting to veer to the side. It's a big king. My shiner rig worked," I triumphantly exclaimed as my voice wavered between adolescence and adulthood.

I tussled with the big king and eventually plopped it in the fish box.

"Got it. Yes! That was so awesome!" I proclaimed with a fist pump.

"I'll be darned...Way to go!" Dad said.

Maybe I should have left well-enough alone, but I had to try again. My shiner rigs remained untouched the rest of the day, but nothing could take away the satisfaction of having my little scheme pay big dividends.

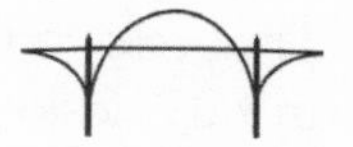

One of our main goals of the season was to improve our king catch. We were making some progress, but we still had a long way to go. On August 9th we ventured out 14 miles to the legendary Rockpile to chase a rumored congregation of kings. Our enthusiasm was short lived though. The trip left us demoralized by moderate swells, a nasty chop, 100-foot visibility fog, and no big ones for eight hours of misery. Feeling downcast and in an effort to regroup, we went down to the boat after dinner to try to glean some intel and prep the gear for the next day. A fellow doryman named Bob had some success catching some big kings in the same area and shared that all his fish were on whole herring rigs. Filled with hope, we re-rigged all of our gear before sundown and prepared to rise early.

A greasy-slick ocean greeted us on our morning commute. With barely any wave action, we zipped back to where we left off the day before. An hour later we merged with the offshore flotilla on a small area of aquatic real estate. We were totally dialed in on landing some smileys as we deployed our new armaments below the surface. Fishermen often referred to them as "smileys" because their value made you smile. As fast as you could say Jack Robinson, Dad's port deep spring sprung to life.

"Whoa, I got one pounding my deep, Terry. Look at that fish hammer that spring!" Dad announced. Then while cranking up his line from the deep water, he turned and met me with a sneaky grin, "We're in for a big day. I can just feel it."

Soon after Dad plopped a large king in the box, the cowbell on my deep spring started clanging aggressively as the spring stretched in helter-skelter fashion. "Get your side back down quick, I got another good one pounding down deep," I urged him. In ten more minutes, we had two large kings in the boat. It was evident that our effort and resilience was paying dividends. "That trip to the docks last evening sure as heck paid off, didn't it?" asked Dad. "Ready for some more action? Let's head back through that spot. Did you write the LORAN numbers down?"

"Yep, got 'em right here. Let's make a turn after we pass this troller and have a repeat performance," I responded.

Even though we lost a few that day, our final king tally was nine. Seeing the money fish come aboard, we put away most of the coho gear in favor of targeting the big ones. While our tally that day wasn't off the charts, we felt we had earned some fishing cred among our peers.

A thin veil of fog slowly drifted in around midday and added to the mystique of the day. By late afternoon the fog bank was becoming thicker and the fish went off the bite for a couple hours. With a full one-hour trek home ahead of us, we decided to put the gear in the boat while there was still some visibility.

About 20 minutes into our departure, we noticed a small troller with one pole up and the other down, which was a signal that the vessel was broken down. With the water being so incredibly calm, we motored alongside and chatted with two guys on board who said that their battery had died. Fortunately for them, we had an extra battery, so we were able to get close enough to loan them our spare. Even though they were able to fire up their engine, their alternator was failing. We had notified the Coast Guard of the situation, and they instructed us to escort them to the buoy line for a rendezvous with one of their lifeboats. While our first priority was to help the fishermen in distress, the downside was that the small troller was agonizingly slow. As a result, the one-hour trek became two and the waning light began to weigh on our minds.

After a successful hand-off to the men in blue, we needed to act fast as we had never navigated back to port in total darkness.

"Okay, we need to get in quick before it's pitch black. The course we have penciled in our chart book will take us straight through the jetties from the Whistler," I read aloud. "Our LORAN reading is right on the spot."

"Alright, Ter, keep your eyes peeled for the green and red cans and their lights in the buoy line. If we're between them, we'll split right between the jetties and be in." Dad instructed.

Like we had done several times before with good visibility, we nailed the foggy crossing with precision.

"There they are, Dad. I can see the silhouettes of the jetties on each side of us," I shouted as we gave each other a quick high-five.

Perhaps as some kind of award for our navigational performance, when we emerged from the fog we were greeted by a brilliant extravaganza of lights on the Yaquina

Bay Bridge and the illuminated backdrop of the Newport bayfront. It had the feeling of when Dorothy and her friends finally arrived in Oz and stood amazed at the Emerald City's splendor. All day long I had songs from the new Alan Parsons Project album *Pyramid* playing in my head. The LP's atmospheric tones fused intricately with the harbor's ethereal misty splendor, making the experience all the more magnificent.

With great gusto, we delivered our catch, docked the boat, and stopped at the bayfront diner to celebrate our epic adventure. Putting some kings into the box added a few extra skips to our steps. Before inhaling my well-earned greasy burger and fries, a call home to Mom was a priority. As always, her genuine enthusiasm about our adventuring put even a wider smile on my face as I giddily recounted our foggy quest over drenching restaurant chatter in the background.

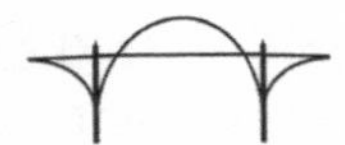

Still racing with adrenaline, we eagerly charged out the next morning to the same locale with plans to blow the roof off the previous day's score. Instead of a blow, it was more like a puff, and the routine settled back into very ordinary scratch fishing. Fortunately, we had Tom as a dory fishing friend, and his capers were anything but ordinary. The wind was light with gentle swells and clear skies. With just a fish coming aboard now and then, Dad decided to hail Tom on the CB to see if he had any action going on. "*Honyok. Honyok.* Tom, are you busy?"

There were a few minutes with no response before suddenly, Tom burst through the airwaves with a frantic reply, "*Carolyn Kay,* Bruce, this is *Honyok.*"

"Hey, Tom. Just wondering how the fish catching is going. It has slowed here."

"Oh wow…! I just had a battle with a huge halibut,

Bruce. I mean, this thing was gigantic. It was moving my whole deep line around like a toy and pounding the davit. I was able to get a good look at it before it finally broke off," he said, hyperventilating. "That was a monster fish. I haven't even checked my other lines to see if I caught any salmon in a while."

"Wow. Sorry to hear that you lost that one. I can't wait to hear more about that at the dock, Tom. Alright, I'll let you go to get your gear in the water. Talk to you later. *Carolyn Kay*, out."

A few hours after Tom's halibut hullabaloo, Dad decided to give Tom another shout on the CB to check on his general welfare and to see if he ever found any more fish.

"*Honyok, Honyok*, this is the *Carolyn Kay*, Tom, you busy?" Dad transmitted.

"Hey Bruce!" Tom replied in an exasperated voice again. "I just had a huge shark on!" Taking a breath he continued, "My starboard float line looked like it had a salmon on it. I was about to bring it in when the whole float bag started traveling across my wake in front of the port float, and it kept going. That's when I saw its huge fin. It happened so fast. It traveled all the way to the port side so far, that the line's stainless cable crossed my body and pinned me to the console on my neck! I was watching all this happen and the big thing was practically strangling me! I could see enough of the shark to notice the cable was wrapped around it. It actually started rocking the boat and was scaring the daylights out of me. It bent my davit and I was worried I was going to capsize, but then, all of sudden the cable broke and it was gone. I've never seen anything like it." Needless to say, Tom's fishing day was done. Aside from a little bit of neck abrasion and a very elevated heart rate, he was okay, and he just planned to put his pulverized gear in the boat and sort it out later.

For those who might have thought he was telling a lofty fish tale, there was plenty of evidence of the cartilaginous monster's destruction of Tom's rigging. His normally twelve-inch, tightly wound port float spring, which took some might to pull apart using both hands, was stretched out about six feet. For comparison's sake, imagine stretching out the spring in a ball-point pen as far as you can. The 1½—inch diameter galvanized davit was indeed bent 90 degrees, much like you could do to a pipe cleaner. Back at B Dock, Tom recounted his tale with the same exuberance as he did during our radio call. Even though he had some repairs and a mess to clean up, we all joked about what possibly could have been the local news headline: *"Dory Fisherman Strangled By Shark!"*

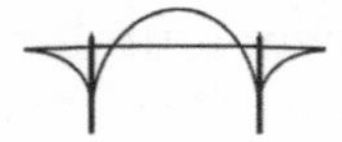

Just like the end of the 1977 season, I was keeping a close eye on the uptown bank readerboard as it tormented me with mid to late-August dates, signaling the imminent return to school. Several days following Tom's escapades with sea leviathans, we embarked on our last sojourn of the regular season. It got off to a blazing start as a king jolted and pumped the port deep spring right after the gear was set. A few minutes later we had a 25-pound chinook in the box before the sun had popped up above the Coast Range. Aside from a few more big late-season silvers, the rest of the day was a quiet finale. A sputtering engine at midday rang ominously like a tolling bell and it was our cue to pull the gear early before ending the season with a breakdown.

Like the flick of a switch, I was back in academia for my junior year. With two season's experience under my belt, I was better prepared for the culture shock that inevitably ensued. My basketball career came to an abrupt end after not making the final cut at tryouts. It was a consequence of fishing all summer and missing hours of valuable Summer League court time. To fill the space, I got a job at KFC as a fry cook. Even though I never did unlock the secrets to their secret recipe, I became adept at their systems much like working on deck. It was a good gig and getting to know a lot of cute girls made it a win.

Our attempts to fish weekends in September for the chinook-only season were met with mostly dismal weather. The big news that month was a storm that surprised a fleet of tuna fishermen far offshore. Sources for marine weather forecasts paled in comparison to what is available today. Caught off guard, at least eight boats sank and many others were in distress. The Coast Guard kept busy with rescues and lowering extra bilge pumps from helicopters to boats taking on a lot of water.

On the last September weekend we struck up a conversation with a doryman who had switched to fishing for albacore tuna. A big school of albies had swung in very close to shore with the warmer water. Just as I was getting back into my routine, this guy started talking about loading his boat up with "bug-eyes," as some called them. My acclimation to Valley life spun backward, knowing that if it were two years in the future, I would be hoisting albacore aboard instead of packing books around or deep-frying chicken wings. A few weeks later, we pulled our boat and put it away for a well-earned winter slumber. The good news was that we had somehow made enough money to keep the operation afloat. Dad and I would be blessed with another winter of sharing memories and full of hope, and we would strategize for an epic 1979 season.

CHAPTER 4

SEASON 3

A BLESSING IN DISGUISE

1979 Setlist
Boston *Don't Look Back*
Styx *Equinox/Pieces of Eight*
Supertramp *Breakfast in America*

Some things that happen are a blessing in disguise. That was certainly true in the spring of 1979. Flowers were blooming in the Willamette Valley after a wet and gray winter, and so was our enthusiasm for the upcoming dory fishing season. In just two seasons, the fishing culture had woven itself into our DNA. It felt like we had been entwined in the industry much longer than we actually had. Amid the euphoria, a watershed moment during Spring Break in our living room with my parents made my head spin.

"Hey, Terry, do you have a moment? We want to discuss something with you about the upcoming fishing season," Dad seriously asked.

"Sure...," I answered, hesitantly.

Ruminations ran rampant in my brain for a few seconds as I took a seat on the couch. *"Well, this is unusual. Mom is sticking around for boat talk, which isn't a good sign. Dang, I hope we don't have to sell the boat,"* I overthought. Dad's next question floored me.

"How would you feel about fishing the dory by yourself?" Dad asked his 16-year-old son who had never fished solo before.

Feeling relieved that fishing was still in our future, I shifted to my reply. "Seriously? I'm not sure. I've never done it. Where are you going to be if I'm fishing the boat myself?" I asked, a bit baffled.

"Well, I connected with this guy from Depoe Bay who has a 32-foot troller. He offered to lease the boat to me. I've mulled this over a lot and talked to your mom about it. If you are comfortable with this, you could fish the dory and I would fish the troller. To efficiently fish the dory alone you would need hydraulics to run the gear, so I'm already looking into that."

Talk about tying your brain in a granny knot. I wasn't sure what to do or what to say. I loved being part of the whole dory scene, and fishing together with Dad. Operating with two boats just didn't make much sense. Dad was pretty serious about this though, and he even got Mom on board, which alone, blew me away.

"Okay, so where's this boat? What's the situation?" I asked two of a thousand questions swirling in my head.

"It's up in Portland right now in a boat yard near the airport along the Columbia River. It needs some work. I'm planning on going up on weekends to work on it. The owner is getting the engine repaired, so I'll be in touch with him on that. The plan is to have it ready on Memorial Day weekend and then run it down the Columbia to Astoria and along the coast to Newport," Dad spilled.

"Your dad feels like it's time to move to a larger boat," Mom interjected.

"I don't see how we can get two boats ready, Dad. How are we going to have time to do that?" I assertively asked.

"Actually, our dory is in good condition and doesn't need as much maintenance as last year. I have already looked into hydraulics and know how to set it up. I'm confident we can have both boats ready before the coho season starts."

I had a lot of doubts, but I decided to go along for the ride on this grandiose scheme. As fast as a big king can bust a 60-pound leader, we began to prep both boats. Fortunately, the work we did here and there over the winter on our dory really did help carve out some time to begin work on the troller named *Sea Fervor*.

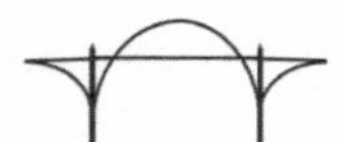

Upon arrival at the Portland drydock we were met with an unpleasant surprise. It didn't take long to realize that the boat needed a major dose of TLC. The rusty diesel engine looked like a toy that a toddler took apart, and the pilot house was a dumpster fire with dog food, mold, and other garbage all over the cabin deck. Some serious caulking was needed in the seams of the hull's planking and paint was peeling about everywhere you looked. The condition of the boat didn't exactly scream confidence that we would ever survive the supposed voyage to Newport. Dad remained upbeat though, at least outwardly, while I became more skeptical with every visit. If anything, the boat was giving me a fever instead of a fervor.

By the time June rolled around, progress on the *Sea Fervor* project was moving at a snail's pace. The anticipated launch date had already come and gone, and nothing had progressed on the engine repair. Something was definitely rotten in the state of Oregon. Dad had arranged to meet up face to face with the boat owner to get a progress report on the engine and discuss other details. The parking lot chat was brief. The owner mentioned something about an engine part not being ready yet, and that was about it.

I didn't hesitate to mince words. "Something's not right here. We're supposed to already have this boat in the water, and the guy seemed like he didn't even have a plan. I think we should drop this deal and just fish our dory," I pleaded. My dad's optimism about the whole deal had started to wane as well. He didn't say much about my proposal.

Later that week Dad decided enough was enough and worked out a settlement deal with the owner, who had strung us along for whatever reason. This brought a huge sigh of relief as we could refocus our energy on the upcoming season with a single boat, outfitted this time with rotator-cuff saving hydraulic gurdies.

The season of 1979 will be remembered as much for state and local groups expressing concerns about the sustainability of the salmon runs as it was for the fishing itself. The projected numbers of returning wild, or native salmon in certain rivers were low. Adding to that, Native American tribes expressed concern about tribal rights for salmon in certain locations throughout the Pacific Northwest. As all the anxieties and data congealed, the all-species season opening was moved to July 1st instead of the traditional June 15th to protect salmon runs. With all our spring season drama still settling, this gave us a little wiggle room to work the bugs out of our new hydraulic system. Along with the realignment of the stars, the melodic, progressive-pop sounds of Supertramp's *Breakfast in America* LP were rocking the charts. They were a perfect match with the coastal ambience and were adding an upbeat tone to the season's new direction.

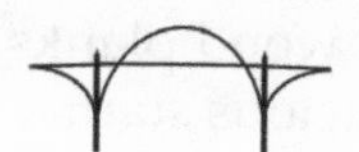

The opening day forecast wasn't very rosy. We set our alarm anyway, but woke up to pouring rain, blustery winds, and a whistle buoy that was hooting like an owl during a full moon. It was always a bad sign when trailer curtains blew horizontally while it was still dark outside. Snotty weather morning wake ups followed a certain ritual. We'd get dressed and drive across the bridge to a landmark called

Chicken Point. This is a state park by the Yaquina Bay Bridge that has a nice viewpoint of the Yaquina Bay jetties, bar, and ocean. The name Chicken Point is derived from fishermen who were too chicken to go out to sea and would go there instead and make up excuses to stay in port. Funny thing was, most everyone from novices to veterans went there now and then. After a stop at the Point, we would go down to the docks, check the boat, maybe chat with someone, and get breakfast. Then it would be a very long day from there if we didn't choose to go back to the Valley for a day or two. A nap, a dive into a good book, and perhaps cooking up some fresh fish likely filled out the rest of the day.

On the first day of July we followed our rainy-day protocol and made all the usual morning rounds. Around 7:00 AM we made our way back to the trailer with the weather still in its unrelenting state. Upon entering I did a little skip and jump onto my bunk and the whole thing collapsed. You could hear the wooden supports crack like a tree hit by lightning.

"Oh no," I yelled out. "I just collapsed my bed frame. Did you hear that crack?"

"You must have eaten too many pancakes," Dad joked. "Well...we have something to do now although I'm not sure what's open since it is a Sunday."

Many stores were closed on Sundays, including the local hardware store. We made a trip to one of the bait and tackle shops on the bayfront and fortunately the owner had some nails, screws, and a few wood planks to make an adequate repair. It was an inauspicious start.

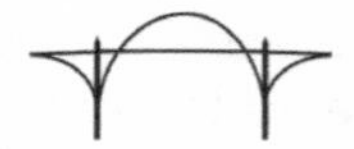

As luck would have it, the weather improved the next day, albeit on an ocean with some big leftover swells from the wet and blustery low. The fishing wasn't great, but at least the price for silvers was an impressive $2.23 a pound, which was about a dollar more than we were used to.

The third day of the season brought an interesting twist. The hydraulic setup we installed wasn't working out so well. The Briggs and Stratton engine that provided power to the hydraulic pump was incredibly loud. It was like mowing a lawn on the deck of the boat. We tried several ways to muffle the sound, but none of our solutions spared our eardrums. A slipping belt on the hydraulic pump was a reoccurring issue, too, and it caused us to lose fishing time trying to troubleshoot it. Eventually, after getting very frustrated with the noise and mechanical issues, we made a little trip up to the bow storage and pulled out the hand cranks that we kept on board. We rigged those old faithful devices while still on the water and used them for the rest of the day. We ended up with a decent catch and it just felt right to be fishing that way.

The next day brought a nasty ocean, and we decided then and there to sell the hydraulics and go back to hand cranking. This was unheard of, but in our case, it turned out to be a good move. It was a crazy full circle we traveled in five short months, resulting with Dad and me on the dory hand-cranking away again in paradise.

Big swells and scratch fishing defined the morning of July 5th. As the day progressed, the fishing perked up. A few big chinooks and several fat silvers at a record-setting high price yielded over $350, which was our largest single-day paycheck. The day was full of special effects. We hooked a huge fish that had to be a chinook that shook and throttled the port davit that supported the trolling wire. Unfortunately, it bent the hook out straight. The springs were jolted again by two very big out-of-season halibut that we released when brought to the surface. Later in the day, we were treated to our second basking shark sighting off our stern beyond our float bags. The best news of the day though was learning from the workers at the fish company and the talk on the radio that we were one of the top producing boats. For the first time, fishermen were asking us for advice.

It was nearly a perfect day, but I managed to spoil that at the gas dock. Upon our approach to the dock I was handed a very short rope to tie up the boat. I heroically grabbed the rope, jumped from the boat to the dock, and then realized I was poised on the edge of the dock at a 45-degree angle over the water. Gravity prevailed and I plunged into the bay. Of course, it seemed like nearly everyone we ever knew, including the cute gas dock girl, happened to witness my spectacle as I crawled like a wet seal on the pier. I just muttered to myself, "way to go, Terry," and tried to brush it off as no big deal. Of course, the next morning several fellow small-boat fishermen made sure to recount the episode for all to hear on the CB radio.

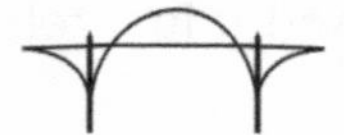

By our third season, Dad and I had developed our system that was a fine-tuned machine. When there was a problem on board, most times we knew the right steps to take action and what our roles were to be. We were starting to develop our own philosophies and techniques though. Sometimes conflict would ensue and would go down something like this:

"I think we should steer west out to 35 fathoms. I heard the guys on the radio fishing outside us all had lines going with fish," I would state.

"We ought to tack 10 mikes south," Dad would counter. Mikes, which stood for microseconds or millionths of second, were a unit of measurement on the numerical read-out on a LORAN. "There were some fish there an hour ago."

From there, the silent course corrections would commence. I would steer west, then he would reach back and adjust the wheel to the south as he pulled his gear. It would go back and forth until we either caught fish or one of us relented. The same thing happened with fishing gear and trolling speeds. It sucked to get in an argument on a small boat at sea as there wasn't anywhere to go. Like any good team, we had our "creative differences," but the more time we spent in close proximity, the more we learned to respect each other and roll with the tensions that arose now and then.

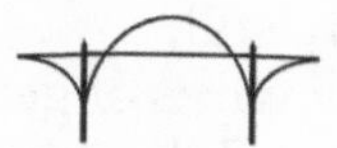

After two-and-a-half seasons, we had already seen our share of what the wind could do. One midsummer morning delivered the most out-of-the-ordinary wind encounter we ever experienced. The sky was overcast and we were greeted by one of the flattest oceans you could find. It was like a millpond. Being it was a Saturday, the sport fleet boaters had arrived en masse from every nook and cranny.

"Holy cow, Ter. Look at all the sport boats pouring out of the jaws today," Dad observed. Keep an eye out for some of these boats cutting in front of you. Some of these guys have no clue of what they're doing."

They were indeed pouring out from the jetties like lava from a volcano and subsequently were plunking their gear down right out past the buoys and transforming the entry to the port into a clogged artery. The word was out about a large school of coho that had been parked out front of port and was generating some red-hot fishing.

"Let's head out a few more fathoms than the puker fleet before dropping our gear, Dad. It's like a traffic jam here."

"Good idea. We would be dodging boats left and right," Dad agreed.

Some of the weekend warriors, also known as "pukers," "pilgrims," or the "Tupperware fleet," had very little maritime common sense evidenced by their poor navigational and decision-making skills. It was comical sometimes when we caught a fish and one of these boats would dart in behind us right in our wake as if we had a huge school of fish following our boat. Sometimes their gear would get tangled up in ours as a consequence of invading our bubble.

"How does the 27-fathom line sound to drop the gear? We're out of the main mass of the fleet, although it looks like there are some more coming this way," I inquired.

"Sounds good. I have a good feeling there's a lot of fish still here, so we better get the gear in the water," Dad agreed as the air remained eerily still.

We dropped in a few wires of gear while a number of boats populated our space. Like it had been for the past several mornings, silvers started slamming the gear hard.

"Hey, I have fish climbing on this wire going down. There are at least two, oh, there's another… and, whoa, another hit. I think there's at least four on my side!" I proclaimed.

"Okay, get yours set and take the wheel while I get mine down. They're smacking mine, too, Ter. Once I get mine down, go ahead and pull yours. We're going to load the boat today."

There were indeed four fish hooked on my side's gear, plus two more. With a half a dozen in the box, I started to send my gear back down for another serving when we were suddenly blindsided by a southerly windstorm. It was as if someone had flicked the switch of a giant fan on high and blasted it directly at us.

"Whoa, what in the…? Where did the wind come from?" I shouted.

"Wow, Ter, look at it. It's already starting to cap out. This is crazy. I don't think we're going to be able to fish this very long. Nuts! There are fish everywhere, too," a disappointed Dad shouted back above the roar and whistles of the sudden southerly blast.

We went from pulling in fish on a mirror-like ocean to having the boat begin to crab sideways over our deep wires with whitecaps instantly frothing as far as the eye could see. A few minutes later it was absolute chaos with boats still attempting to fish and others frantically tossing in their gear and hitting the throttle to get out of dodge. Another six fish were plopped in the box from Dad's side. We tried to fish a little longer, but the wind kept cranking up.

Befuddled and disappointed, we decided to pull gear and get out of the mayhem before it got too nasty, and to avoid a bar that would soon resemble a jammed highway at rush hour. It was a good call. A few hours later, we started hearing some harrowing tales of those who tried to stick it out and got their butts kicked. We had already endured our share of snotty ocean pastings in our short career.

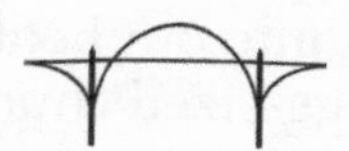

By the time mid-July rolled around, we had nearly 100-day trips to sea since our maiden voyage in 1977. Throughout that span, we were fortunate not to have witnessed or been in close proximity to any harrowing events where boats went down or lives were lost. Our streak ended on a calm July morning while motoring between the docked shrimp boats and the bay's breakwater enroute to another day of fishing.

"Sounds like it's another smooth ocean. Where do you want to drop the gear today?" Dad asked above the puttering outboard.

"Oh, let's head south like we did…" I started to reply before a huge explosion just 40 yards off our starboard near the shoreline reverberated through the port docks.

"A boat blew up! Over there, by that dock! It's on fire!" I pointed out and yelled.

"Hold on, this looks bad, Ter!" Dad said as punched the throttle, bringing the boat to a plane in a no wake zone enroute to a possible rescue or recovery.

As we arrived on scene a minute later, the remains of a burning hull of a small troller belched acrid black smoke that smothered Port Dock 5. Amongst some floating wreckage, a figure's bearded face protruded out of the water several feet away from what was his floating home seconds earlier.

Looking at the man's motionless expression, I was convinced at first that the blast had taken his life, but then saw his eyes shift to assess the situation.

"Dad, there's a guy in the water right over there. It looks like he's alive," I yelled.

"Get ready to help pull him aboard. I'm going to pull alongside," Dad instructed.

Seconds later, a small fiberglass sport boat that was also nearby rushed to the scene at the same time and cut in front of us. In the ensuing rescue, they managed to pull him aboard and then backed into our boat with a crunch. The fender bender took an egg-sized chunk of trim out of our hull. This was of little concern to us at the time given the circumstances as we were focused on saving the man's life. Just after the sport boat crew pulled the bewildered and numb soul on to their craft, the Coast Guard 44-footer's flashing lights and siren broke through the bedlam in their quick response to the scene.

So after a boat blows up and a man is rescued, what are you supposed to do? It didn't sit well to just spin around and head out the jetties as if nothing happened, so we hung around the scene for a bit in the event that the Coasties wanted to talk to a witness or something. Seeing the situation was under control and that we weren't being summoned for any information, what else was there to do but go fishing? Throughout the day our ears were turned to the CB banter for an update. The local news reported that the explosion was caused by a faulty propane stove. Miraculously, the poor guy was not in critical condition and was expected to make a full recovery. The episode was a good reminder how quickly things could turn sour in the industry.

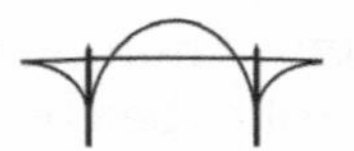

The rest of July was a mix of scratch fishing and some very good coho action as the catch totals ranged from $125 to

$500 a day. This was hands down much more profitable than the past two seasons. We took advantage of the situation and fished whenever we could, even if it meant just a few hours in the morning before the weather went to worms. We were also catching more chinooks, too, but a real banner day for those big ones still eluded us.

Fishing nearly every day was a problem in the laundry department as there was no time to visit a laundromat. It came to a point where our fishing clothes smelled like a fish-processing plant, and the trailer aroma was even more pungent. There were several occasions when I laid out my dirty socks and began culling the two that were the least soiled and damp to wear for the day.

When there was time to run a load of clothes, laundromat trips often were a source of entertainment. On the Newport bayfront, there used to be a laundromat right next to a noisy, gruff tavern. While we never actually ran a load of clothes there, the word was that in order to protect your laundry, you were best off to sit on the washer to keep others' hands out of it. For a short time, there was a laundromat a block away from highway 101 that was an odd duck. The facility was likely used to be a small retail store and was run by an unkempt guy in suspenders. In an effort to "entice" customers, he laid out flattened, opened packages of popular brand potato chips and corn snacks in the window dressing. Awkwardly, while I waited for my clothes to dry, his toddler son ran around the building stark naked while his father was seemingly unphased. The most notable laundry facility was located along the main highway. It was normal by laundromat standards. Once though, according to the story told, a doryman was out of clean clothes during a torrid salmon bite and decided to run a few loads late in the evening. With no one in the facility late that night, he decided to peel off the clothes he was wearing and wash them, too. Of course, he was spotted washing his whites and darks in his skivvies, and the cops paid him a visit. Being it was the 1970s, he was able to explain his way out of any trouble. He happily left later on wearing some clean duds and carrying a basket full of freshly washed duds for the next week or so.

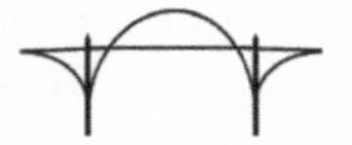

We continued to drill hard for decent wages in the month of August. With the price per pound continuing to hold steady, it was still worth the time and effort to poke your nose out on the ocean for even a few hours on rough days to make $100 to $200. One scratch day was extra special. We had gathered reliable intel the evening before about some chinooks caught close to port and that trolling whole bait was the way to go. Drawing from prior experience, we put in some extra elbow grease before nightfall, and re-rigged our gear for the onslaught we hoped would occur the next morning. It was a quick jaunt out to about 25 fathoms "straight out from the jaws" meaning a straight course out the jetties. Hand cranking was so much easier in shallow water. You could run through the gear fast and have lots of energy to spare. This was one of those days where Dad and I were operating in total congruence with our whole system and our bait rigging strategy.

"Alright, Dad, inch up the RPM's slightly. I want to give this bait a perfect rolling motion," I instructed.

"How's that?" he replied.

"Perfect speed. Take a look at the action on this one."

"Oh, that looks good. I'd devour that if I were a king."

With our tantalizing bait, we pulled a *Carolyn Kay* record of ten chinooks with a 15-pound average. It turned out that we were one of the top chinook producers of the day and were the topic of conversation on the airwaves.

"Hey, Bruce, what secrets do you and Terry have going on over there? Every time I pass by, you both are hoisting a king aboard!" Terry on the *Blue Angel* called out on the CB.

"Yeah, they are highlining today," added Larry on the dory *Ramrod*.

It was a high honor receiving compliments from those two fishermen. If there was an all-star dory team, *Blue Angel* Terry and *Ramrod* Larry would be in the starting lineup. As it happened quite frequently, the fish made a quick exit the next day and the weather deteriorated, but what a great feeling it was to seize the moment!

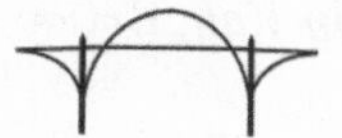

Just like in 1977 and 1978, tell-tale signs of the season winding down started to appear like a slow meticulous drip. Fishermen would decide to hang it up for the year one person at a time and return to their alternate worlds. The docks would start to get a little quieter and fewer boats would leave the harbor. One of those was Tom who announced he was heading back to Utah, which probably meant we would never see him again as he would be off on another venture of some sort.

The waning of the season didn't mean there weren't fish to catch though. The season's final productive coho-catching day was on August 20th. It was one that started slowly, but with the ocean so nice, we felt obligated to make a long day of it. Late in the afternoon, we were working some very active tidal rip lines with the *Blue Angel*. Terry was one of the hardest working dory guys around, and as the years passed by, he became one of our closest fishing friends. He worked as a truck driver for a freight company in Portland and used his vacation time to fish. At times he brought his oldest son, Chris, along with him to be his crew member. Terry loved the Beach Boys and would often have his stereo blasting to create his personal endless summer. He claimed that whenever he played Beach Boys songs, he would catch fish.

"Wow, look at all these rips forming, Ter. There could be a lot of bait fish congregating," Dad pointed out.

"I'll drive right down the rip line, cross over to each side, and do a few sharp turns to make the gear look tantalizing," I replied.

"Oh, I have one on my deep line!" Dad announced as his spring bounced and gyrated in classic coho fashion. "Oh, another climbed on... and there's another! This looks like the hotspot."

"I have a couple on my side bouncing now, too! I'll steer. Go get your fish first, Dad."

"*Carolyn Kay, Carolyn Kay,* Bruce, Terry, you busy?" hailed *Blue Angel* Terry.

"Hey, Terry, what's up?" I answered back.

"You might want to slide this way. I have slips bouncing on both sides, and...there goes another on the float. I put in a Beach Boys tape," Terry announced. The term slips just was another term for silvers or coho, aptly named because they are so slippery and wiggly.

"Thanks, Terry. We have several slips climbing on, too. Okay, let's drill this area. Gotta go pull a side," I said as I ended the conversation.

While we were pumped about the fish catching, we were treated to some spectacular wildlife performances, too. In the rips, where currents were colliding violently below us, the surface was erupting with baitfish like a bubbling cauldron. Mixed in with the feeding frenzy, scores of porpoises were swimming, jumping, and sounding all around us.

"Whoa! Check out those porpoises, Dad! Look at 'em all around the boat!" I shouted.

"Amazing! I sure hope none of them get tangled in the gear though. They are awfully close," Dad said.

Thanks to echolocation, they didn't pose a problem with all the hardware we were dragging through the water. We did hear a few suspicious, un-salmon-like bell clangs on the springs though.

If landing doubles and triples of silvers, and being entertained by the porpoises' swift, agile, and graceful maneuvers wasn't enough, the evening's next special effect amplified the ambiance.

"What in the world...? Is that a school of salmon on the

surface? Look at all of them. There are fins cruising all over that side of the rip!" I proclaimed.

"Drive right by them and let's see if they hit the gear. Get ready!" Dad said with great anticipation.

Upon closer examination as we trolled aside the unphased swimmers, we became less enthusiastic when we noticed the shape of their fins. They weren't salmon—they were salmon-sized jack mackerel. We later confirmed this when we caught one on an egg wobbler spoon. Nevertheless, their presence along with the other sea life, illustrated the density of the rip's ecosystem. Topping off all of the splendor, an epic sunset was posing to cap off the evening.

"Hey, *Blue Angel*, Terry. Are you busy?" Dad transmitted.

"Ya?" answered Terry in his trademark reply.

"Are you still catching? It's starting to taper off here with one now and then. Boy, that was an active rip."

"No kidding. Porpoises, all those mackerel and several handfuls of silvers. It's one now and then, Bruce. I think we're going to start putting the gear in the boat. We don't have much daylight left," Terry said.

"We'll do the same and we'll run in with you, if you don't mind."

"Good idea, Bruce. I think it'll be dark by the time we reach the jaws."

Running in the dark still wasn't part of our usual protocol, but with the evening reaching sensational levels, we bent the rule. Both of our boats passed between the jetties as the last rays of sunlight slipped below the horizon. Dad and I were exuberant as our eyes met the glowing panorama of city light.

"Wow. That's quite a sight, Terry!"

"It's pretty cool. That was the best evening bite we ever had."

"It sure was. We'll remember that one for a long time," Dad affirmed.

Near the end of the season, my Uncle Steve drove from Madras—a Central Oregon town positioned near the desert canyons and the clear-flowing, pristine Deschutes River to join us for a few days. He had tried to fish with us a year earlier, but the screaming northwest winds put the kibosh on that. Steve, who was and still is an optometrist, is an extremely innovative guy who has a wealth of outdoor experience. We were anxious to have him aboard and share a taste of the dory culture.

He was supposed to arrive around sunset, but as the evening wore on, Dad became concerned that he hadn't arrived yet. We didn't have a phone in our trailer so the worry just mounted. A bit later we received a knock on the trailer door from the owner of the trailer park. Dad answered the door and received some evening-changing news.

"Hey, Bruce? Your brother called. He was in an accident. He was hard to understand but he left a number for you to call," the trailer park owner relayed.

Dad used the payphone in the park to return the call and discovered Steve had an encounter with a deer in the road and had gone off an embankment in his tiny Honda Civic on the very curvy Highway 20 between Corvallis and Newport. Amazingly, he dodged the many trees on that embankment and ended up in a patch of blackberries near a creek. Some people who lived nearby heard the commotion and ventured out to check on the situation. They hacked their way through the brambles where they found him and took him into their home. Upon hearing this, my father decided to go to the rescuers' residence and preferred that I stay put until he could figure out what the next steps were.

It turns out that miraculously, he wasn't hurt badly, which was a huge relief after a tense several hours. Steve stayed at his rescuers' home while Dad returned early in the morning to give me the update. He suggested that I fish the boat solo while he helped his brother take care of matters related to the accident.

"I'm going to help Steve tomorrow with his car and take him to Corvallis to get checked out by a doctor. There is really no need for you to come along unless you really want to. Why don't you go ahead and fish the boat yourself tomorrow? It's going to be a flat ocean and you've more or less run the boat yourself at times while I have been napping. I'll make sure you get off to a good start before I hit the road in the morning, and I'll let some of the dory guys know to keep an eye on you."

Relieved that my uncle was going to be fine, I was jazzed with the notion of my first solo run. As I headed out between the jetties that morning, my father watched nervously from atop Chicken Point where he had a good view of my departure. It was a chaotic morning with a hodgepodge of boats pouring out of the jaws at varying velocities creating wakes that intersected and merged. Even though I was white knuckled and was harboring butterflies in my gut, I was also immersed in an endorphin rush. The good vibes came to an abrupt halt when the high-pitched outboard motor's alarm pierced the air on the outbound commute. Much to my father's fears, he watched our boat suddenly throttle back to an idle and noticed the deck light brightly illuminate the boat. Concerned, I scrambled to the stern and hoped it would be a simple fix. Dad just helplessly watched from Chicken Point as I tilted the engine up as the boat was bobbing all over the place from the crisscrossing wakes. Luckily, it was as I suspected. I had run over a patch of seagrass and some of it had wrapped around our outboard's water intake port, causing the engine to overheat. About two minutes later, Dad breathed a sigh of relief as I cleared the intake ports of grass, extinguished the deck light, and headed out to the fishing grounds.

"*Carolyn Kay, Carolyn Kay,* Terry?" Dad hailed.

"Hey Dad."

"What happened back there? You okay?"

I briefed him on the episode and reassured him all was well.

"Alright, be careful and have a great day. I'll give you a shout when I get back in town."

"We'll keep an eye on him for you, Bruce. He'll probably scoop us all today anyway," interjected *Blue Angel* Terry.

It turned out to be a great day for the rookie solo doryman. The ocean was like glass all day long and I put about a dozen late-season silvers in the box. Even better, it was a huge confidence booster knowing that I held my own compared to the other dory guys. This just fueled my ambition to eventually run my own dory.

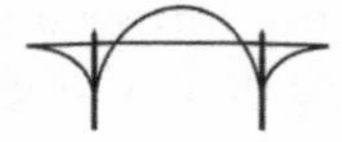

Having been part of the dory scene for three summers, some of the dockside community knew I was approaching my senior year. Their awareness brought about the inevitable bombardment of post-high school questions. "So what are your plans after high school? Are you going to college?" When I said "No," everyone's facial expressions clearly revealed a response that scored about a 3 out of 10 on the future-plan rating scale. I had taken architecture classes for several years and had considered pursuing a career in that field, but my interest started to wane. Between the disconnect with my secondary schooling and my infatuation with the fishing scene, college wasn't even a blip on my radar. I really didn't have a clue of what to do once graduation rolled around other than fish.

Even though the end-of-season blues were tugging at my heart once again, I had a few things to look forward to. A new high school was opening up in Salem for my senior year, so I knew that would provide a dose of renewal. I also finally got my own ride—a 1971 robin-egg blue Datsun pickup purchased with the money I had saved frying up chicken at KFC.

Missing the water on a spectacular sunny September afternoon after I was done with classes, I spontaneously fired up the Datsun for a coastal cruise. Boston's latest album was cranked on high as well as *Equinox* and *Pieces of Eight* by Styx as I glided southbound on Highway 101 toward Newport. The coast weather was in full splendor with warm temps and sunny skies that had a hint of autumnal haze on the horizon. Being back in my element provided some headspace to give thought about the year to come and life beyond graduation. One thing was clear, the fishing scene and coastal culture had captured my heart so much that I could not imagine parting with it. The challenge ahead was to figure out to what extent I wanted it to be part of my life, and how I would make that happen.

CHAPTER 5

SEASON 4

ROLLING WITH THE CHANGES

1980 Setlist

Doobie Brothers *Best of the Doobies*

Supertramp *Crime of the Century*

Jeff Beck *There and Back*

The Eagles *The Long Run*

The Who *Who's Next*

The Kinks *One for the Road*

Yes *Drama*

As the new decade rolled around, Dad began needling me hard about my post-high school trajectory. With college off the plate of options, I had given thought about diving headlong in the fishing industry as a deckhand. This meant finding work on a crab boat from November through at least April. Even though the fishing culture was rushing through my bloodstream, I had some misgivings about going all in as a teenager. It's a tough environment and completely different from day fishing on a dory for salmon. You want to be sure to hook up with a reputable skipper and crew. I had become quite observant of some operations that were sketchy at best and a poor influence for an eighteen-year-old guy. There were no guarantees that I would find a good situation.

On January 23, 1980, I heard Dad gasp and sigh as Jimmy Carter announced the reinstatement of the Selective Service for a military draft registration amidst the tensions between the Soviet Union and Afghanistan. With his anxiety of me potentially being drafted in military service, his future-plan questioning sessions intensified.

One morning soon after President Carter's address, Dad lobbed a lofty loaded question. "Hey, Ter, your mom and I have been talking. What would you think about joining the Coast Guard after high school?" My father and I had marveled at the amazing seamanship and boatmanship skills that the Newport Coast Guard demonstrated daily, whether they were performing rescues or engaging in training. "If the draft gets implemented and you're not in college, you would be amongst the first to be chosen. Enlisting in the Coast Guard would allow you to choose which branch you would like to serve. You would learn all sorts of great seamanship skills and save money for a dory after your four-year tour is complete."

His exhortation backed with laser eye contact sent my head reeling as I didn't see that one coming. "Well, maybe. I haven't ever thought about that. What if I couldn't fish for those four years though?" I questioned.

"If you got stationed along the Oregon Coast, I bet you would be able to squeeze in some dory fishing."

What if I don't though? I thought. This where the rubber was meeting the road—the reality of me transitioning to adulthood.

"You've got a lot of changes in the coming year and you're going to need to make some decisions soon." Dad's forte was to fixate on time-sensitive decisions and he didn't often let go. "You've seen some of the characters on the docks that are deckhands on crab boats. While there are some good boats to work on, you can get mixed up with some tough customers. Think about it. You'll need to decide soon," he emphasized with heavy urgency.

All of Dad's bullet points in his presentation made good sense, but I needed some some time to marinate on that information. My parents had gifted me plans for a 24-foot super dory of my dreams from the same builder as the *Carolyn Kay*. A stable four years of income would certainly help make that dream come true. There were so many facets that brought concern though, most notably, would my fishing career be placed on a four-year hiatus? Would I ever actually resume it? Thoughts of adapting to military life and possibly being stationed many states away percolated in my mind when my head hit the pillow each night. With patience not being my dad's virtue, this just added to my anxiety.

As spring approached, Dad spontaneously asked on several occasions, "Well, have you made your decision yet?" This annoyed the hell out of me and usually ended up in either an argument or at least created some awkward tension since I wasn't sure what to do. My head was reeling with possible scenarios about post-grad options. I'd picture myself around the damp, gray, misty docks in mid-winter as a crabbing deckhand, or working in a slimy, smelly fish-processing plant endlessly fileting bottomfish. Then I'd shift to a scene of seeing myself at a Coast Guard station in some far-away place. More than once, the possibility of our fishing career fading into nothingness during my four-year tour-of-duty crossed my mind.

Even though I wasn't too keen to admit that Dad was right, his assertions had a lot of cred. I knew diving into the year-round fishing scene wasn't for me, at least at eighteen. Something nagged at me about needing a stable foundation. Before Dad could ask again about "my decision," I made up my mind. I would enlist for four years, take the leap of faith that I would get stationed in Oregon. This would allow me to save money for my super dory, and, after my commitment, perhaps take a swing at full-time fishing. After a couple trips to the recruiting office in Eugene, I was all set to report to boot camp in Alameda, California on January 5, 1981. With that weight off my shoulders, I could focus on graduation and the upcoming fishing season, which I was looking forward to more than ever.

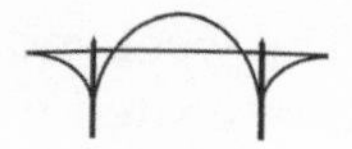

Every winter, the Trollers Association held clinics in the Portland Metro area on weeknights at random pizza parlors for guys like us who needed a fishing fix now and then. There would be gear demonstrations, season regulation updates, and gear raffles. Those sessions were great opportunities to reconnect with our dory friends, make new connections, and learn new strategies. One of our goals was to become more adept at catching chinooks. These gatherings were fuel for some great conversations on the car rides home between Dad and me as we'd engulfed not only slices of pepperoni pizza but whole servings of new information with great enthusiasm. When the Pacific Fisheries Management Council announced the coastwide seasons in the spring, we learned the coho season would start on July 16, two weeks later than the previous year. The chinook-only season would open as usual on May 1, so our game plan was to have the boat ready in May and eagerly put those new tactics to the test.

Spring of 1980 was electric. Sounds from the Eagles new album, *The Long Run*, were permeating the airwaves all across the dial. The buzz at school among my friends and classmates about our fast-approaching graduation was intensifying while Mt. St. Helens, just a few hours drive north from our home, woke from its slumber. It was creating rumblings in the newscasts that echoed from our AM radio in our boat dry storage as we feverishly prepped the *Carolyn Kay*. By May 3, the boat was back at Port Dock 7, this time across the way at the C Dock and ready to put those new chinook tactics to the test.

Something Dad and I had failed to factor in during the winter strategizing sessions was wind—lots of screaming northwest wind. Every weekend in May was filled with wind. We also had something else to deal with—ash! St. Helens blew its top on May 18th and scattered volcanic ash all over the Northwest. The weekend following the eruption, we arrived to find our dory coated with a thick layer of the gritty material. This prompted an unexpected washdown and it wasn't the last time we had to perform the ritual as the restless mountain belched a few more times that year. To add insult to injury, we didn't catch any fish on those cold, bumpy oceans and got tangled up in a crab pot. It was humbling and it became more interesting.

The fish gods and northwesterlies must have been in cahoots in June, too. We had to travel far and take a beating to finally find some kings off of the north end of the Pile. A stiff 12-knot breeze greeted us along with some vicious currents to make fishing 50 fathoms a full-time, two-man show.

Unlike the month of May, we were finally getting a few chinooks.

"Fish!" I yelled above the droning outboard and wind in my ears. "It's another king. Hopefully I can get this one in the box, too. It's a lot of work cranking up this deep. Definitely a good workout." Soon after, it was flopping on the deck.

"That's a nice fish, Ter. Nice job getting it in the boat," Dad complimented. "Wow, it's getting nasty out here. It's tough keeping this boat straight when you pull your gear with all the currents and this northwest blowing. I'm not sure how much longer we're going to be able to stick it out. We have a long trip back to port, too."

After a few more fish and another tack north, the wind really cranked up a level. It was time to put the gear in the boat and get out of dodge.

"Alright, Ter, you have a good course for the trip home?"

"Yeah, I'm good. I think we might get a bit wet with some of the whitecaps hitting us broadside, but we're far enough north not to get beat up too bad," I remarked.

About 15 minutes into our trek, I suddenly pulled the throttle back. "What in the world? Look ahead, Dad, there are branches everywhere."

"Holy cow. Okay, one of us is going to need to stand up in the bow section to be a lookout. We definitely don't want to run over any of this debris." Dad instructed.

"You know what I think this is?" I surmised. "I think it is debris from the Mt. St. Helens eruption. It must have flowed out of the Kalama and Toutle Rivers and down the Columbia. It's probably been floating down the coastline for the past few weeks."

We were faced with having to navigate a labyrinth of detritus in a steady northwester that had the potential to mess up our day. There were hideous tree branches that resembled serpent-like tentacles and occasional boat-puncturing deadhead logs that bobbled vertically between the waves threatening to impale passing vessels.

"Slow down. Turn to the port. There's a big one off to the starboard. Stay clear of that one!" Dad shouted as he took the first lookout watch. "I'm getting drenched up here. I'm going to switch with you in a few minutes," Dad added as we bucked into some big wind chop while trying to steer around St. Helens' landmines.

It took 45 minutes and a few turns each on lookout before we finally cleared the wooded maze unscathed. We had seen the news of the blast and experienced the ash, but our tour of the driftwood helped us realize the gravity of the devastation.

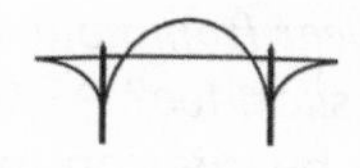

After getting repeatedly pummeled in the chinook-only season, we decided to take a pause until the all-species season started on July 16. There was a newly instituted 15-day moratorium beginning July 1st where no fishing would be allowed. It all had to do with state, federal, and tribal concerns about wild chinook and coho run populations in a number of rivers from Washington to California. It was becoming highly complex and controversial. Like it or not, there wasn't anything we could do about it, so we planned to use the time to make sure the boat was in prime condition and to enjoy some spectacular Valley summer weather.

During the pause, I decided to take a drive down the Southern Oregon Coast to Brookings, which is a stone's throw from the California-Oregon border. My mission was two-fold: enjoy the freedom of cruising 600 miles round trip in my own rig and investigate the fishing amenities in Brookings. Blessed with great weather, my cassette player was cranked and filled my truck cab with the aggressive guitar-driven sounds of The Who and The Kinks, and for a little bit more melody, the Doobie Brothers. Aside from spilling an entire 32-ounce Dr. Pepper on my lap somewhere around Bandon, it was a heavenly, care-free trek along the scenic south coast.

Each year in Brookings there was a special fishery during the first half of November for huge kings that took place right out front of the port. Since I wouldn't be in school, it was something that I wanted to leave open as an option for the fall. Brookings is regarded as one of the safest bar crossings along the Oregon Coast, and it provides quick access to the ocean. While finding my way down to the docks, I happened to drive by the Coast Guard station and noticed a few of the guys out in the parking lot in uniform playing hacky sack. My thoughts instantly shifted from fishing to my impending service to our country. This got me wondering, *What I would be doing a year from now, and where would I be? Would I be playing hacky sack, too?* As the summer wore on, these thoughts weighed heavier on my mind, and with each passing day, I learned to savor what would turn out to be an epic summer.

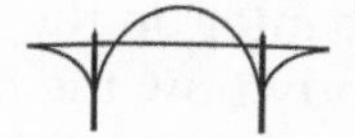

The feeling was electric on the port docks in Newport. Dorymen that we had become acquainted with during our first three years appeared out of the woodwork one-by-one with high spirits and freshly rigged and painted boats. Looking down the row of boats on B Dock and the adjacent A Dock, it was a welcoming site to see the likes of Terry's *Blue Angel,* Larry's *Ramrod,* Randy's *Pineapple,* Wayne on the *Zorba,* Jerry on the *Dory Duz,* and several others poised and ready for action. Fishing with Terry was always a joy. He was quite the strategist who always was upbeat and happy to share valuable fishing intel. We were looking forward to more great adventures on the water with the *Blue Angel.*

Larry was a pharmacist by trade from the Corvallis-Philomath area, which is an hour east of Newport. His boat *Ramrod* was a red dory with blue trim that lived up to its aggressive name. Larry was great to team up with as he was very tactical in fishing an area and working a patch of fish whenever the opportunity presented itself. Eventually, Larry traded his dory stripes for a larger trolling vessel and continued his reputation as skilled fisherman. Sadly, his troller sunk off the coast of California. He had leased out the boat and it was run up against some rocks near the shoreline.

The Newport and Pacific City dory fleets would agree that dory fishing in the 1970s and 1980s would not have been the same without Randy. This skilled doryman and shop teacher from Hawaii fished a yellow with blue trim coho-catching machine aptly named *Pineapple.* Most memorable were his conversations on the CB radio with fellow dorymen. His chart-topper would have been any of the many morning broadcasts about his noodles. Randy always started his mornings off with some ramen, which he typically broke out after he set his gear. It was common knowledge that fish-catching didn't officially start until Randy had his noodles. After many of the dory guys had their gear in the water, banter on the radio would start and someone would ask Randy how the fishing was going. He'd respond with something like, "Nothing in the box, but I haven't had my noodles yet."

Wayne was another doryman with rock star status. He owned the *Zorba,* a blue-trimmed yellow dory that had a small cuddy cabin over its bow and was moored at a marina a mile upriver. He was a high school science teacher and it was always interesting to hear his scientific perspectives. Water temperature was important data in the fishery, as 52 degrees F was the sweet spot for salmon fishing. When the cold northwesterlies would blow for days, the water temperature would plummet. This was great for the sustainability of the salmon stocks as it generated upwelling under the surface and made nutrients for salmon more accessible, but as far as fishing, the salmon would scatter to seek warmer water and fishing was often dismal. Wayne went above and beyond in an effort to determine the water temperatures at different depths. He put on his biologist hat and took the anal temperatures of coho salmon to gather the necessary data about the water temperature at which fish were caught. He later reminisced, "I don't know how accurate it was or if it helped catch more fish, but it gave me something to do on the scratchy days!" Wayne was also a fellow "hand cranker," as he too, had yet to cross over to the hydraulic side of the industry for pulling in gear. Cranking by hand still earned you a badge of honor in the early 1980s. Wayne continued to be a mainstay in the dory fleet up through 1983 and then permanently moved his family and the *Zorba* to southeast Alaska.

Jerry on the *Dory Duz* was a very friendly, even-keeled, clean-cut guy who was known as a highlining doryman. He always seemed to know where to go and could scrape up fish even on the leanest of days. His home port was Pacific

City, but every now and then he would travel down south to join the Newport scene. Interestingly, his boat was named after a minor character in the novel *Catch 22*. To this day, Jerry still fishes for sport offshore of Pacific City and sometimes Randy joins him when he is on the mainland.

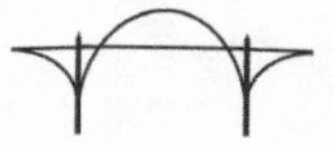

The coho season started with a bang and we put 33 silvers in the box out in deep water on a foggy, windy day on the north end of the Rockpile. Catches thereafter during the first two weeks tapered a bit and averaged around 15 silvers per day. Chinooks were few and far between and the northwest wind was showing its bravado in a big way as cold mornings and hissing whitecaps were the norm in late July.

The 1980 season served up an unexpected arrival. Tom showed up with plans to lease a legendary fish-catching Pacific City dory named *Wonder*, instead of his steadfast craft, the *Honyok*.

"Hey, Tom!" Dad greeted. "Good to see you. We were wondering if we would see you again."

"Yeah, I got the opportunity to lease this boat with hydraulics. It's a real fish catcher in PC. I'm hoping it will be more profitable than my boat," Tom replied.

With Tom back in the fold, it was a guarantee for more camaraderie and adventure. During a coho bite just south of Newport, we discovered that we had left our day's provisions in the car. By early afternoon after eating the leftover bread onboard, we were looking at our bait with hungry eyes. About that time, Tom radioed us to let us know that fishing had hit a lull.

"Hey, Bruce. I'm going to head in for a few hours, get some lunch and rest, and then head back out in the late afternoon for the evening bite. Do you need me to pick up anything?"

Dad and I looked at each other. "Have him get us some

hamburgers, Dad! We can rendezvous on his way back out," I pleaded.

"Hey, Tom, can you pick us up some burgers and we'll touch base with you later. We left our groceries in the car," Dad said.

"You bet. No problem. You want fries with that?" Tom both joked and seriously asked.

When it came time for Tom's burger delivery, there was still a horde of boats fishing and it was like navigating a maze to find us. We never made the meal rendezvous. Much like our first-ever voyage, we ended the day famished. Tom, on the other hand, had one of the better onboard meals of the dory fleet that evening!

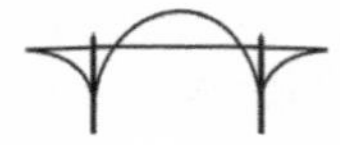

Toward the end of the month, Dad had to go away for a few days for a work conference, so I invited my friend, Greg, to come fish with me while Dad was away. I met Greg when I was in third grade at noon recess. We happened to be among the last few stragglers to finish our lunch that day.

"What do we do with our lunch boxes?" Greg asked, mumbling.

"You're supposed to put them in your class box before going out to recess. I think they took them back to class," I answered, expertly.

"Well, I guess I'll just take it to recess," Greg stated, still mumbling, as he proceeded to carry it around on the playground while we just walked around. The next thing we knew, we were best friends and spent hours playing basketball, board games, having sleepovers, and avidly following the Blazers and Oregon State Beavers basketball teams.

In the summer of 1975, my friends and I noticed he was always tired and had very little motivation. By fall, a doctor's visit revealed the cause of his ongoing fatigue. Greg was diagnosed with leukemia and immediately admitted to the hospital for treatment. This was devastating and we nearly lost him. Greg was a warrior though. He battled the disease into remission a year later, during a time when few in his condition did.

After a healthy, normal tour of high school, he experienced a relapse when his cell counts became abnormal soon after graduation. Once again though, Greg defied the odds and was back in remission by late July. We had tried to have Greg fish with us a year prior, but windy weather squashed that opportunity. With his health improving, he had the green light from his family to give a few days of salmon trolling a whirl. However, when Greg came over, the cruel prevailing northwesterlies had no mercy for even those who endured hardships, and much to our disappointment, we were unable to fish together for a second straight year. It wasn't the last attempt to get Greg out on the water in 1980 though.

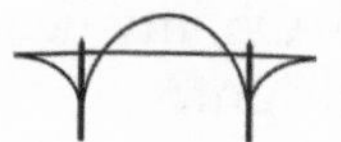

Of course as soon as Greg went home, the weather began to cooperate. Dad and I finally got in a few good days fishing in decent weather for a change. Dad had his share of aches, pains, injuries, and unfortunate events, but he was tougher than nails. I had seen him get nasty knife cuts, stings by jellyfish tentacles on the gear, and endure sciatic nerve pain on windy, choppy days. One incident on a calm, sunny day along the 35-fathom line topped all of those.

"Hey, you pulled three slips off that line, Dad. Nice job. I think we're up to 30 now."

"Yeah, this has been a good run here this afternoon. Once I get this deep back down, let's head back through that spot and see if we can keep this going."

"Sounds like a plan to me," I replied as I kept the boat on a steady southerly course as Dad deployed his gear.

"Ohhh!" Dad cried out while at the same time the hand

gurdy he was cranking downward, which had a brake mechanism, started freewheeling, assisted by a 30-pound lead weight plummeting to the depths. The handle whipped around and nailed Dad square in the forehead and laid him flat on the deck.

"Dad! Dad! Are you okay?" I shouted. No response. "Oh my gosh, Dad!" I thought the impact had killed him on the spot. Several thoughts went through my mind, most notably, "Should I call the Coast Guard? What will I tell Mom? Should I try to revive him?"

Moments later I heard him moan and start to stir as a few bells jingled, signaling fish on. "Dad, talk to me. Are you okay?

"Ohhh. What happened? What's going on?" He asked, dazed.

"The gurdy freewheeled and hit you in the head," I informed him. "I thought it killed you at first. Can you sit up?"

"I think I can get up. Oh, my head hurts. Give me a few minutes. I think I'll be alright."

"Are you sure? I think we need to get you back to shore and see a doctor. I can pull the gear while you rest up in the front."

"No, no. I think I'll be okay. Just give me a sec."

In typical Dad fashion after a near-death experience, he dusted himself off and jumped back into the task on hand. In today's world, he would have been in concussion protocol, but in 1980, he just kept running gear the rest of the day. We pulled about a dozen more fish and finished the day without further incident.

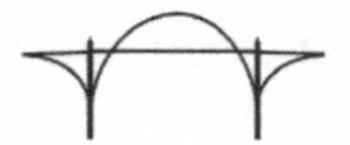

The stars aligned a few weeks later for Greg to get another shot to go fishing. As usual though, on the first day of his visit, the wind unexpectedly was blowing hard at sunrise, making for another day on the docks. Greg was probably wondering if we actually ever really fished and that we just made up all the fishing tales. The next morning everything came up smelling like roses, and we were greeted with a flat ocean and sunny skies. Dad had decided to take a few days off the water, likely and most unselfishly to give Greg and me some space to hang out together. He was always quite perceptive about stuff like that.

"Hey, we finally made it out here! It's flat as a pancake and the forecast is great! I think we'll head out near the Rockpile where the water warms up a bit before we drop gear," I proclaimed.

"This is awesome. Sounds good to me!" Greg replied.

The real estate where we dropped gear just felt incredibly fishy. It was emerald green and there were rips everywhere. In less than five minutes, the bells were clanging on both sides of the boat.

"Whoa! We dropped in on some fish, Greg. Those springs dancing around and bells clanging signal silvers on the lines. If a chinook hits, you'll know the difference with big, long aggressive tugs. Go ahead and take the wheel while I pull the gear. A little later you can pull some fish aboard."

By the end of the day, Greg was running one side of the gear and pulling fish aboard. On top of that, we had one of the top small-boat scores with 29 silvers and 4 big kings. The only thing that went wrong, and it could have gone way, way wrong, was an embarrassing incident at the gas dock. I had pulled the boat's drain plugs while running full throttle in the bay to drain water out of the boat, which is what we did from time to time. The only problem, much to my chagrin, was that I forgot to put them back in.

"Alright, the gas tanks are all full. We can cast now and head to the Port Dock," I said.

"What's with all the water in the back of the boat?" Greg asked.

"Oh, crap! I forgot to put the drain plugs back in! Quick, untie the bow line. I'll get the stern. We're going to head full steam up the bay. You take the helm. We'll go until the water drains out and then I'll put the plugs in! I can't believe I forgot to do that. What an idiot!" I said, being sure to chastise myself for my blunder.

Greg and I fished a second day, but the fishing was notably slower, so we headed in early. He was pretty wiped out from the previous day and from his recovery process. On the final day, he was invited to fish more comfortably on a 26-foot boat owned by our former high school PE teacher and her husband, complete with a warm, dry cabin. It was a blessing to share that experience with Greg as he loved fishing, and it turned out to be even more cherished in the years to come.

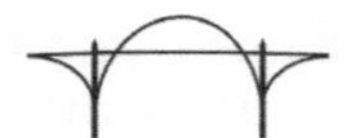

The textbook sales business started pulling Dad away from the water in the latter half of August, so I ended up fishing solo for several days. This came with mixed feelings as I certainly missed the camaraderie and help, but at the same time, it was an opportunity to exercise my independence and face the challenges of fishing by myself.

My summer solo tour began on a foggy morning. I nudged my *Crime of the Century* cassette by Supertramp into the tape deck and made the dark drive to the docks. I was confident in my navigation skills, so I didn't hesitate to set a course on a flat ocean out to the North End of the Rockpile. With the Davies-Hodgson penned melodies spinning on repeat in my head, I cruised at maximum RPMs to the work site. The morning's fishing turned out spotty at best, but I did put a few kings in the box.

About mid-afternoon, I was shaken out of a spring-watching trance as my port deep spring started pounding aggressively. There was little doubt that it was a monster king, and it was more than ready to go head-to-head with me. I suspected it had chomped down on our trusty Little Joe 120 plug. After letting it soak as it was pulsating the metal davit and cable from the depths, I started cranking it up.

"Hang on there big king. Whoa, this is a big pumper," I said aloud to myself as I felt it tug on the gurdy handle.

I brought the spread to the surface and noticed it had indeed taken the plug, which was on a very long leader that allowed for more stretch and shock absorption. The fish in typical chinook fashion veered 90 degrees to the port side and gave me a look like, "I dare you!"

"Alright. Here we go. Come to the boat. Don't go crazy on me. No, no, not toward the prop wash!" I yelled out to the fish. Managing the monofilament in hand-over-hand fashion, I kept it over the side rail and out of the prop. I leaped over the extra gas can and met the fish on the starboard side as we continued our battle.

"Okay, so you want to do battle on the starboard side. That's fine," I continued my dialogue. "Oh, oh, stay away from the prop," I said as I leaped over the gas can again and back to the port side. "Okay, I'm bringing you aboard."

After one more surge, my foe started wearing out. Noticing its pause, I made my move, handlined it to the boat, gaffed it, and plopped it on the deck. It was without a doubt the largest salmon we had ever brought aboard.

"Yes! Oh yeah!" I cried out.

Talk about an endorphin rush. I forgot who I hailed on the CB, but I was so hyped, I had to tell someone, as I was nearly hyperventilating with a soprano voice. With only one deep line in the water during the ensuing battle, the boat had been making several wide circles in some open space away from the other boats. I was literally shaking for several minutes as I put the gear back down. A couple more nice-sized kings came aboard that day, but they were nothing compared to the hog that weighed in dressed out at 29 pounds. The glory concluded that foggy evening when I delivered my catch to the fish company amongst a chorus of oohs and ahhs.

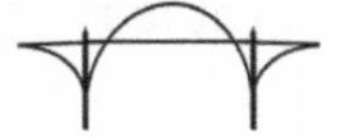

Earlier in the summer, my father crossed paths with a young guy named Brian. Dad introduced us and we became instant friends as we both were obsessed with the whole salmon trolling scene. It turned out Brian and I were the same age and he was from Silverton, Oregon, which is very close to Salem. During his senior year of high school, he purchased a blue 20-foot Harvey dory with a little cabin that covered the bow. Amazingly, he moved to Newport, finished up his coursework while bunking on his dory, and earned his diploma. I was blown away that he pulled this off seemingly with ease. It didn't take long to figure out Brian was one of the most brilliant and innovative people I had ever met.

Brian and I kept in touch throughout the summer, mostly on the docks and CB radio as we both were on the water as much as possible. As more and more fishermen were calling it a season, Brian and I started fishing together more in late August. We worked the water hard to scratch enough fish to make it worthwhile. On one very snotty ocean when few were catching much, we started drilling a spot on the south end of the Rockpile. We caught a dozen or so each, which doesn't seem like much, but it was significantly better than most had been doing. With a small taste of success, we were dialed in on heading to the same spot the next day to pump up our teenage egos a bit more. We doubled our scores from the previous day. It was pretty cool to be a couple of high-liner eighteen-year-olds who were scooping the saltier older men of the small-boat fleet. We'd hear them say on the CB, "I don't have anything going on here, but those two teenagers on dories sure have been catching fish somewhere around the Rockpile."

Unfortunately, those were the last days to write home about for the 1980 season. A few days later while we were fishing in different areas, I overheard Brian on the radio inform another one of his fishing comrades that he cut his hand with a knife and was heading in. It turned out to be a couple of sliced tendons, which abruptly ended his season and earned him a big hermit-crab-claw cast up to his elbow. The remainder of the coho season just paid for the gas.

Despite the lackluster late-season catches, the time on the water was wonderful. It was the beginning of a special slice of time, sort of like my gap year although it just lasted a few months. I used the opportunity to take a deep dive into the catalog of the progressive rock band Yes, which included their newly released *Drama* album. The sea was flat as a countertop and blue sky was abound. To quell the fishing boredom, I made up for my lack of reading in high school and devoured the *Lords of the Ring* trilogy while trolling. I even tried some kite flying, but in a time when I wished for a slight breeze, there were just intermittent puffs of wind.

Fall chinook fishing was as underwhelming as the late-season coho catches. There just weren't enough fish nearshore to make it worthwhile. I needed an excuse to keep the boat in the water and hang out there in the fall. Brian returned to town, complete with his mega-cast, looking for something to do as well. He planned to get a job on the back deck of a crab boat and learn that trade if his hand healed up in time. So, with time to kill, we devised a plan to commercially catch Dungeness bay crab in Newport in October and November. This was legal and some dories did this quite successfully in smaller bays up and down the coast. The major fish companies did not buy the bay crabs, so fishermen had to secure their buyers, such as fish markets and restaurants that wished to make fresh crab available while the ocean crab season was closed.

We ventured uptown to a fish market, talked to the manager, and much to our surprise, she agreed to buy bay crab from us. We were pumped and eager to put the operation in motion. It's not like this now, but if you knew where to go along the bayfront, you could get all the free crab bait you needed. The local fish companies would have huge bins that were full of fish carcasses now and then. You just had to keep your eye out and be ready when you saw them open their street-side doors. The only other problem solving needed was what to do about live tanks for the crabs we caught. This was easily solved with a couple of large plastic trash cans we purchased at Payless, and we poked holes in them and attached a rope harness to each for retrieval. The plan was to submerge them at the dock, hopefully full of crabs, until it was time to deliver the crustaceans to the market.

Soon thereafter, we were on the water crabbing the flood tide. Brian became the official helmsman since he still was nursing his injured limb, and I was deemed the crab ring puller. It was a good workout and we hauled in a lot of commercial-sized dungies, as the locals call them. The boat was equipped with a deck light, so we even pulled rings in the dark, which proved to be a whole different world in the late hours and was a blast. We filled two large trash cans after just a couple flood tides, and were already counting all the money we would pocket. Life was good.

With great pride and enthusiasm, we loaded our first big haul of crabs, trash cans and all, in the bed of my Datsun pickup and motored up the hill from the bayfront to deliver to the market along Highway 101.

"Just think how much money we can earn doing this!" I declared.

"Yeah, 80 crabs in just two tides. That should be $150 to $200 dollars. We can do this all fall," Brian added.

Upon arrival, with dollar signs dancing in our heads and shining in our eyes, we summoned the manager who came out to inspect our bounty. Anticipating that she would give us glowing reviews and accolades, instead she managed to suck the wind out of our sails with just eight words as she pinched their legs, "Oh, I'm sorry, these crabs aren't full enough." What she meant was that there was not enough meat in the shells. Commercial-grade crabs must be very firm both in the shell and the legs. We should have known better, but in the thick of our exuberance, we figured the crabs we harvested were good enough.

"I know you both worked very hard. I'm sorry. Maybe you can find someone else who will buy them from you?" she added.

While we maturely accepted the rejection in person, being teenagers, we profusely grumbled on the ride back to the docks with our rejected crabs.

"I can't believe she's that picky. What a ripoff!" I vented, even though we both knew she was right. This brought about the next conundrum. What to do with the crabs? We ended up submerging the crabs back in the bay in their makeshift live tanks. In an odd turn of events, we sold our catch for a pittance to a guy Brian knew upriver in Toledo who must have had a craving for fresh crab. About as quickly as our mastermind operation came together, it skidded to an abrupt halt.

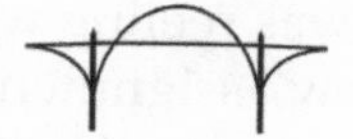

Jeff Beck's instrumental album *There and Back* had become a mainstay on my playlist. The melodic jazz-rock fusion tones fused marvelously with the moody late-fall feeling. The long, atmospheric guitar notes on the track, "The Final Peace," had their way in signaling that it was time to hang up the carefree summer and fall I enjoyed so much. The stormy November weather was just around the corner, and it was prudent that I focused on cardio and mental focus for boot camp. I also just wanted to be with my family from that point forward while I had the chance. A week later, the boat and I were back in Salem. Brian needed a place to stay, so we let him crash in our trailer while he healed up his hand and worked on securing a deckhand position.

On January 5th, I departed the Eugene airport along with three other guys from Oregon en route to Alameda,

California for three months of basic training. What my fishing future held for the upcoming year, as well as the next four, I had no clue. My headspace was consumed with the changes and challenges that were ahead of me. Coast Guard boot camp was an unforgettable experience. While it required a lot of physical endurance, it was even more of an intensive test on one's mental stability. They were very tuned in to see who would crack under pressure.

Even though for a while it seemed like my basic training experience would never end and pushed me harder than I ever experienced, I came out unscathed on the other side. I found that keeping an even keel and remaining level-headed was crucial with all the mind games a recruit has to endure. As luck would have it, I got stationed in Coos Bay, Oregon, which is a couple of hours south of Newport and a little more than a three-hour ride to Salem. I'm not sure who was more excited, me or my parents, since it was close to home. My first assignment was on the *Citrus*, a 180-foot former buoy tender converted to a cutter that focused on law enforcement. My mind was reeling with so many unknowns ahead of me with my new assignment. It also left me wondering that, maybe, just maybe, I'd still be able to find a way to carve out some time to get some trolling in with Dad for the 1981 season. I was anxious to dive in and see how it all played out.

CHAPTER 6

SEASON 5

STILL IN THE GAME

1981 Setlist

Foreigner 4
Heart *Dreamboat Annie*
Journey *Escape*
Quarterflash *Quarterflash*
Rush *Moving Pictures*
Stevie Nicks *Belladonna*

Living and working on a 180-foot ship with about 45 other men was unlike anything else I had experienced. Being the new recruit, at times felt like I was being fed to the lions as I was subjected to pranks and other initiation rites of passage on a daily basis. It all subsided in a short time for me though by remaining calm and cool while being the subject of their fun. For those unfortunate souls who resisted, the crews' shenanigans dragged out much longer.

At least the practice of spending a lot of time at sea was a piece of cake compared to that of some other crewmen. While getting underway on my first patrol, I was surprised to see some crewmen frantically dash to the head (the ship's restroom) to pray to the porcelain gods. I had never been seasick on any boat, and I ended up with a perfect record on the ship, too. In a weird twist of fate, it turned out that we conducted boardings of fishing vessels on our 10-day patrols. These took place at many of the prime Oregon Coast fishing grounds and included foreign processing boats as well as local trawlers and trollers.

On a few patrols that spring, we deployed Zodiac boats to inspect some salmon trollers from various ports, including Newport. I was serving on lookout and helm duties at the time, and I recognized several of the boats that we were boarding. Knowing some of the people who fished those boats, I tried to throw in a good word or two to the officers to make the inspection experience easier for the fishermen. The captain and executive officer picked up on my familiarity with the fleet, sometimes asking what I knew about this boat or that. Much to their disappointment, I didn't have any dirty intel to share about any of the boats I observed. The hard part was looking through the "big-eye" spyglass while on lookout duty at all the trollers engaged in their work on deck. Occasionally I would catch a glance of someone on deck throwing a big king in the fish box. While it was great to have such a close view of the action, it was like having that chocolate cake in front of you, but not being able to take a bite. In the meantime, Dad was pressing on by getting the boat ready for the season while I was figuring how I could get some time off to join him.

Much to my surprise, I was able to take about ten days of leave and I was still in the game for the opener. I figured being a new guy on the ship meant very little time off, but it all worked out so that Dad and I were able to kick the season off in normal fashion. It was a bit ironic though as the ship I was serving on was going to be on patrol during that time. The possibility existed that our dory could be boarded by my crewmates. I got to thinking how awkward that might be if they happened to find us in violation of anything. Not wanting that thought to become reality, we double and triple-checked to make sure everything from the boat registration to safety gear to fishing gear was all in order.

A perk popped out of nowhere that summer, too, which worked out marvelously to my advantage. Still fresh from boot camp, my rank aboard the ship was seaman apprentice. Aside from my general deck duties while in port, one of my responsibilities during the summer months was to work in the ship's galley, where meals were cooked and served. I didn't cook, but instead washed dishes and did all sorts of grunt work for the cooks, or subsistence specialists as they were formally titled. The perk was that I got more time off than working on deck. It was a big win for me as it gave me some extra dory days.

Aside from going home on a weekend here and there before the season started, I wasn't available to do much of the boat prep. However, Dad weaved his magic and somehow took care of business to have it ready to roll for the July first opener. My leave started July 2nd, so Dad fished the first day solo in miserable weather for one measly fish. It was a dismal way to start a season. The first-day report didn't phase me though as I slipped out of my military state-of-mind and slid right back into fishing mode. I was primed and ready for a few weeks of new adventures and stories to tell.

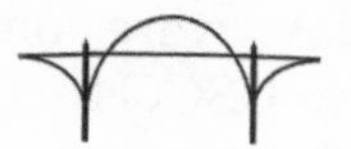

It was a great feeling cruising north on Highway 101 for the opener, and I had some freshly cultivated tunes locked and loaded in my tape deck. Foreigner, Journey, Rush, and Stevie Nicks fused with the treks along the coast highway and made the summer commutes all the more memorable. Stevie's *Belladonna* LP was one of those albums that just instantly became ingrained with the entire spirit upon its release in mid-summer. The depth of its melodies and instrumentation synced to perfection in capturing the essence of the moody coast hues. Many of the album's tracks accompanied vivid coastal sunsets that painted the sky on the northbound drives.

The first week's fishing was slow and the weather deteriorated to the point where we took a couple of days to head to the Valley for some family time. Upon our return, we persevered through a hard-fought all-day derby that yielded 23 silvers, 2 pink salmon, and a king.

Hoping to build on a respectable score, we ventured out to the same spot the next morning. After pulling the first silver and ready to pull dozens more, we got all four of our lines tangled in a crab pot. This took us out of action for a few hours as we dealt with lost gear as well as the quagmire of monofilament that was knotted and looped in the most unimaginable weavings and webs. We weren't the only ones who were dealt a bad hand as another dory around us met the same fate. All things aside though, we managed to scrape up 13 silvers, which seemed like a fitting number considering the day's events. The fish gods must have had some pity as we were blessed with an 11-pound king to quell our frustrations.

The following week was a mixed bag of results, which included a couple of labor-intensive coho-catching days in the 30 to 40 fish range. With such a short time frame, my mindset was to grind it out for all it was worth. During this stretch, 11 to 13 hours days were common when the weather allowed. Fortunately, my USCG brethren never paid our boat a visit, although I did overhear on the CB of some fishermen who said the ship was in their neighborhood conducting boardings.

After putting in a full day on the water on July 15th, I bade farewell to my Dad and hit the road to travel south for two hours along Highway 101's winding path. Quite frankly it was a rather somber and sobering moment. The summer season always seemed endless, but this time it ended abruptly. I had never had to pull up stakes in the middle of the action. I was so grateful that I was able to sneak away for a few weeks, but like anything you love, you always yearn for more.

As I made my sojourn south on highway 101 in the fading light, I could see the small villages of tranquil anchor lights of larger trollers just a mile or two offshore. They were nestled in coves and behind capes along the coastline. I envisioned the fishermen settling in for a night's rest and with sights set to rise early for another day in paradise. Admittedly, my veins were coursing with jealousy.

Arriving in the town of Coos Bay late in the evening, I saw the red aircraft lights on the ship's mast as I rounded a corner on the highway through town. I always looked for them to provide reassurance that the ship did not leave port without my knowing. As I retreated to my bunk in the crew's berth, I swallowed a dose of reality and mentally prepared for the next day's deckwork tasks and training.

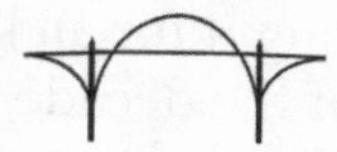

After my departure, Dad worked his tail off and had a mixed bag of success, adventures, frustrations, and mechanical mishaps, all of which are quite the norm when you are on the water daily. He fished a lot with the dory guys along with a couple of highliners in fiberglass boats. Scores ranged from 10 to 50 fish, with some chinooks thrown in for good measure here and there. There were also big schools of hake and small black cod to work around. While the hake always wreaked havoc on the gear with their razor-sharp teeth, the black cod masses were harmless but occupied every hook intended for salmon. Blue sharks often made a midsummer appearance, and like hake, inflicted torture on monofilament line and occasionally chowed down on salmon hooked on the gear. On a few occasions, silvers had to be hauled in hand over hand as fast as possible, complete with a dorsal fin trailing close behind, to keep them from becoming an entree for the apex predators. Dad also was treated to a surprise visit by a transient orca. Perhaps it was the one that made a drive-by in 1977 and thought she would see what he was up to after all those years?

It was during the 1981 season that Dad established a life-long friendship with Dennis, more commonly known as Denny, who lived close by in Salem. Instead of a dory, Denny owned a fiberglass sport boat, the *High and Dry*, that was adapted to fish commercially for salmon. They usually fished the same areas that summer and in subsequent years as well. Denny was incredibly helpful and quite innovative. Together, the two of them launched a renaissance era of boat and house projects. During the offseason, they teamed up to build workbenches and other furniture for each other, and then there were boat projects. These included fish troughs, fish boxes, and gearboxes. Perhaps Denny hit his most creative stride with PVC pipe. He was a master of creativity with the white plastic tubing, and his talents rubbed off on Dad who also started using it for all kinds of household and boat projects. For most of the decade, we would spend a lot of time teaming with Denny on the water. On days when the weather was not cooperating, we shared good times with him and his two sons, Curt and Ken, dockside.

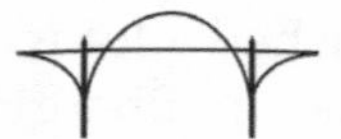

The timing of my mess-cook duties on the ship continued to be the gift that kept on giving. I was able to squeeze in four more trips, which included a 50-plus fish day. The culture shock of transitioning from fishing boat to ship continued, but it did get easier. It was a bit comical, too, as some of my shipmates couldn't comprehend why on Earth I would spend my off days and leave time on the ocean.

"Hey Boot," they'd ask, addressing me with what they called new Coast Guardsmen fresh out of boot camp. "You're going to spend your day off on the ocean? You're crazy!"

I just shrugged it off and left it to them looking at it from a whole different perspective than I, which was justifiable. When I was unavailable for dory duty, Dad recruited a special guest to tag along as deck help. One of the former owners of our boat, Steve, joined Dad for a day and it was a special treat of having a good friend aboard. Later, Dad had to go for a work conference for a week in early August, so things worked out where Steve leased the boat for that time and did quite well.

By the end of August, the season quota for silvers was met and the coho season shut down, leaving just chinooks to catch. Earlier at the midseason mark, we reached Dad's monetary earnings goal, and in our logbook, he wrote, *"Made the goal. Will take home some money to Carolyn."* I'm sure Mom was happy to see that, and I know it made Dad happy that all the effort could be applied to doing something nice for her. Dad adored Mom and worshiped the ground she walked on. He always beamed when he was able to do something special for her such as buying her some nice jewelry. Even though the coho derby had come to an end, I was hoping to squeeze in a couple more trips. Those plans never panned out though between weather conditions, ship duties, and due to the sudden downturn of my friend Greg's health back in Salem.

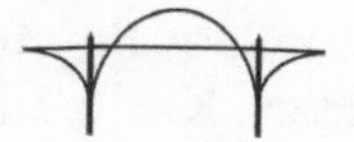

With Greg's health declining, I seized a weekend off to visit him in the hospital. Quarterflash's debut album was receiving heavy airplay in my rig, and it accompanied another indelible life event during my three-hour trek home. Ruminations ran rampant in my mind as I processed the possibility of losing one of my best friends. Upon my arrival, I met up with his brother and father who were emotionally drained.

"He's not doing well at all, Terry," Greg's father said with great sadness.

"His older brother frustratedly expressed, "He's only 19 years old..!"

It was not easy to hear that news. I was invited into his hospital room to visit. My heart was beating like a drum as I knew it was likely our last conversation. I wasn't quite sure what to say, but before I could say more than hello, he grabbed my hand tight and looked me straight in the eyes, which I know was Greg's way of letting me know that time was short. Following that deep moment, we dived back into our usual conversation topics before he needed to get some rest. As I made my way to my truck, I held on to a thin thread of hope that he would rally, like he had done before, but my gut told me otherwise.

On the morning of October 23, 1981, around 9:00 AM, I was back on the ship working on deck, when I was summoned to the dock shack to take a phone call. I never got calls, so I knew for sure what was coming. It was my father phoning in to say that Greg had passed away that morning. Feeling numb, I went back to my duties on deck, but I was emotionally shaken. I wasn't quite sure what to do next. I needed some space to process it all, but unfortunately, the deck of a ship wasn't very conducive for that. My friend, Karl, noticed I was out of sorts and I let him know what happened. He had met Greg in early September when Karl and I marathoned it from Coos Bay to Portland and back in one day for a Kinks concert. Karl had some seniority and went to bat immediately to get me approved for some leave for the funeral, which I appreciate greatly to this day. After some unnecessary harassing by a few superiors questioning my hair length, my request was granted (with the provision I would get my hair cut) to attend his funeral. I set aside my feelings concerning their insensitivity, packed my seabag, and hit the road.

The drive home was a surreal moment. The autumnal sun blazed in all its morning glory while traveling along and around the twists and turns of the stunningly beautiful Umpqua Highway. This stretch of highway that connects the Coast to the Valley is saturated with the greenery of an abundant mix of pine, hemlock, and cedar trees, all while following the path of the Umpqua River's jade green to clear rushing water. Heart's *Dreamboat Anne* was coursing through the tinny speakers inside the cab of my Datsun pickup as Side Two's acoustic melodies resonated with my heavy heart and melded with the sunbeams that gleamed through the tree branches.

Almost like it was scripted, immediately after Greg's service, Oregon's blustery autumn weather moved in for the long haul. The *Carolyn Kay* was tucked away for its offseason slumber, and Dad and I settled back into our responsibilities. It had been a year full of a lot of new adventures as well as some highs and lows. I felt blessed beyond measure to have been able to get some unexpected quality dory time on the water. Much like the fall of 1980, I ended the season with few answers and a boatload of questions as to my whereabouts when the next fishing season rolled around.

CHAPTER 7

SEASON 6

WITHDRAWAL SYMPTOMS

1982 Setlist

Alan Parsons Project *Eye in the Sky*

Asia *Asia*

Fleetwood Mac *Mirage*

Kansas *Vinyl Confessions*

Throughout the fall and winter, I dashed off to Salem now and then. I had a lot to share about what life on a ship was like, and I engaged in some strategizing with Dad for the 1982 season. Those conversations were full of "ifs" since I didn't know for sure what the next year held in terms of where I would be stationed. My career goal in the Coast Guard was to become a Boatswain's Mate (BM), which was a jack-of-all-trades rating. The duties of Boatswains (or Bosuns) range anywhere from soup to nuts. They operate boats, work in buoy operations, investigate oil spills, perform a myriad of shipboard duties, and more. To earn my Boatswain's Mate rating, I had a couple of options. The first was that I could remain on the ship in Coos Bay and work on mastering and demonstrating skills on the job along with many hours of correspondence coursework. The second was to go to school in Yorktown, Virginia. A vast majority went the latter route, which usually was accomplished in a much shorter, yet intensive time frame. I balked at first at this idea. I had come to like the ship and crew, and I had embraced the Coos Bay-North Bend community. I had also settled into a comfort zone as I was close to home and there were opportunities to keep fishing.

Eventually, I was convinced that remaining on the ship would lead me nowhere and that the only way to move forward was to head east. So, by late March of 1982, I was in the air on a route that would take me to Yorktown. This decision was a game-changer. It meant I would finish school in early June, have a few weeks of leave at most, and then spend a few days relocating to a new duty station, which at that point could've been anywhere. The fishing season had been announced. With the data pointing to low numbers of wild-stock coho, the season was going to start on July 1 and be very short. In my world it meant that, unless I was relocating to another spot on the Oregon Coast, I was going to miss the whole fishing season. This was some hard news to swallow, but it was my reality and I had to own it.

I graduated third in my cohort as a Boatswain's Mate Third Class, which I figured would score me a great duty station. However, I learned there was a glut of BMs, and that there were no openings on the entire West Coast. So much for any possibility to step aboard our dory.

This left me wondering where I should request to be stationed. I figured Florida would be a change of pace with pretty girls, sunshine, and chasing drug boats. As fate would have it though, Florida was unavailable, too. The person filling the slots thought they were doing me a favor by stationing me in Southeast Texas, which he said was as close as he could get me to Florida. I could tell by my parents' reaction when I called home that they were bummed about my assignment. After consulting a map to verify the town of Port Arthur's existence, location, and whether Texas truly had a coastline, I accepted my destiny and made plans for a quick trip home.

The all-species salmon season that Dad would be facing solo was going to be the shortest by far in our six years. Before leaving for the Lonestar State, I did get a chance to drive over to Newport, which included being able to pay Brian a visit. It felt good to be back, but there was a pit in my stomach as there was a buzz of activity at least among the larger boats that were fishing chinooks and halibut. It felt weird knowing that I would not have any part of it. With that reality soaking in, I just had to distance myself from the whole fishing scene. My time was better spent at home with family and preparing for a long journey to the region known as the Golden Triangle. I was able to help get the boat ready while at home. It was good to at least contribute to that ritual even though there was a lot of work left for Dad to do on his own.

Despite a rather somber farewell to my family, my spirits lifted in anticipation of the grand road trip I had mapped out. The first days were a piece of cake, but the further south I traveled, my ride's comfort level deteriorated rapidly in my non-air conditioned 1971 Datsun pickup. My final night of sleeping in the back of my rig was at a KOA camp in Kingman, Arizona. I couldn't even crawl in the canopied bed until nearly midnight without it feeling like a pizza oven. My trip through the Grand Canyon state delivered some additional nuisances with the highway biting off a big chunk of my tire tread and my radiator petcock valve leaking. By the time I got to New Mexico, I didn't think twice of forking over some bucks for an air-conditioned motel room. At least I had some fresh news tunes from the Alan Parsons Project, Asia, Fleetwood Mac, and Kansas to take the edge off of the monotonous long highway stretches. Tired, cramped, and sweltering, I arrived in the Port Arthur city limits. I was greeted with a highway drive through the heart of the Texaco refinery flanked with adorning flame-belching towers. One thing I knew for sure, I was in for a life-changing experience.

My parents always were going the extra mile to help me in my transition. Dad sent some gear down to me to tie. He likely already had enough gear tied up, but he knew it would help fill the void and allow me to have a hand in the season, even if it was so menial. My mother one-upped my dad a few months later. She was concerned that I wouldn't have a cake on my birthday, so she baked one, carefully packaged it, and sent it via U.S. Mail. Of course, when I opened the package the cake looked like it met a paint shaker as I am sure it was flipped, tossed, and jostled during its trip to the Deep South. When I called to thank her, she asked, anxiously, "Did it stay in one piece in the mail?" I said, "Well, not exactly, but it sure tasted great!"

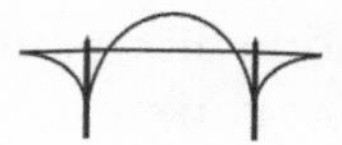

On July 1st, I was 2,417 miles away from Salem logging hours to get locally qualified to run boats for my new duty station on a very warm, hazy, and humid morning. As the diesel engines hummed and we cruised at a slow, steady, and non-eventful pace on our patrol on the Intercoastal Waterway, I wondered, *"Where did Dad choose to fish on the season opener? How many fish did he have in the box?* I had no way to get a hold of him at the moment and would just have to wait to talk to Mom via landline in hopes of getting a relayed report. The withdrawal symptoms raged like a storm. Adding to my mental tug of war, there was no one around whom I could relate to how I was feeling.

While I was anguishing in salmonid separation, my transition to my new duty station was lackluster at best. For whatever reason, I just couldn't get in sync with my new assignment and life in a whole new culture. The duty station was a far cry from the camaraderie on the *Citrus*. Part of the disconnection was my failure to embrace my new community. The southern lifestyle, the heat, the humidity, the flat terrain, hordes of mosquitoes—I wanted no part of it. This just jettisoned me into a depressing spiral throughout the summer. The drinking age in Texas was 18, so I dabbled in the rock and roll night club scene to try to perk up and fit in with the local vibe. While it was all cool and new in the beginning, the luster wore off quickly as it was more of just a hub for post-high school locals, headbangers, and endless covers of Billy Idol and Quiet Riot.

Fortunately, I got to hit the reset button. The Coasties sent me to a marine environmental safety class in Yorktown, Virginia. The autumn Virginia weather was so Oregonesque. When I wasn't in class or working out in the gym, I was taking in the lush greenery while running the forest trails and paths through the historic battlefields. The respite was a perfect remedy for renewal. After the schooling and a few weeks back home, my Lone Star State assignment's trajectory was on a much better course.

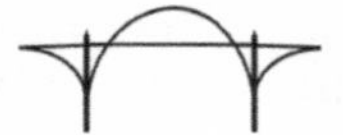

Dad had the boat back at the Port Dock and couldn't help noticing it was strangely quiet with the season opener only a few days away. It was a sure sign that times were changing, and it made him wonder what the future held for the industry. He gathered some intel from some charter boats, whose season had opened earlier. They were putting fish in the box north by the Yaquina Head Lighthouse, so that became his plan of attack. It turned out to be a good plan with 33 coho and 4 chinook for his efforts in dense fog. He heard some radio chatter about a big school of fish fifty miles south offshore of Florence. Typically coho pointed their snouts northward, so his gut was telling him that south of Newport would be a good bet to drop some gear soon.

His second outing was nothing short of epic. Dad followed his hunch and he took a left out of the jaws on a nice ocean to Seal Rock (also known as Seal Rocks). This landmark is referred to in a singular and plural sense since it is the name of a community and is a cluster of large rocks located just offshore ten miles south of Newport. After a half-hour delay due to the highly improbable situation of having the stainless wire on both float lines break while deploying gear, fish started climbing en masse on his deep lines. He ended up just fishing four lines off each deep wire that loaded up immediately. Realizing he had plopped in on a gold mine of fish, he just worked those two wires repeatedly. With fish piling up, they needed to be gutted, so he'd clean six, pull four, in that pattern for a long time. The wind was blowing 15 miles per hour from the south, so it was challenging to steer with just two lines in the water, dodging boats, all while tending to fish cleaning and catching. Later Dad noted that had I been there, we could have boated 150 fish, which some boats did. All in all, though, an utterly exhausted Dad tallied 92 silvers and 1 chinook, which shattered our personal best.

The next morning my father was faced with one of those "how do I top yesterday" mountains to climb as he headed out to see what the fish gods had in store for him. He was aching from the countless contortions the prior day's rodeo served up. This included the thousands of revolutions both arms experienced cranking up and down the thirty-pound lead weights, complemented by the drag from the boat's movement, current, and lines loaded with salmon.

With the fish moving north, he headed straight out from the jaws and plunked the gear down in the 40 to 45 fathom line. No sooner did he drop a few lines, the derby commenced again, and it was like the movie *Groundhog's Day*. The only difference was that later in the day he started to get a little worn out and he started to get sloppy. On days like that you are in constant motion and there are no lunch breaks. It makes it easy to forget to hydrate, which just makes decision making all the more difficult. In a little bit of irony, he did happen to notice that the ship I was stationed on the prior summer, the *Citrus*, was nearby patrolling the waters, sending law-enforcement teams on the inflatable boat to board fishing boats. Fortunately, they didn't conduct a boarding of his boat as he had his hands full enough. At the end of another long day though, he produced another epic score of 75 coho and 2 kings.

Despite some very sore hands, he got his second wind the following morning and ventured out to the madness once again. When fish show up in large numbers, you have to make the most of the window of opportunity, even when your mind and body try to convince you otherwise. It was another great performance at the workplace for 70 and 2. The fishing slowed down later in the day though, and the consensus among the fleet was that the fish were moving offshore. They sometimes took a detour to the north end of the Rockpile where all sorts of feed congregates amongst all the crazy currents and rock formations below the surface. So, the plan for the next morning was to point the boat's bow toward the North End.

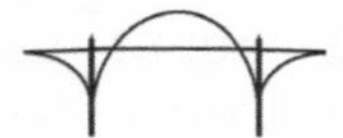

In the morning light, the trip across the bar generated some new gray hairs. The crossing was met with some huge long-period swells. Few things humble you more at the moment when all you can see are water mountains while you float on a small chunk of wood in the trough of some huge rollers. Following his lumpy seaward trek, Dad's gear became entangled in a crab pot before luckily breaking free with minimal gear loss. Once order was restored, a visitor dropped by for an up-close and personal check on his well-being.

"Oh, crap! Stay away from the gear!" He said aloud as the gray whale came close enough to make eye contact. "Go away. I'm catching fish here," As with the other whale drive-bys, there was no harm, no foul by the curious marine mammal as it continued its northbound commute. After a few flurries of action, the bite tapered back to reality and the final day's tally ended with a respectable catch of 47 silvers and a handful of chinooks. Supposedly there was another big coho school heading up the coast. With the springs going dormant for a few hours in the late afternoon, Dad headed in a little early. He hoped that some extra rest would pay off big time in the event that the freight train of coho arrived in Newport waters.

Some of the dory guys made it a late night at the local watering hole and weren't up with the chickens. Fortunately, Dad had quit drinking in 1977. He shared this to me while on a drive home from a basketball camp in Pullman, Washington I attended during the middle of our first fishing season. This caught me off guard because I had no clue he had a problem. As far as I could recall, there never was any kind of toxic situation at home where he was drunk and out of control. He explained that he drank a lot while alone, and he didn't want it to interfere with our family. Years later, I appreciated his abstinence for another reason. I had witnessed several situations in our fishing career where the wheels fell off for fishermen who turned their attention to the bottle instead of catching fish. For most of the transient small-boat fishermen in the salmon industry, many an hour were spent alone when the weather ran foul. Combined with alcohol dependency, excessive idle time created a slippery slope toward disaster. Dad's sobriety most likely preserved our place in the industry as he avoided the temptations of going out with the guys in the evenings.

Being the early bird that he was, Dad went with his gut and ran solo down south toward the waters off Alsea Bay, about 15 statute miles away. The Alsea River bar is extremely shallow as there are no jetties, so very few boats cross it as it is often barricaded with large breakers. The fishing offshore in the area at times was very productive though, and on this particular day, Dad hit the hotspot and had it mostly to himself. Another dose of blood, sweat, and cheer yielded 52 coho and a couple of kings. One of the chinooks was 14 ½ pounds and was so stout that it was shaped like a football. Waking up fresh and clear-minded and making the early morning run to the Alsea was a total win. As it turned out, it was the last of the high-octane coho fishing, and there were murmurs about the season coming to a close much sooner than anyone thought.

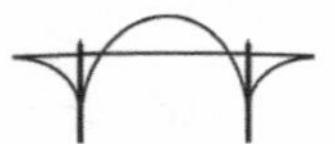

With such good catches early on, Dad had visions of a banner season, possibly grossing $15,000 to $20,000 for 30 days of effort. When Dad called Mom from the Port Dock payphone to say hello and give a fishing report, she would urge him to go back out and make more money! However, this dream would soon fade as the word on the docks was that the coho quota was being filled at a rapid rate.

The next day's action south of the bar was slow and ended at 10:00 AM with a sluggish troll against the brisk northwest wind that started ripping early. His entries in the fishing log stated, "Tough sledding...I'm exhausted and discouraged. My hand and back hurt, but mostly I'm pissed off!"

Even though the news of an early closure was discouraging, the upside was that my sister was on her way to be Dad's deckhand for a couple of days. The timing was perfect for his spirits. The second to last day turned out to be a decent hard-earned scratch of 24 silvers. Jen's crowning moment on the boat was helping Dad in a crab pot crisis. As it always does, the boat suddenly pivoted out of the blue while humming along at its peaceful pace. The humming was replaced by moaning stainless cable and metal springs that uncomfortably screeched for mercy. After attempts to work free from the crab pot that had ensnared the gear became futile, Dad was nervous as hell and took the costly fork in the road of choosing to cut the stainless cable to escape from the captor. This meant all gear on the wire would be lost. The next thing you know, Dad outfitted Jen in oversized rubber rain pants and three-quarters extended her over the side of the boat.

"Alright, Jen, I need you to reach out over the water with these cutters. I'll tell you where and when to make the cut. I got a good hold on the suspenders on your rain gear, so don't worry, you won't end up in the water!" Dad instructed.

"Alright, Dad," Jen said, following his lead.

"Okay, Jen, now cut the cable below close to the waterline."

"Got it! Like that?"

The boat recoiled and sighed with relief upon its reprieve.

"Great job, Jen. We could have sunk the boat back there. We were nailed to the ocean floor," Dad announced as he pulled her back on board.

After pausing for a moment, Dad added in a hushed tone of voice, "You don't need to tell your mother about this."

Even though he didn't lose his cool, Jen could tell that Dad would lose some sleep at having to part with the wire, lead, and eight spreads of expensive gear. The episode from Jen's lens was a bit different though as the exhausting day concluded with a KFC dinner that she described as "heaven!"

Someone must have filled in the fish that the season was ending soon. Most took an early vacation for the season's final day. While Jen started the day off a bit sleepy as can happen when you're just boat riding and not catching, she jumped into action when a few fish started showing some interest. With the clock ticking away that day toward season's end, an official-sounding CB hail from the Coast Guard echoed like it was originating thousands of miles away and announced the season would end at noon. All boats were instructed to pull gear at that time and head to port. Dad was sorely disappointed as it was only July 12th and this meant the fishing for the summer was for the most part, finished. He was dejected as his early-season dreams of paying off debts with banner-season fish income were dashed. Sure, there would be the chinook-only season continuing soon, but with the king catches mostly being a handful or less per day, it would be hard to justify spending too much time, energy, and resources in that direction.

It was an interesting dichotomy. Even while hearing my father's frustration about the abruptly lopped-off season and unmet goals, the 1982 season still seemed like Utopia to me. From my sweltering perspective in Southeast Texas, I would've given anything just to have been there for a day or even an hour. My father's emotions were still on a roller-coaster, but I was already looking ahead to 1983 and dead set that I would be there front and center on opening day. The next season was far away from every fisherman's mind though and the stability of the coho fishery was in murky water at best.

CHAPTER 8

SEASON 7

CHILD'S PLAY

1983 Setlist

Stevie Nicks *The Wild Heart*
The Kinks *State of Confusion*
The Police *Synchronicity*
U2 *War*
Zebra *Zebra*

Over the winter and into the spring, weather forecasters were talking about a phenomenon called El Niño, which means Christ Child, a term coined by Ecuadorian fishermen long ago. It has to do with a phenomenon where the waters of the Pacific start to become unusually warm around Christmastime and the simmering effect creates climatic changes that wreak havoc around the world through the rest of the year. I had never heard of it before, but by late spring, it was starting to gather momentum in the news.

The El Niño of 1983 has been regarded as one of the most severe in recorded history. As for Oregon, the winter of 1982-83 was warmer and drier, and it was catastrophic for the Oregon salmon season. According to a fisheries article in sciencedirect.com, the average weights of coho and chinook landed that year were the lowest since 1952 when that statistic was first recorded. Also, only 42% of the coho predicted to return to the rivers to spawn reached their destination. These climatic effects posed some very challenging times for the salmon fleet.

Despite the gloomy predictions that were floating around with all the El Niño talk, I was on Cloud Nine as I had scored over two weeks of leave time for the fishing season. I was more than ready for a break from Southeast Texas's challenging climate and the constant aroma of petroleum. While Michael Jackson, Prince, David Bowie, the Eurythmics were saturating the airwaves and MTV, a new Irish band captured my interest. I was all in with Bono and U2 after seeing their video for "New Year's Day," and I bombarded my eardrums with their album *War*. I added their first two albums to my collection for a larger dosage of The Edge's signature echo-driven guitar riffs. I was also fired up about a new band named Zebra from New Orleans. The first blistering spin of side one from their debut album blew me away and it was getting heavy reps all summer. Along with the lads from Ireland and the trio from NOLA, my cassette player kept warm with new tunes from the Police, Stevie Nicks, and the Kinks. I had these primed and ready for my 1983 fishing set list.

Being stationed in the heart of the oil industry, one of my primary duties was piloting a 15-foot and a 32-foot patrol boat on two major rivers that fed into the Gulf of Mexico. Both waterways were major thoroughfares for tug and barges as well as large oil and chemical tankers from all over the world. They were always taking on or offloading products at the numerous refineries littered along the river shorelines. Way too often, there would be spills and another one of our main duties was to investigate. Some were quite small and easy to control. Others were massive and required a cleanup contracting business and an armada of workers and equipment. Occasionally, there would be a spill-and-run incident, which left us with the mission of solving the mystery of whodunnit. It was quite fascinating and provided a portal to meeting many interesting people and boarding some amazing crafts. As a nineteen-year-old, I found myself having a Norwegian breakfast with an oil tanker captain while discussing cleanup of a small oil spill. On a routine inspection of a tugboard underway on the river, I enjoyed a quick and delicious spicy Cajun sausage, beans, and rice lunch with a burly tugboat crewman who kept a close eye on the TV and the latest developments on the soap opera "General Hospital." Seeing all the pollution helped me appreciate the beauty and purity of the Great Northwest.

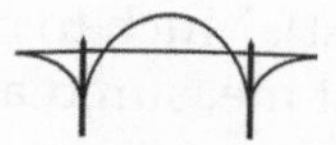

A few weeks before my arrival, Dad was getting the boat prepped and ready for trailering to the coast. This coincided with his textbook sales job melting down as there were some major internal issues within the company. Even though Dad excelled in the sales business, his position was eliminated. It was partly a relief to get away from a toxic work environment, but the pressure of launching into a new career understandably brought a lot of anxiety. On the day after his textbook sales career came to a close, Dad focused his energy on fishing and took the boat to Newport, with mom in the passenger seat this time around. Once the boat was launched and moored, Dad sensed an eerie quiet on the docks. The abrupt ending in 1982 and the dark cloud of El Niño hovering above had dampened the enthusiasm.

My arrival on June 30 was met with a classic soggy day in Newport, where the rain just found a way to trickle down my neck, no matter how much armor I had on. Nonetheless, I was very fired up for the season and I didn't let a short-lived, low-pressure system spoil my return. The doom and gloom of the El Niño reports were also far from my mind. We had heard dire predictions about seasons and fishing before, and not all were accurate, so our approach was to just go fishing and find out for ourselves.

On opening day we were greeted with the pitter-patter of rain on the metal roof of our trailer. Every year we parked it under a very large coastal pine tree, so when the rain eventually made its exit east over the Coast Range, the tree limbs would continue their little rainstorm for an hour or two. It paid off to step outside to get the weather scoop rather than to just peek out the window. The rain squalls and southwest wind didn't deter us, and we trolled around for an hour as the weather went to worms quickly. Those 60 minutes were sobering. We just caught one little raggy silver and the water temperature was a balmy 57 degrees (warm for early summer on the Oregon Coast). Much to our surprise, we had a little albacore tuna that measured about 8 inches hooked on a hoochie-flasher rig. When some fishermen overheard us talking on the CB to another boat about the incidental tuna catch, they thought we mistakenly identified it as a mackerel, which were common to catch at times. I knew the difference between an albacore and mackerel, and was 100% certain it was a miniature tuna. While it doesn't seem like a big deal, it turned out to be a harbinger of bizarre sightings and experiences to come for everyone by the season's end.

The next day brought about more crappy weather, and to add insult to injury, word on the airwaves went viral about the coho price being $0.90 per pound, contrasted to $2.33 per pound in 1979. This certainly created a different perspective when it came to deciding whether to fish in marginal ocean conditions. When the price was good, dorymen were much more inclined to risk having their fillings jarred loose as they pounded their way offshore on a snotty ocean to scratch up some fish. With the price per pound so low, it made you think twice about if it was worth heading out in inclement weather.

The weather improved in the afternoon, so we decided we might as well go out and plunk the gear down since we weren't making any money sitting at the dock. Much to our surprise and delight, we nailed 24 silvers. With 2 medium kings added as a garnish to the day, we were pretty pumped that we kicked ourselves in the butt and made the effort to go out. As the euphoria began to wear off, we analyzed the fish ticket to notice that our catch grossed a whopping $99.40, and the coho weight average was a measly 3.5 pounds. That was about a pound lower than usual for that time of year. With reports of low weight averages everywhere, the terms "rags" or "raggy" became commonplace to describe silvers as they were slender and had a malnourished look to them.

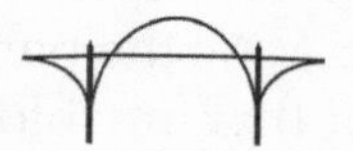

With six seasons under our belts, we had exponentially improved on our techniques, and Dad and I were mostly in agreement when it came to fishing philosophies. Like all great rock bands or sports teams, conflict arises when individuals work long hours together, sometimes in close quarters. We were not an exception to this in 1983. During scratch fishing, you start to strategize on a different level. You draw upon previous experience with water temperature and color, the weather, the time of year, location, and so forth to figure out how to cajole more salmon to slam your gear. After a few flurries of fish one morning, the switch turned off and was followed by a mind-numbing drought. Dorymen constantly watch their springs on the trolling poles. They naturally stretch with the rhythmic motion of the waves, but usually, you know instantly when something is on a line. No matter how much we ran the gear, we couldn't coax any gullible salmonids to wiggle a spring. This led us into some dialogue to revise our game plan.

"Well, what do you think, Ter? We could troll south where we had that little clatter earlier," Dad suggested.

"I heard guys getting a few fish outside us in 35 fathoms. That's better than anything we have going at this depth," I retorted with my idea.

"Yeah, but we were out there earlier and didn't have a bump," Dad replied.

Without agreeing to a decision, Dad said, "I'm going to pull my side and change up the gear. Our gear isn't enticing them today."

While I steered offshore to deeper water, Dad ran his gear. Very subtly, I noticed Dad would reach over and give a little turn of the helm to the left, turning us south. I'd move the wheel slightly to the right to resume my offshore target, then Dad would move the wheel his way as the boat would slowly veer south. This silent steering wheel war ensued for several awkward minutes. As the pattern continued, the tension mounted. On top of that, my blood pressure was rising as I brooded about Dad's choice of gear he planned to switch out. I felt what we were using would rise to the occasion once we found some fish, and I had no confidence in what he was sending down the wire. To make matters worse, we started a small throttle speed war. He would decelerate and I would accelerate. Finally, I lost it.

"Would you just stop it! What's wrong with heading out a few fathoms? We're doing nothing here?" I shouted. "And why are you changing out all your gear, suddenly. It's been working. Fishing is dead for almost everyone!"

"We already spent time out there earlier and we didn't get a bump and I'm going to shake things up on my side. What we're doing is not working!" Dad said in an infuriated tone.

Dad was a nice, jovial, and helpful man who was a delight to be around. But, when things got under his skin, he became a volcano ready to blow.

"Hey, we trolled all over down south for nothing, so it doesn't make any sense to head down that way! And when you slow down our troll speed, my gear doesn't work right either," I countered.

Dad didn't say another word, but he was really pissed off. As he brought the gear aboard to switch it out, flashers slammed in the gear trays. A new round of silence set in. I just continued steering west, hoping that my side would suddenly erupt with a double or triple in the deeper water, and thus, prove my idea was the best. That didn't happen though, so there we were, several miles offshore on a 22-foot boat at odds with each other. The frustrating part was that there was nowhere to go. A little part inside me just wanted to jump over the side and swim to shore. This was years in coming. This moment of divergence was a product of my emergence in adulthood and independence combined with each of our stints of fishing solo since the 1980 season. It felt poisonous and spat in the face of all of our wonderful collaboration since we started the whole venture, so finally I spoke out.

"Look, I'm sorry for shouting at you! I just felt like you were putting down all my ideas," I apologized.

"I'm not trying to put down your ideas. It just felt it didn't make sense to head out to where we trolled around for nothing. We can give it a shot, though. With it being so slow, it's a good time to experiment, too. What do we have to lose?" Dad responded.

He had a good point about it being a good time to be innovative. I felt like a jerk for being so stubborn.

"How about we just swing it around and troll the 25-fathom line? The water will still be warm enough and maybe we could scratch up a king or two. Can we just put this behind us?" I said with a smile and an extended hand.

We shook on that note and it was greener pastures from there on out. It was also the last confrontation of that level we ever had.

The next three days ranged from a dozen silvers to 30 and only included a couple of medium kings. We still had not quite reached the $100 mark in a day, which had been quite easy to do the past several years. The coho were consistently averaging an underwhelming 3.5 pounds each. To try to match what the fish were eating, it was common practice while cleaning fish to inspect the stomach contents. Often when cleaning fish caught in a frenzy, we would gawk at some of the stomachs and intestines that would be plugged and bulging at the seams with needlefish, shrimp and crab larvae, squid, and sometimes large herring. In 1983 though, the stomachs were more like uninflated balloons. There was very little feed in the area due to the lack of upwelling and northwest winds. In other words, the fish were nearly starving. The El Niño prophets were proving to be dead-on regarding the effects that were said to occur. About a week into the season, it was evident that this was the new normal for 1983.

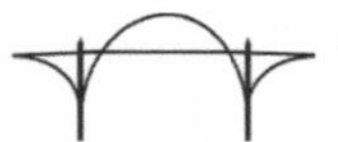

Brian had been fishing Dungeness crab in Alaska that summer, and he had just returned to town. It was great to see him as it had been quite a while since our last visit. Dad wanted a day off, and he saw Brian's arrival as an opportunity to get some well-needed rest. As he had done before, it was his nature to give me a day on the water to run the boat and have a friend along.

The next morning Brian and I ventured north and scratched out 22 silvers and 5 kings. We fished intensively on relatively calm seas and through some dark rain squalls. Meanwhile, Dad was on the beach putting on his chef's hat to make an awesome pot of stew. When we arrived back at the trailer, we were greeted with the wafting aroma of Dad's culinary masterpiece, and he was gleaming with anticipation for us to sample his main entree. The day concluded wonderfully and it was just another example of Dad's generosity and unselfishness.

The last week of "my season" included some decent days of up to 40 fish, which helped us exceed $100 a few more times. On my final day, we got a tip to troll out to the south end of the Rockpile. Whereas a week earlier we were enjoying the strength in numbers of the dory fleet, this particular day was eerily quiet and barren with few boats in sight. We nearly had the fishing grounds to ourselves. While it was certainly hard to leave knowing that my two-week respite was nearly over, the sting was a bit less painful seeing that the season was shrouded in a cloud of dreariness and it was threatening to smother any remaining hope.

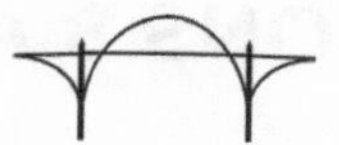

When Dad resumed solo, the fishing tapered off dramatically. El Niño was leaving its indelible mark. Fish were becoming scattered. Aside from a couple of 20-fish days, scores typically were in single digits, barely paying for the gas. Adding to this, some days were infested with blue sharks, and on one occasion Dad pulled up three chinook heads on consecutive spreads. The blue menaces were routinely severing expensive monofilament and gear and often uncomfortably patrolling the perimeter of the boat for hours, undoubtedly attracted to fish blood trickling out of the kill box drain. To add insult to injury, the northwesterlies finally started to rev up and made for some rough fishing conditions. Dad had reason to hold his head high though. Through all the frustration he endured, he earned the badge of honor of being among the top producing dories.

By mid-summer Dad needed to get aggressive on finding a new job, and my mother finally told him it was time to come home. With his career likely to change, he felt that this was to be his last lengthy season and that I would be running the show once my tour of duty was over. With 1982 being such a short coho season followed by the climate-ravaged 1983 season, it left us both with a lot of concern and doubt about the shape of the 1984 season. After being locked in on resuming full-time salmon fishing, it was starting to feel like I was losing grip on a dream I had been holding onto so tight for several years.

CHAPTER 9

SEASONS 8 AND 9

THE DARK SEASONS

1984 Setlist
Bruce Springsteen *Dancing in the Dark*
Jackson Browne *Hold Out & Lawyers in Love*
Huey Lewis and the News *Sports*
1985 Setlist
Don Henley *Building the Perfect Beast*
Supertramp *Brother Where You Bound?*
Tears for Fears *Songs from the Big Chair*
U2 *The Unforgettable Fire*

Having successfully scored two weeks of summer leave in 1983, I was confident I could take two weeks in 1984 to get my fishing fix. Meteorologists were predicting El Niño to subside, which meant the North Pacific wouldn't feel like bath water and the salmon wouldn't look like withered rags. As we both feared, any optimism we had was punched in the gut after the new year as there were many rumblings about a total summer shutdown coast-wide for coho. When the seasons were set in the early spring, it was official. There would be no coho coming aboard the *Carolyn Kay* in 1984 and it left us with a big decision. Would it be worth our time to fish a chinook-only season all summer?

Before hearing the gloomy news, I already had plans for taking a few weeks of leave in July again and had purchased my plane tickets. Each time we talked about the season on the phone, I could tell by Dad's tone that he was less than enthused about the whole situation. I am quite sure he would have been fine just sitting the season out. Being halfway across the continent, my perspective was blurred and distorted as I had visions of us throwing kings in the boat over both shoulders. In yet another example of Dad's generosity, he put the boat together enough so I could get a much-needed fishing fix and at least say we gave it our best shot. Since the end of the prior season, he had started a new job providing estimates for a home heating and cooling business in Salem. The learning curve was steep, but he burned the midnight oil to learn the trade and was beginning to be quite successful. In his new gig, summer time meant catching air conditioning unit sales, so the thought of dropping the boat in on a wing and a prayer for kings wasn't very palatable. Thus, the caveat was that I would mostly be fishing solo with Dad playing a cameo role in the whole operation.

My arrival in Newport was a flood to my senses with the sounds of sea life, savory bayfront aromas, and the chilly northwest breeze. This was a stark contrast to the hot, humid petroleum-infused gulf air of Port Arthur that I had yet to get used to. While it felt great to be back on the Oregon Coast, my first trip back to the boat docks was lackluster at best. It was like a ghost town. There was hardly a dory to be found. Most of the larger boats were tied up. Those who were fishing were having to venture far offshore to escape the frigid nearshore waters that hovered in the high forties. Coastal upwelling of cold, nutrient-rich water from the depths was in full force, courtesy of non-stop northwest winds. It didn't take long to realize that we should have sat this one out.

Despite being one of the only small boats crazy enough to give it a go, we ventured out the next morning to take a look. Dad decided to take a day and fish with me before plunging back into the HVAC world. By the time we pounded out past the buoys, the ocean was capping as far as the eye could see. Against our better judgment, we dropped some king gear spreads along the 25-fathom line in the clear, super-chilled North Pacific waters. We didn't say it aloud to each other, but we both knew we were trolling in a desert.

"Boy, it's going to be a short one today, Ter. That wind is already whipping up good. It's going to be hard to hold a course when we pull gear soon," Dad announced.

"Yeah, I hate to say it, but I agree. The water is freezing, too! I get why the trollers have been having to go way offshore to have any success. Hopefully we get a bump or two on the gear soon before it totally blows up out here," I replied.

About an hour later, Dad suggested the obvious, "I think we should put the gear in the boat. There's nothing here and we're going to get our butts kicked soon. There will be better days as we know."

Dad was right. There would be better days. Not in 1984, though.

Later in the afternoon, Dad headed home and I stayed in Newport in hopes that the wind would die down. With the Willamette Valley in a heatwave, it set up a classic Oregon Coast summer scenario of brisk northwesterlies for several days as air from a high-pressure system raced down the coastline. My time was spent just reading and relaxing along with some Springsteen, Jackson Browne, and Huey Lewis to fill the space. After three days of hearing the wind whoosh and watching the trees sway to and fro under beautiful sunny skies, I threw in the towel and headed to enjoy the splendor of the Willamette Valley's beautiful temperate summer weather with the family.

Before flying back to Texas, I made one last trip to Newport with Dad to retrieve the boat. He didn't have the time or drive to give it a go later in the summer. Upon our arrival, the wind was still screaming, the docks were still barren of small boats, and the only fish to be found were still far offshore. If there were any doubts about our decision, they certainly were erased.

My head was swirling on my Houston-bound flight. My grand plan of salmon fishing on a brand-new dory was going down in flames, and it was disheartening to say the least. It wasn't making much sense with the industry becoming a shell of what it used to be. With half a year left to serve in the Coast Guard, I needed to rethink my game plan.

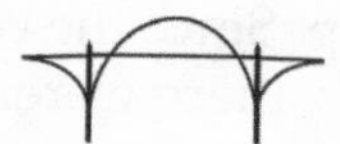

Six months later, Port Arthur, Texas was in the rear-view mirror. I hit the road in my fully loaded 1982 Toyota pickup as I headed toward the Great Northwest. New Don Henley and U2 tunes were primed and ready to keep me company on the long trek westward. I was able to tack on some leave time before my discharge date in January, so that meant I could depart earlier than originally planned and be home for Christmas. It was a great carefree trip that took me through the desert southwest, up the California coast, and north on Highway 101 before heading east to Salem. I reached my destination with a day to spare before the Willamette Valley was blanketed with snow.

Between July and December, I did a lot of brainstorming on how I could make a living on a dory. This even included researching fisheries in California, which in those days involved a lot of phone calls, but nothing turned up very promising. I also decided that ultimately I wanted to fish full time, which meant becoming a deckhand on a crab boat and being available for other fisheries.

After Christmas, it was time to get down to business. My first venture was commercial crabbing on our dory on Alsea Bay, just south of Newport. A few dory guys typically drilled hard for crabs there in the fall prior to the commercial season, so I thought, why not give it a try in January? While the weather after the turn of the new year was nothing short of spectacular on the Oregon Coast with stunningly clear skies and balmy day-time temperatures, the crabbing was dismal. There were very few commercial-sized crabs because the ocean season had started. Most of the keepers were being scooped up by the big boats offshore. I should have realized this, but I was too wrapped in the euphoria of being back in the Northwest. After a week of dodging sandbars on cold, dark nights and repeatedly hand-pulling crab rings that only yielded disappointment, I folded up shop and headed back to Salem to regroup. Since the commercial crab season had started in December, there weren't any deckhand jobs open, so I just had to keep my eyes and ears open for any opportunities.

To avoid draining my savings, I took a temporary job driving a truck for a local newspaper in Salem and delivered bundles of papers to individual carriers in the wee hours of the morning. Just when I got the hang of the route in an unfamiliar outlying town, some good news came my way. My fishing friend, Brian, informed me that there was a deckhand job open on the boat in which he was working, named the *Challenge*. The boat was owned by Mike, one of the most successful fishermen in Newport. Since I didn't have the luxury of time to give a proper two-week notice, I announced my departure and set to work to find a place to live. I found a great little mobile home on an elderly couple's property in Toledo, which is a few miles outside of Newport. Soon thereafter, I was embarking on my first venture on the deck of a crab boat.

It was great to get back to the Pacific and to have a steady post-military job. Spring ocean crabbing is much like scratch fishing for salmon. The catches aren't nearly as big as they are when the season opens, but if you work hard and have a skipper who knows the area well, you can still make a few bucks. Throughout the spring and early summer we ran crab gear from Newport south to Florence with Brian running the crab block, which is hydraulically powered and pulls up the crab pots. I baited pots, and we both sorted crabs right and left. After my first full day of crabbing, we had finished running several hundred pots in assembly-line fashion. Even though my bunk was near the loudly humming generator, I managed to fall into a short, but stress-laden level of sleep. My entire night's "rest" was immersed in a dream where I was still working my tail off on deck. In my land of nod, crab pots were continually coming up and off the crab block as I was scrambling around the deck. It was like I was going through an intensive physical training circuit workout during the REM stage. Needless to say, I woke up utterly exhausted as I was mentally pulling pots all night long. The upside was that we caught quite a few dream-state crabs during my slumber.

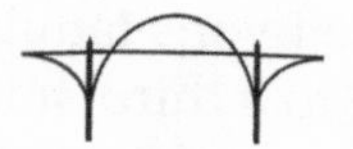

When it's rainy and windy in the winter and early spring along the Oregon Coast, you need to make sure you have plenty of hobbies. Newport was much smaller in 1985 than it is today, so on days of inclement weather there wasn't much to do. When the boat was tied up, I'd eventually make my way from my rented mobile home to Brian's place, which was just a few miles away, and take in heavy doses of basketball on TV. This was all fine and dandy, but Brian's wife, Kari, was thinking it would be for the greater good for me to have a girlfriend to hang out with rather than being their guest couch potato. Long story short, she slipped me the number of a former department store co-worker named D'Ann who she thought I might enjoy meeting. Since I was kind of a quiet guy, Kari doubted I would actually follow through with a call, but something told me that maybe I should.

Even though I was nervous, the next time we were blown

into port I took a leap of faith and rotary-dialed ten digits that would ultimately change my life. During our hour-long chat on the phone, we hit it off great and much to my surprise, she was open to seeing me, in person! I explained that my days off were totally dictated by the weather, so it turned out to be a Tuesday a week later that I drove to Corvallis for our first date. Upon meeting her for the first time, she was everything Kari described and I knew I didn't want to blow this opportunity. What I found amusing a bit later was that my rather clean-cut, slender appearance was a bit of a shock to her. She had me pictured as the stereotyped fisherman you would see in a movie—a short, stout guy with a bushy beard, and beer gut.

Even though Corvallis is a college town, there wasn't a whole lot going on that evening. If you don't believe in miracles, you might after learning that she agreed to see me again after enduring two hours of the movie *Police Academy 2* and some fancy dining at the Lyons family restaurant.

The second date led to a third, and it wasn't long before I was filling the gaps in our busy spring fishing season by making day trips to Corvallis and then steaming back to Newport so that I'd be on the boat early the next morning. D'Ann's schedule was hectic, too, working 6 AM to 3 PM at a stock brokerage firm, but occasionally she would sneak over to the coast for a few hours to dine out in Newport before making the dark, curvy trek back to the Valley. Her coastal experience growing up was quite typical of a Valley tourist—visit the popular attractions, get sandblasted on windy excursions on the beach, and eat chowder at the famous Mo's Restaurant. I had a blast showing her the peeled-back layers of the coastal vibe. She experienced eye-opening glimpses of dock life, meeting some rather eclectic locals, dining at some of the more off-the-beaten path eateries, and some of the stunning, out-of-the-way coastal nooks and crannies. The new Tears for Fears album had become a fixture in my tape deck, and the song "Shout" quickly became a shared favorite song.

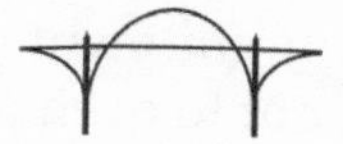

As the crabbing waned a bit, we filled the gap with three halibut seasons, which were each about a week long. The amount of preparation for halibut fishing is enormous. There are hundreds of lines, or gangions, to tie, a whole deck to convert from crabbing to longline fishing, loading up with ice and bait—the list goes on and on. While it was amazing to catch big flat slabs of up to 150 pounds, it was some of the hardest work I had ever done. When you are not pulling up the gear, you are cleaning fish, icing fish, cutting bait, and baiting hooks. Since the season is more like a derby, sleep is very low on the priority list.

After a few days of two-hour rests, it's all I could do to maintain focus. Once, after a short respite in my bunk, I was so groggy that I instinctively reached in the adjacent fridge, popped open a can of Pepsi, and chugged it while lying prone for a fuel-injected caffeine and sugar rush in order to function. It was a fascinating fishery though, and aside from the targeted species, we never knew what we would catch. On the hooks were many species of rockfish, black cod, skates, and sharks. It was not an experience for the squeamish. During sets at night, we had to pull the gear quickly as slime eels and sand fleas would invade the catch. Slime eels, in particular, are like something out of a horror movie. They find their way into the fish through any possible orifice and then begin to devour their victims from the inside out. We knew they were present when we would pull a normally plump rockfish and it would collapse on the deck like a wilted balloon. The worst was yet to come as one or more slime eels would suddenly slither out of the deflated victim on the deck, and true to their name, would coat everything in contact with layers of stringy, slippery, and sticky goo. After the final halibut trip in 1985, I plopped down on the couch, spun side one of Supertramp's new album *Brother*

Where You Bound, and then woke up 15 hours later.

Since I had made a commitment to Mike to work on the deck of his boat, I chose not to even give thought to breaking out the dory for the 1985 season. All coho fishing was shut down again for the summer, and when late spring rolled around, it was apparent that very few small boats would be participating. Working on deck of the *Challenge* was a great opportunity to learn many facets of the local industry from a rockstar skipper. I soon realized I had landed one of the primo deckhand jobs in port, and it would've been crazy to let it go for a short stint trying to chase kings on the *Carolyn Kay*.

To fill the void between halibut openers and occasional late-season crab trips, we took a stab at purse-seining for squid of Heceta Head, north of Florence. In the mid-eighties, schools of squid were everywhere, and they would rise to the surface from the murky depths in the evening like aquatic phantoms. They were attracted to the light from the glaring beams of the deck lights while we were crabbing. Seeing this, our skipper Mike got all excited, purchased seine gear and a skiff from a boat owner who was willing to sell, and we made two trips with a crew of four to go figure out how to catch them. We plugged the boat twice fishing from dark to dawn and had a blast working out the kinks in the operation. It was almost comical as we brought the squid to the surface and started brailing them. They would squirt ink in every direction, and en masse, they sounded like a symphonic net full of farts. With blasts of ink jettisoning in every direction, we invariably became inadvertent targets and soon looked like we were transforming into raccoons. While we found we could easily fill the boat with jet-propelled cephalopods, the price per pound hovered only around a dime. Even though it was still marginally profitable, the fish company could only take on a certain amount of our tentacled product per week, so our seining venture ended with two trips under our belts.

While on one of our final runs through the crab gear for

the season, we noticed several of the larger salmon trollers were dialed in on a chinook bite off the central coast near Yachats (pronounced Ya-Hots). Mike wasn't wild about salmon trolling as he saw other fisheries as being more profitable, but with the catches being so good during a lull between halibut openers, we slapped on the salmon gear to join the party. I was all in on this as I was able to get my trolling fix.

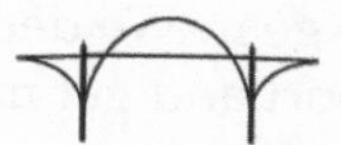

My tour on the *Challenge* opened a portal for me to gain first-hand intel of how the "big boys" of the trolling industry fished. On the docks, I tagged along with Mike, who knew everyone, for visits to the boats of highlining salmon fishermen. From these dockside chats, I was able to glean incredibly valuable fishing secrets. Unbeknownst to anyone, when I arrived home, I furiously jotted down every detail I could recall. Seeing those trollers catching a bunch of big kings so close to the beach sent my mind reeling as I pondered, "Maybe, just maybe, I'll be able to try out these new nuggets of knowledge on the *Carolyn Kay*!"

We couldn't have asked for better conditions for chinook chasing. The first trip off Yachats under sunny skies and calm seas was filled with steady action with kings engulfing hoochie and Hotspot flasher combinations in the shallow 25-fathom waters near shore. It was a blast to see some of the new-to-me gear setups in action. I continued to be amazed by Mike's success, too. It didn't matter what species we fished for. He always came up as a highliner.

We made a second trip just a few miles south of Newport, just beyond the nearshore reefs in 22-25 fathoms. The fish were congregating up against the reef line and chowing down on an abundance of bait fish that were stacked up. It was a challenging and delicate balancing act presenting the gear through the main vein of the school, but yet keeping clear of the jagged pinnacles that could wreak havoc on the gear. Fishing was solid with good-sized kings on each tack north and south. Unfortunately, one deep line snagged the rocks, which placed heavy tension on the wire and sheared the pin that held the metal davit in place. In an instant, it walloped me square on the forehead and knocked me onto the deck hatch cover. Mike bolted out of the wheelhouse to check on my well-being. Even though things went dark for a moment and my head felt like a shaken snow globe, I was able to help retrieve the gear. We decided that it would be best for me to head to port and get my head checked out. Surprisingly, a doctor's visit revealed no concussion or concerns other than a nice welt as a badge of honor.

We wound up early fall fishing with a couple of butt-kicking albacore tuna trips. The first took us 100 miles off the coast of Grays Harbor, Washington. Our adventure got off to a very rocky start for the first two days with a brutal northwester that pounded the boat so much that the onboard mini-fridge door came flying off its hinges. It was so rough that both of us became queasy, even though neither of us typically dealt with seasickness. Adding to our nausea, we only had one fish to show for our effort. The water calmed down though, and then we got into several schools of big cold-water albies with doubles and triples coming aboard regularly. It was during those moments on deck that I experienced what some fishermen refer to as "tuna fever." Hoisting 20 to 30-pound albies in rapid fashion got my tuna blood running. The dory fisherman in me could help daydreaming of a *Carolyn Kay* voyage with the boat plugged with albacore.

When the fishing tapered off for the fleet, we pointed the boat home but kept the gear in the water for a spell just in case we happened to bump into another school. The sky and water was blue and clear, and the seas were dramatically calmer than our arrival route. I was enjoying the ride on the back deck while keeping the tuna jigs clear of seagrass when our trance was suddenly interrupted.

"Hey Mike, there are some whales off our starboard bow. Check it out. It looks like they're headed this way," I shouted to him in the wheelhouse. About a minute later, I shouted again, "Whoa. They're getting closer. They look like orcas. If they keep their course, they'll swim under the starboard side." In no time at all, the whales were within ten yards as I hollered, "Mike! They're swimming under the boat! They're huge!"

"Yeah. I can see them on the color machine!" Mike shouted from the helm.

The mayhem was followed by several loud whooshes behind the boat.

"Oh my gosh! You have to see this, Mike. They're right in the prop wash. Three of them just behind the stern jigs. I hope they don't get hooked. You've gotta see this." I emphatically yelled out.

As he came out on deck, we watched our three cetacean visitors veer from the stern to port side until they disappeared in the distance toward shore. It was an adrenaline-pumping encore to a trip that turned out way better than it started out. Word on the radio from other fishermen who encountered them was that they weren't orcas, but false killer whales instead. After a subsequent tuna trip off the windy coast of Northern California, we wrapped up fishing for a few months for some R & R and then prepped for the winter crabbing season.

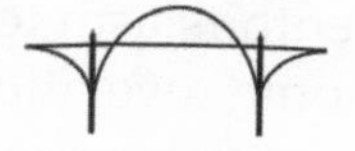

December 1st came quickly, and we were back on the water pulling pots. Brian had taken a job in Alaska, so I moved to running the crab block and Mike hired a new deckhand named Tim. He was an experienced salmon fisherman and had his own troller. We hit it off very well and formed a good deck team. The season started with a rare coastal snowstorm, but high pressure moved in like a mother-in-law and blessed us with many days of blue skies and calm seas. Crabbing was lights out! We would run through all the pots, plug the boat and then some, unload, then rinse and repeat. During a delivery, the skipper of another crab boat was in awe of skipper Mike and him repeatedly finding the Mother Lode.

"Amazing…absolutely amazing," he muttered and shook his head from his flying bridge.

December is like a crab derby with all the local boats and some transient crabbers, many of which just fish in December when the highest volume of crab is harvested. It was "go big or go home," so we fished every day possible. Tim and I both had major sinus infections but powered through with our antibiotics knowing the weather would eventually afford us some rest. Needless to say, D'Ann and I didn't see much of each other before Christmas.

The spring of 1986 was a season of change. Crabbing had dialed back to more modest catches, and the halibut seasons had been moved to summer. The encouraging word from the Pacific Fisheries Management Council stated that coho fishing was being restored, in moderation. The short of it was that boats could harvest 50 coho a day, plus a 2:1 ratio of coho to chinook thereafter. This released generous quantities of dory dopamine, as I eagerly anticipated the opportunity to wake the *Carolyn Kay* from its long slumber. Working with Tim led to several discussions on deck about king-catching strategies. The knowledge he shared was like gold and amplified my enthusiasm to put it all into action.

Tim and I also had some revelations about our career ambitions. Another salmon fisherman we knew was trading in his troller for a dory, and also going back to school to earn his elementary education degree. Tim was pondering a move to education, too. The more we talked about it, the more it appealed to me. By May, Tim had enrolled in the University of Oregon's Ed program and returned to his troller to fish the chinook season. After some soul searching, research, and heart-to-heart talks with my mother and D'Ann, I put the wheels in motion to enroll in a community college near Corvallis to pursue my elementary education degree. Adding to this move, I stepped down from my job on the *Challenge* and went to work to get the *Carolyn Kay* all dressed up for the regenerated coho season. Leaving Mike's boat was a difficult decision as it was one of the best deckhand gigs in town. I realized though, that while deckhanding was a great adventure, it wasn't something I wanted to make a career of. Nor was diving all-in fishing my own larger vessel year-round. I decided to follow a different call.

The year had served up an exciting new trajectory. My relationship with D'Ann was going great and the academic world was on my horizon. There still was space to keep my feet in the salt, and The *Carolyn Kay* was about to ride again after two seasons of darkness. I couldn't wait for Dad and I to see those springs dance again.

CHAPTER 10

SEASON 10

REGENERATION

1986 Setlist

David Sanborn *A Change of Heart*
Hiroshima *Another Place*
Mike + the Mechanics *Mike + the Mechanics*
Nu Shooz *Poolside*
Peter Gabriel *So*

Life felt like it was in perfect balance. The *Carolyn Kay* was back where it belonged at Port Dock 7 along with several other dories that suddenly emerged from a long period of stasis. Al made a few appearances, and it was good to hear his jovial and hearty voice. The late spring buzz that was ever-present in the 1970s was reverberating on high volume across the waterfront. Amid the return of the nostalgia, Steve and Rozy of the *Pisces II* were noticeably absent. Steve became heavily immersed in the king crab industry and other fisheries and their boat never re-emerged after the lean seasons of the first half of the 1980s.

Along with the positive vibe flowing through the marina, a new mix of tunes cascaded from my truck stereo, carving a new soundtrack for the regeneration taking place. Mixed with the usual serving of classic rock standards, a sprinkling of new sounds spiced up the playlist. Upbeat techno-pop from the Portland band Nu Shooz, the debut album by Mike and the Mechanics, and some cool smooth jazz sounds from David Sanborn and Hiroshima flowed from the Toyota's door panel speakers.

In May and early June, Dad made some trips over to my place in Toledo where the boat was stored to help me outfit our dory for its reemergence. The respectable catches of kings near shore by trollers and a few dories motivated us to get the boat in ship shape in short order. With Dad's diminished availability to fish and the industry's health still in question, I abandoned my dream to build a brand-new dory. I already had access to a good craft, and it made little sense to go into debt.

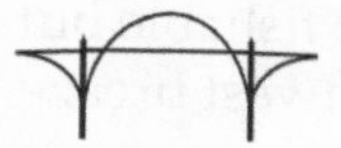

The first day out on the water was a wonderful reunion. Fishing solo, I motored the *Carolyn Kay* just past the whistle buoy out to 25 fathoms on an overcast morning with a light breeze from the southwest. Just like riding a bike, the process of setting the gear came back like a snap. I instinctively clipped spreads of five to six fathom lines sporting brass spoons and hoochies powered by Hotspot flashers. I was more than eager to put all the intel I had gathered in the past year to the test. One important detail I applied that I learned from Tim and others was that they never baited their hoochie gear, and they trolled like bats from hell at high RPMs to give the rigs action. Conversely, among many of the smaller boat fleet, not baiting hoochies was trolling heresy. It was my aim in 1986 to debunk that theory.

With the gear finally set, I started a hopeful troll south. Our past ventures in the early chinook-only season were far from stunning. Even though I was brimming with hope with the new gear tactics, scars from the past cast a lot of doubt on 1986s maiden voyage. Within the first hour though, a pumper on the starboard deep line started ringing spring bells. After pinching myself that I had a fish on, I pulled the gear and boated a plump large king. Adrenaline was coursing through my veins in seeing that it had attacked one of my new gear spreads. Two more larges were boated that day on the new set ups, and I was floating on Cloud Nine.

Back at the Port Dock, I stuffed coins into the Port Dock payphone and gave my dad the latest play-by-play of the day and how the new gear worked. With occasional wind gusts whooshing in the phone speaker, I shared my long-distance enthusiasm with D'Ann. Her whole reality of my fishing career had been in seeing me as a deckhand. While she had seen our boat, browsed through some photos, and heard my stories, the whole dory fishing drill was all new.

A few days later, Dad became reacquainted with his sea legs. It was one of those fishable but semi-snotty and cloudy oceans with a stiff southwest breeze. It served as an excellent workout for regaining balance needed to keep upright in the boat. Before Dad stepped aboard that day, I knew how things were going to go down regarding the new gear. If it didn't produce right away, he was going to question the lack of bait aboard the boat and the swift trolling speed.

"The three kings I boated a few days ago were on these C-28 and C-29 hoochies. Just so you know, I didn't bait a single one and they produced. I trolled a few hundred RPM's faster than usual, too, just like all the big guys. So far so good!" I said as I pointed out the gear in the gear trays.

"Really? No bait?" Dad inquired.

"Nope. I didn't even bring any aboard and don't have any today."

"Well, we'll see how it goes," Dad said in a less than convinced tone.

A half-hour after we had trolled with no bumps or bites on the sloppy ocean, Dad was transmitting a few doubting signals my way. I was praying that the springs would start hammering soon so the doubt didn't fester. Fortunately, four large kings were boated that day, and I could see the evidence was nudging Dad toward becoming a convert. A few things became apparent after that day. There were some chinooks near shore. Second, the new approaches to king fishing were working, and lastly, it was a blessing to fish with Dad again. We fell right back into our synchronous roles and operated like a well-oiled machine.

Even though our fishing genes were reawakened, high pressure sent a welcoming party for the occasion. Our old foe, Northwesterly, took the stage, cast its meteorological spell, and stranded us on terra firma. Big strong summery gusts whooshed through town, rocked trees, and flapped flags with gusto. While it was nirvana for kite flyers, it was a test of patience for dory fishermen.

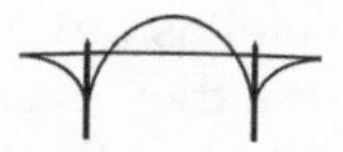

Eleven days later, the wind relented and the dory guys gradually emerged from the shadows back to the salt. I managed to pull five kings, again just south of the port close to shore. The king catches were far from lights out, but it was encouraging that putting a handful of big ones in the box was becoming the norm.

On the evening of June 23rd, I ran into a dory fisherman named Jake at the Port Dock parking lot. He was a nice guy and a savvy fisherman who owned a blue and white dory. We lived polar opposite lifestyles, but like many acquaintances on the docks, fishing was the common ground. Jake shared a tip about some of his troller buddies who toughed it out in the northwest slop and had some big king scores down south off Seal Rock. This news was gold and was just what I needed to hear to keep the momentum going. He was heading that direction in the morning… and upon hearing his hot tip, so was I!

The next morning's sunrise was glorious and the ocean

was like a soft pillow with just enough swell to provide balance and harmony for a perfect day. With the throttle wide open and the silhouette of the Coast Range riding shotgun with me, the flat bottom of the boat glided over gentle crests and and through the troughs. A symphony of jingling bells affixed to the trolling pole springs sounded like Santa's sleigh. Seal Rock began to emerge through the misty beach haze and signaled that I was close to my targeted area. The conditions became more ideal upon seeing numerous tidal rip trails. This phenomenon is where opposing currents meet and create a churning wash of biological material, some of which floats on the surface. This creates a haven for fish to feed and for fishermen to follow. Mixed among the thin foamy quagmire in those rips were velella jellyfish. These little mariners have a flat circular base and are each equipped with a sail that extends vertically at a right angle. Westerly winds and swells drive velellas out of the offshore currents toward the shoreline where they eventually wash up en masse on the beaches. With Seal Rock in clear view to the south, I decided to start setting the gear along the 30-fathom line and see if those rumored kings were still in mass quantities. There were hardly any boats around. I wasn't sure if it was a good sign or a bad one.

In 1986, a new regulation was established for all hooks to be barbless. This was created to protect coho, which had to be released during certain parts or conditions of the season. To do this, we simply took out a pair of pliers and pinched the barb on the hook down. While this wasn't a fail-safe method for coho survival, it did help quite a bit. It also meant it took extra precaution to not lose fish. Fortunately, chinooks exert a heavy pull, so it wasn't too much of a detriment by not having the barbs as long as you kept heavy tension on the line.

Moments after setting the gear down, despite setting spreads more designed for kings, armadas of coho started climbing on everything I had to offer. However, mixed among all the silvers were some kings. To minimize coho mortality, along with not having to expend energy to catch and release them, I reduced the number of spreads per wire. This helped although there were still coho everywhere. Had it been a wide-open coho fishery, it would have easily been a 150-fish day, and they were decent-sized for it being so early in the summer.

Not long after I had boated a few kings, Jake arrived on the scene. He motored about 15 yards away and yelled, "Anything happening yet?"

"I just put two larges in the boat. I think the fish you talked about last night are here. There's a mega-school of silvers here, so I'm not running a lot of gear. Look at my springs, there's silvers hitting again. Ooohh! A big one just hit that deep line."

"Alright! I'm going to get my gear down. Go get your fish. Talk to you later!" he shouted as he motored a short way down south.

Large kings and mediums kept engulfing the new gear and the springs were always pumping and jiggling. The cool part was that it was just Jake and me on a large parcel of salty real estate. By noon it was apparent that this was going to be the day to shatter our boat's personal best king score.

"Hey Jake. How goes the battle over there?" I hailed him on the CB.

"Yeah, it's been pretty good. Definitely getting some good ones here, between the creek and the rock."

"Alright! Let's keep drilling this area. I owe you one for this tip."

We probably should have remained more covert as more boats slowly trickled into our hotspot. On the radio I heard someone say, "I'm not catching much out here on the Pile, but I heard a couple dory guys nearshore down south somewhere catching some."

The ocean remained angelic throughout the day. When it seemed like it couldn't get any better, I was treated to a bonus prize. As I was pulling gear through a field of velellas, an aqua-colored translucent Japanese glass float about the size of a soccer ball passed right under my nose as I was pulling gear. These were rare finds and were mostly found when the velella schools were present. I quickly threw out a cup to mark the spot, and saved the location on the LORAN. I made as tight of a circle as I could without tangling the gear, very unlike I did on our first day ever fishing. Passing by a second time, I snared the cup and the prize. While it wasn't of much value to a glass float collector, it added to the awesomeness of the day.

The fishing finally tapered off in the early evening, so I called it a day with a *Carolyn Kay* best of 24 kings. I made sure to give a big thanks to Jake on the CB for the tip and hoped for the chance to buy him lunch sometime. After completing the rituals at the fish company, gas dock, and tucking the boat away, I set my course for the Port Dock pay phone to share the news of the day with D'Ann.

"You sound excited. So how was fishing today, Terry?" D'Ann asked.

"It was one of the best days I've ever had on the water. I caught 24 kings and a Japanese glass float. The ocean was flat. It was an amazing day! It was a nice payday, too."

"That's awesome! Are you heading out tomorrow to the same spot?"

"I think so. It slowed down a bit this afternoon, but there still should be some fish there. The weather is supposed to stay calm for a few more days. I want to get as much time on the water this week before we head over to Madras for my grandparents' 50th anniversary."

When I hung up the receiver, I promptly dialed up Dad and filled him in on the banner day.

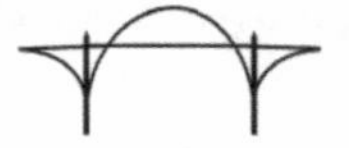

The big school of fish moved on but each of the next few days brought a respectable catch. Mother nature served up more magnificence on June 27th. On a mirror-pond ocean

I noticed a few trollers making some tacks just south of the whistle buoy in 22 fathoms of water. I decided to plunk the gear then and there. In no time I put a big one in the box and then another followed on the next pass. My grandparents' 50th wedding anniversary celebration in Central Oregon was the next day, but with fishing so close to shore, I was able to make a full day of it and seize a rare moment. By late afternoon I had scratched up 10 good-sized kings. While it was hard to leave a good fishing hole behind, I was anxious for our family gathering in Madras. Many extended family members were planning to attend, and I was stoked for a whitewater raft trip down a wild stretch of the Deschutes River.

The time with family was wonderful, and the rafting trip was epic. We went with a Native American guide service that led us on a unique whitewater adventure. Our voyage took us down the Deschutes River, which flows through majestic high desert scenery. At midday, we pulled out on a beach and were treated to an amazing buffet all set up in the desert sagebrush. The highlight was their fry bread, which was made on the spot and was the perfect carbo load after some riveting runs through some gnarly rapids. It was refreshing to enjoy a quest on the water that wasn't salty for a change.

Following the family festivities, it was time to dial back into fishing mode. For the first time in a very long time, the docks and the radio chatter were abuzz and euphoric about the all-species season. I had fished the chinook-only season in June mostly solo, so it was a special gift to have Dad back in the fold for the opener.

Only the gentlest of swells greeted us as we emerged from the harbor, just to remind us that we were still guests of the Pacific.

"Terry, it's so good to be back and to be able to put some silvers in the boat. I can't wait to drop the gear." Dad exclaimed exuberantly. "Where are we headed, skipper?"

"I think we should just head straight out to 30 fathoms,

put the gear in and see what happens. The charter boats have been knocking 'em dead out front all week. I think there are silvers everywhere, and we know there are a few kings around close to shore, too,' I suggested.

"Alright, Ter, ready when you are!"

Our gear trays were armed with a platter of hot pink spoons, tantalizing short-spread hoochie-flasher combos, and some of the steadfast king gear down deep. No sooner than we had started setting the gear, the metal davits supporting the trolling cables that ran through pulleys from the gurdies started pulsating wildly as did the trolling wire in the water.

"Holy cow, Ter, at least three fish have hit my gear sending it down," Dad announced.

Moments later I echoed his observations, "Yep, I have at least three or four on, too." Let's get all our gear down and then things are going to get crazy."

For the next couple of hours, it was a matter of just taking turns pulling the deep lines back and forth. While one pulled, the other cleaned fish and steered. Finally, we took the time to pull the floats and peel off the fish that were hanging there for a few hours. We didn't need to drop them back in. By 9:10 AM, we had caught our 50-coho quota. We hadn't boated any kings at that time, so we were not allowed to take in any more coho with the 2:1 ratio rule. Suddenly we were hit with a totally foreign scenario. We were kind of dumbfounded. We looked at each other and asked the same question, "Now what do we do?" The ocean was ideal, the fishing was red hot, and it was barely even time for a mid-morning snack.

"We could troll for chinooks in close, maybe south of whistle buoy. Maybe there won't be silvers all over the place there," I suggested.

"We might as well give it a shot. Nuts, Terry, we could easily catch 150 to 200 silvers today!" Dad replied emphatically.

To put things in perspective, it took us 17 days of fishing

to catch 50 silvers in our first season, which was a direct result of very poor coho runs and two guys who didn't have a clue. Still spinning from our odd predicament, we headed east to the 22-fathom line. We set the deep lines with four to five spreads each of long-leader king gear and hoped the silvers would just turn the other way. It didn't take long for the bells to start jingling and jangling, but the music they made was not the sounds that kings compose. The silvers were thick in the shallows, too. It just didn't make sense to cull through so many silvers to scratch up perhaps a king or two. As that reality set in, we pulled the gear and set our course for a short ride home. It felt so wrong, but it was what it was. We were one of the first boats to deliver that morning, which if nothing else was a testament that we were doing things right. Little did we know at the moment, but it was a situation we were going to need to come to grips with several more times during the season.

The next day wasn't quite as lights out for coho, but it was still pretty steady. We were catching a few kings, so there was this balancing act that demanded some quick recall of basic math fluency. Say we had 50 silvers and 2 kings. This would mean at that moment we could retain 54 silvers, but then could only pull aboard chinooks, which meant for each chinook boated, we could keep two additional silvers. On several occasions that season we would reach the maximum number of silvers, have to release a few that were on our lines, then catch a few kings, and then keep a few more silvers. It was madness and far from perfect, but at least the management council attempted to provide a season. The season's second outing yielded a solid 48 coho and 6 king score.

On the third day of the season, we found ourselves in king country. After catching a few big ones right away and hearing of others doing the same, we switched out the coho gear and targeted the money fish. We figured if the king-catching action died off, we could troll out to deep water and load up on silvers and get our fifty or thereabouts.

We put 11 big kings and 29 silvers in the box, which netted more cash than if we just loaded up on coho.

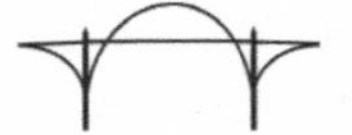

After a few lackluster coho days with just a few kings sprinkled in, 50-fish derbies became the norm for nearly every remaining day of the coho season. Sometimes we would hit the quota and be in port in time for a late breakfast whereas other days we had to work a little harder. In addition to having Dad aboard for half the season, I was able to convince D'Ann to serve as a deckhand when fish were practically jumping in the boat. The idea that we would likely just fish through mid-morning was certainly more appealing to her than an all-day shift. As expected, each line had doubles and triples stacked minutes after the gear was deployed. This was a total win as I had her back in port before the breakfast menu shut down. Even though she had some concern about sea sickness, it never happened. Aside from taking a short nap once I had the gear down, she was a real trooper. She took on the helmsmanship duties while I ran gear and cleaned fish. When I asked her if she wanted to fish a third day, she answered quickly, "No, I have a perfect record. I think I'll end my fishing career on a high note."

While many days were carbon copies with coho catches in the fifties and some kings mixed in, there was one day that broke the mold. The sky was blanketed with the classic pillowy coastal summer stratus clouds that merged into a flat-calm ocean in a blurry horizon line. The thick insulated atmosphere made for a comfortable morning with no wind and moderate temperatures. While fishing wasn't as chaotic as a five-alarm fire, there was some steady coho action with a few kings sprinkled in. There was no doubt we were well on track to have another good score by midday.

Resting on top of our steering console keeping the compass company was a desktop barometer. It was cased in cheap wood and was paired with a thermometer. The instrument had been on board for some time, and I largely ignored it. Before leaving the dock each morning, Dad would lean forward in the console sort of hunched over and would always twist the dial to mark the pressure reading. Then he would tap the glass lens a few times to make sure the barometer dial wasn't sticking. The basic skinny on barometers is to get your butt into port if the barometric pressure reading takes a nosedive. An extreme drop would indicate gale conditions and all hell would soon break loose. This was very rare along the Oregon Coast in the summertime though.

Around mid-morning, we had the boat on a west tack and were trolling through a patch of silvers. We put a few in the box, and as usual, we headed back for another helping. The CB radio chatter was filled with an upbeat vibe as everyone was enjoying the calm conditions at the workplace. Dad was at the helm and instinctively proceeded with his "tap-tap-tap" on the barometer lens. I hardly even noticed, but moments later I became well aware of my father's meteorological musings.

"Holy cow, Terry! The barometer dropped a lot in the last hour! We need to point the bow for home. It's going to blow today!" Dad said emphatically.

"Looks good to me, and I haven't heard any weather reports of wind. I think we're fine," I replied, slightly annoyed.

"I've never seen it drop that much. Something big is going to happen," Dad emphasized once again.

"We'll be fine. We're not that far away, and we're catching fish," I again replied, a little concerned that Dad was quite serious about wanting to pull the plug on the day.

Taking it a step further into embarrassment from my point-of-view, Dad hailed *Blue Angel* Terry on the CB and described the data he mined from our simple instrument along with his hypothesis.

"*Blue Angel, Blue Angel.* Terry, come back to me when you have a moment."

"Hey Bruce! How are you doing over there?" Terry replied.

"Oh, it's been a steady scratch most of the day. We just put a few in the box a few minutes ago."

"Good deal. Yep, same here. I think if we make a day of it, we'll have a good score."

"Have you heard of any reports of wind today on the VHF radio, Terry?" Dad inquired.

"No, I sure haven't, Bruce. It's been a great ocean all day, too. I'll check though and get back to you."

"Dad, it's fine out here. If there was bad weather we would have heard reports from several boats by now. No one has said anything," I complained.

"*Carolyn Kay,* Bruce."

"Yeah, Terry, go ahead,"

"I checked the VHF and the forecast sounds good, Bruce. No big wind today," Terry reported.

A few other guys from the fleet chimed in with similar replies. The fact that we were even having this conversation was making my skin crawl, and Dad's broadcasted prognosis made it worse. I despised going in early.

Thus, the steering wheel war game resumed with me edging it seaward and Dad adjusting it homeward, all in a civil, nonverbal power struggle. I feared that fishing that morning would hit a lull and that Dad would pounce on that stretch of inaction as a reason to head for the barn. And that is exactly what happened.

"Well, it seems like the fish have gone off the bite. We haven't had a bump in an hour," Dad said as he tapped the barometer glass again. "Wow, it went down a bit more. I think we need to put the gear in the boat, Ter."

"How about we troll toward the beach? Maybe we'll find some fish on the way there. If it does blow up, at least we wouldn't be far away," I countered.

After a half hour on our eastward troll with no fish, Dad finally won out and we put the gear in the boat. I was really steamed as I felt like we were leaving a potentially solid fishing day behind. Following our early departure from the Pacific, we delivered our fish. As we offloaded, I could still hear some of the guys on the CB pulling a few fish again and there still wasn't a puff of wind to be felt.

By the time we parked the boat though, it was a different situation. Wind ripples appeared on the water in the bay, and with the radio still crackling, there was some banter about the ocean getting sloppy.

A few minutes later, someone else hailed, "Wow, it's getting pretty wild out here. It's cappin' pretty good everywhere. I'm probably going to put the gear in the boat soon."

"Yeah," another chimed in. "There was nothing in the forecast about this wind."

With each report, I become more and more humbled. The situation got worse from there, and conversations over the air were more tense with the weather deteriorating. By late in the day, most boats were tied to the dock. One fiberglass day-boat from the Port Dock 7 moorages was trying to cross the bar on the ebb and was having a terrifying time. A large shrimp boat happened to be coming in and was able to create a calmer lee for the smaller boat to take advantage of and sneak safely across the bar. The wind, which seemed to materialize out of nowhere, blew all night long up to a gale force. Needless to say, the shame of going in early dissipated, and I had to let go of my pride and admit that my dad's "overreaction" was completely justified. This was further reinforced by Terry on the *Blue Angel* who commented later, "You sure called that one, Bruce!"

From that point on, I found myself doing a little "tap-tap-tap" on the barometer glass after cranking up the engine. Father knows best!

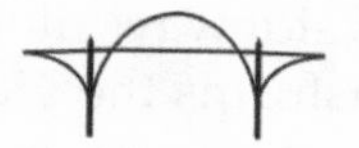

The remaining days of the coho season were quite predictable with scores between 50 and 54 silvers with some kings thrown in here and there. Dad took advantage of every gap in his schedule to sneak in some fishing time. Even though we had transitioned through nearly a complete role reversal with me taking on a majority of the expenses and running the boat more often than he, our relationship and teamwork continued to be rock solid.

It was mind-blowing for both of us that over a few weeks, we had adopted the mindset that 50 silvers per day was the norm, and anything less was a disappointment. On July 24th, it was announced that the quota for our region had been reached and that the coho season would close at midnight. After the 52nd and final coho had been brought aboard that day, my thoughts shifted to, "Now what?"

The morning of July 25th was absolutely stunning with a flat ocean and deep blue horizon, all mixed with the sounds of Peter Gabriel's "So" LP filling my pickup cab. It felt weird to not be out there filling the fish box up with salmon on such a pristine sea. After loading up on some pancakes the size of hubcaps at a small local eatery, I made my way to the docks to give the dory a bath and to do some tidying up.

I took a few days off to get some R and R in Corvallis before diving back into the season's next phase. When I got back on the water again, I found some kings hanging in tight to the reefs just off the beach making for some very welcome close-to-port fishing. In classic fashion, high pressure moved in, the valley heated up, and the northwest wind cranked the volume and added black fog for good measure. Black fog lives up to its sinister name. With the northwesterlies serving as propulsion, it crawls sideways along the surf line like a dark phantom and transforms the view of the breakers into a ghostly blur. This particular weather system cast its spell on the salmon fleet for ten days, pretty much obliterating any enthusiasm on chinook fishing. It seemed like it would never end. With that, I decided to just enjoy the nice valley weather again and spend quality time in the warmth of the summer with D'Ann.

In the 17 months that we had been together, D'Ann had worked wonders to expand my horizons. I was meeting new people, attending her work-social functions, dining out in new-to-me establishments, sporting new clothing, and dashing off for spur-of-the-moment creative excursions. She would come up with ideas like driving up to Mary's Peak on the afternoon of a cool, crisp, and clear Christmas Eve. It overlooked Corvallis and the Coast Range in spectacular fashion and was an out-of-the-box place to exchange our Christmas gifts. I loved her spontaneous spirit and all the new pathways that life with her was carving out.

We had reached the point in our relationship where I knew she was the one I wanted to spend the rest of my life with. I was wracking my brain trying to figure out how and where to pop the big question. Thinking back to my Coast Guard days in Coos Bay, my mind zeroed in on the stunningly gorgeous, forested headland, Cape Arago State Park. It used to be my getaway from the raucous ship life. One day we decided to just drive down the coastline to Coos Bay to show her where I was stationed and to do some sightseeing around the Cape Arago area. While gazing out at the sea on our stroll along the Cape's walking trail, I asked her to marry me. Fortunately, she said, "Yes!" Needless to say, this kicked the wedding planning in gear. With March 21st being the target date, along with an upcoming move to Corvallis, I had plenty on my plate when not trying to catch a few kings.

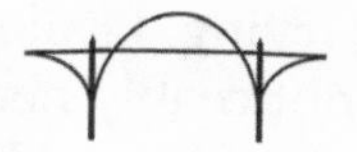

Just before all hope for the remaining season was lost, the wind began to subside. During the season I had gotten to know a skilled fisherman named Mark who owned a dory named *Lady Scarlett*. Mark received some credible intel from some larger boat guys that boats were catching some big kings close to the beach off of the Sea Lion Caves and Heceta Head. This was 49 miles south near the town of Florence. For August to be profitable, I knew in my heart that I needed to make the move. One roadblock was that my small pickup was ill-equipped to trailer a dory and Dad needed his Jeep Wagoner for work. Mark and I strategized and came up with a plan to run our boats about half the distance, drop the gear in, and fish our way to Florence. His girlfriend would pick us up, drive us to Newport to get our rigs, each equipped with a canopy that would serve as shelter for however long we stayed down there.

The Florence king fishing scene had been a well-kept secret for some time. Aside from the fishing, the area was flat-out beautiful with a myriad of coastal pine trees and towering dunes. There were some cons though that anyone interested in fishing there needed to know. The northwest wind often screamed down that way, at least five to ten knots greater than Newport when high pressure set in. Also, reaching the ocean required a winding downriver five-mile odyssey. The most talked about hazard was the bar. It was shallow and known for being treacherous, especially during ebb tide when the river behaved like a pressure-assisted toilet repeatedly being flushed. It was common for breakers to form and block any transit to or from the port.

I had heard enough talk over the past year about Florence to know what I would be getting myself into. I both relished and anguished the challenge as I dealt with the pros and cons like a ping pong match in my head, but I pledged to go forth with the venture. I knew one thing for sure, I would regret not trying. I called Dad to let him know my game plan. He was noticeably nervous about the whole ordeal, but he was encouraging and had confidence that I was making the right move. Regardless, even after making all the preparations for the journey, I didn't get much sleep the night before Mark and I cast off.

The next morning's sky was plastered with multiple

shades of gray. While it didn't have a threatening presence, it wasn't particularly inviting either. The northwest wind was just a whimper and the fog had backed off several miles offshore. Light winds and good visibility highlighted the marine forecast. While there was some comfort in that, I was keeping a hairy eyeball on the conditions.

Mark and I crossed the Yaquina Bay bar and hung a hard left to begin our southerly sojourn. The LORAN had been a problem child that summer, likely due to condensation, and it had the habit of losing its signal made evident by the flickering digits of the digital display. I was praying that it was fully up to the task, especially if that fog bank decided to pay a visit. Mark didn't have a LORAN, so I knew he was relying on me for that critical data.

We set our gear down off Cape Perpetua, which was about the halfway point, with Mark about a quarter mile south of me. I had visions of us being the boats that hit the jackpot, trolling through a big school of kings and plugging our fish boxes as we made our way to the new promised land. Unfortunately, there were hardly any signs of life on our southbound troll, although Mark was able to drum up a stray large king. With the realization that we were trolling through a desert, I spent time checking gear and examining and memorizing the chart to the entrance of the Siuslaw River. Having a clear mental image and knowing the correct compass course was a priority in order to be able to split between the two Siuslaw River jetties with precision. I also took note of the shallow spots where some sharp stacked swells could pose some hair-raising moments.

Sometime within the first hour of trolling, the fog started advancing toward shore. "Oh crap! You are going to move in despite the forecast! Of course, you would," I complained aloud to myself. The creepy cloud wall that had been held at bay past noon that day swept in and blanketed the entire distance we needed to cover. As it stealthily moved eastward, I gathered as much visual data that I could before the clouds enveloped us. The LORAN's behavior had been finicky that morning, with some occasional flickers just to instill some anxiety and mistrust. My gut churned as I started to dwell on the reality that we would have to tackle our first port entrance with just a compass, fathometer, and good listening skills.

With no fish in the box, the wind picking up, and very little visibility, I had to fight off the doubt that kept trying to creep into my mind. *"This was a stupid move!"* I thought. Regaining my composure, I reminded myself that I had given my life to Christ earlier in the year. This was as good a time as any to place my predicament in God's hands. I prayed for the fog to lift, and wouldn't you know it, the Good Lord provided. Like the parting of the Red Sea, the fog bank miraculously pulled back a few miles offshore. I radioed to Mark, "Hey, do you see me? I have good visibility here, but I still don't see you."

Mark took a look around and replied, "I'm about a half-mile south. I can see you." Looking that way, I spotted his dory's silhouette against shimmering waves made visible by the sun's sudden appearance.

"Hey, I haven't had a bump since we dropped gear. Have you had any action?" I asked.

"I just have the one large king in the box. No other bumps though." Mark replied.

"I'm glad you at least have paid for your gas bill. My LORAN has decided to behave and I think we ought to run to port while the coast is clear," I added.

"Sounds like a plan, Terry. I'll start pulling gear and will wait for you," Mark agreed.

It didn't take us long after running south before the fog stormed back for an encore performance. It was thick as pea soup and we slowed to a crawl as we neared where the Siuslaw whistle buoy was supposed to be. Fortunately the swell height was minimal so we didn't have any hair-raising waves to deal with. When we reached where the buoy should have been, there was nothing but a cloak of misty aerosol. I mused, *"Is the LORAN messing up again*?" We shut our engines off and listened.

"Hear anything?" Mark said.

"Not yet, but according to the LORAN reading, it should be right in front of us," I replied.

A couple nervous minutes passed as we motored forward at a crawl and then shut off our engines to listen for a hoot or a moan.

Suddenly, a vague noise penetrated the whiteness.

"Did you hear that, Mark? It sounds like it is dead ahead," I announced.

"Yeah, it sounds close," Mark confirmed.

Sure enough, the buoy moaned again as it rocked with the gentle swells and then it appeared like a friendly apparition with open arms. Looking at the chart, we fired up our outboards and pivoted our bows to a compass course that would take us straight through the heart of the bar. While motoring at a crawl, two large rock arms greeted us out of the airy mire on the port and starboard sides of our boats. Just like that, we were on the river where the heavens opened up in a blaze of sunshine. With our throttles punched we navigated the five-mile winding course upriver past the Coast Guard station and the towering dunes. As we cruised under the Highway 101 bridge, a giant wave of relief swept over me as we successfully crossed the finish line of our journey.

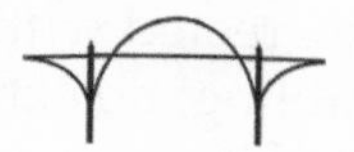

The Port of Florence was a doryman's dream. Moorage was free of charge for transient boats. As long as you didn't mind walking a little further down the dock and maybe tying up next to another boat, it was a killer deal. For overnight lodging, dorymen were given free rein to park their rigs anywhere in the grassy parking area for no charge. Adding to the big savings on living expenses, there was also a crude but serviceable shower facility nearby, which was free to use anytime. Fuel at the gas dock was cheaper than it was in Newport, and the one-and-only fish buyer typically paid ten cents more a pound than did the buyers one hour north. There was even a fishing gear salesman who did business out of his van and showed up once or twice a week with some good deals. In return, the local merchants on the riverfront, which is known as Old Town, just wanted our business. For the next few weeks, I lodged in the Hotel Toyota, more commonly known as the bed of my 1982 Toyota pickup. It was covered with a tinted-glass canopy and bedded with a four-inch-thick green foam mattress where I rolled out a sleeping bag. The scene there was much like the early days of our fishing career where there was a sense of simplicity and newness.

While the typical drill in Newport was to get up early and head out at first light or shortly thereafter to get in "that morning bite," Florence was a whole different ball game, and it took some getting used to. The first thing you needed to know, the tides ran the show on the Siuslaw River. When the ebb tide flowed like a fire hose and collided with swells of four feet or greater, chances were that you weren't crossing the bar unless you were content with risking your life. Therefore, fishing out of Florence required patience, which I found I had very little of.

My baptism in the Florence fishing scene took place on my first morning there. I woke up early all fired up to get an early start, only to be greeted with absolute silence. No diesel engines were rumbling, no exhaust fumes mixed with the low-tide aroma wafted, and no one stirred on the docks. *"Where the heck is everyone?"* I pondered. After puttering around between my boat and the truck, not wanting to be the first one to leave the dock, I finally ran into Mark and a new acquaintance, Bill. We decided to chill out at a diner until the tide changed.

It was a joy to get to know Bill. He was a very laid-back guy who had a wealth of experience in the fishing industry. He fished a 22-foot red dory named *Jireh* with black trim that had a cuddy cabin on the bow section. His fascination with boats dated back to age 13 when he built a small eight-foot pram boat with his father. This led to the duo building 10 to 12 more small craft. Later, Bill teamed with his brother in fishing a dory out of Pacific City. Just like us, their initiation in the industry was humbling. While towing their dory to the coast for its maiden voyage, they happened to look through the back window of their rig and noticed their dory was gone. Miraculously, they found their boat uninjured and sitting in the middle of the two-lane highway. A dozen or so people helped them load their boat on the trailer and then they were on their way. Aside from dory fishing, Bill worked as a joint venture representative in the 1980s on Polish, Japanese, and Korean fish trawlers. American catcher boats would trawl for pollock and cod, and then transfer the nets to the processors. Bill's job was to make sure the transfers and transactions went smoothly. He also worked in a similar role with NOAA. It turned out that Bill also had ties to my dad's past. He was a student in my father's sixth-grade class in Salem. Bill recalled the day in class when JFK was assassinated and remembered vividly when Dad shared the tragic news with his students. While waiting for the tide to change, I learned how awesome Bill was with crossword puzzles. During our short breakfast, he proceeded to kick his newest challenge's butt. When mid-morning rolled around, the docks showed signs of life and soon thereafter we untied our boats and headed downriver.

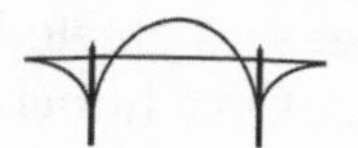

The first day of fishing was underwhelming. I had some kings hitting the gear, but I couldn't get them to stick. Much to my chagrin, I ended up with just one. It was a far cry from what I envisioned. Recharged the next morning, I made amends with myself that I'd return to port with a more respectable score. My second morning in Florence was straight out of a picturesque postcard. There was a hint of leftover fog clinging to the water's surface with a blazing sunrise poised to make its grand entrance on the eastern horizon between the coast range mountains. The bends of the river were flanked with a tree-lined shoreline to the north and majestic sand dunes to the south. In contrast to Newport where the run to the fishing grounds would entail several miles of ocean travel, the trip down the Siuslaw was usually smooth sailing. Better yet, once across the bar, the usual drill was to drop the gear just north of the whistle buoy in 27 fathoms of water and wait for the show to begin.

The second outing didn't disappoint. On a beautiful ocean with out-of-this-world views to the north of the often-photographed Heceta Head lighthouse at every glance, the kings consistently chomped on the gear. When all was said and done, I had thirteen kings to unload at the fish buyer's dock back in port. "*This is more like it,*" I was thinking. I was beginning to understand that this gig was something special and a smart way to complete the 1986 season. Even though the fishing during the first two weeks wasn't lights out, the Florence experiment proved reliable for drumming up a handful of kings or more each time I was able to get out.

Interspersed with this bliss was when a moderate swell would wreak havoc on the bar and make it impassible. This was an exercise in frustration knowing there were fish nearshore, but there was no safe way to get there. After enduring the brain damage of being barricaded in port for several days by a frothing bar, the fleet was greeted with a kinder, gentler crossing and a nice ocean. On a hunch, I swung the helm to the south. Most of the time we fished north, so it was nice to take in some new scenery. Just south of Florence right along the shoreline lies about 32,000 acres of sand dunes, some reaching a summit of 500 feet. It is an absolute haven for ATV and dune buggy enthusiasts. It was even a major inspiration for the *Dune* novel series. With miles of the ever-shifting palette of pale cream to carmel contours painting the backdrop to the east, I set the gear while on a southbound troll. There was barely a puff of wind and just some small pillowy swells. Adding to the mystique, there was some light late-summer fog, but it was the type that wasn't thick as chowder and that you just knew would burn off.

It didn't take long that morning for the springs to start dancing. There was a cool feel to the whole day, too, as there were just a few dories and trollers working the area. In the late summer, it is common for the big smileys to point their snouts toward the rivers and to see more medium-sized kings that we called "feeders" move in. That day, there were several kings in the ten-pound range, and when all was said and done, there were 17 fish to deliver.

Throughout this new venture, I was hoping Dad could take a break from his red-hot AC summer sales to join me. To my delight, he carved out a day on a whim to get a taste of fishing in king territory. After getting the boat tucked away, I met up with him for dinner and briefed him about the area and the day's fishing. He had a motel room reserved so it was going to be nice to be able to break the pattern of sleeping in the bed of my truck.

Since Dad was an early riser, I prepped him for the low-key rollout of the harbor by the late-summer fleet. Being an early riser, I knew he would be chomping at the bit to get underway at first light. As I prophesied, he was ready to roll. We had a quick breakfast and then made our short drive to the Port Dock. Sure enough, you could have heard more noise on the Moon. No one stirred on the docks while the sun was making a valiant attempt to break through the foggy cloak that was draped over the river. Never one to win a patience award, Dad was edging to get the boat underway.

"Well, we're not catching anything here. The fog will probably lift on our way out," Dad declared.

"It's different down here. Let's just wait for the fog to lift. It's tricky to navigate downriver when you can't see and we need good visibility when crossing the bar. Trust me, we will catch fish. You'll see," I assured him.

"Alright, you're the skipper!" he said.

Like clockwork around 8 AM, a few boat engines fired up and there was once again life amongst the old, planked docks and rusty pilings.

Soon we were underway through the thinly veiled fog around the bends of the river on a glorious morning. We skirted by the south jetty in a south-southwest tangent to avoid any middle ground slop on the bar that might be left-over and headed for the very short jaunt to where the action was the day before. A short while later, I throttled back to a troll as we were already at the job site.

"That's so much easier of a trip out than Newport, huh," I stated. "We're ready to put the gear down."

"Wow, Ter, That was quick. This is a special place. Look at the view!"

The wispy fog was still lingering, but it was dissipating into more of a light haze. Offshore a few miles, the dark, black hulls of the foreign trawlers with noticeable rust streaks were patrolling the waters like ominous tanks in crisscross fashion for Pacific whiting. These steampunk-like vessels had appeared daily since I arrived on the scene a few weeks prior, but they never crossed our paths, thankfully. The morning was a fusion of perfection with the brilliant late-summer sky, the gentle swell , the rhythmic puttering of the engine, the sun-stained dunes, and the paradoxical aromatic mixture of salt and carbon monoxide. The ambience added to the unique father-son experience we shared.

"You made a great decision to fish here, Terry," Dad said while also in a similar mesmerized state of mind. And not long after, the fish started biting the hardware that we had prepared for them. What started as a fantastic day only got better. It was a steady bite with only a dozen or so boats in the area. That weak fog bank that hung around like a mild-morning hangover was keeping far enough offshore as if it were uncharacteristically saying, *"I'm going to chill out and keep my distance and let you and your dad have an epic day."* Dad was having a ball, and in a way, it had the flavor of the early days, when everything was so fresh. It was going to be the last day of his season, so we made the most of every minute and wound up with 22 kings in the box. By late afternoon, the fog started to creep toward shore. Not wanting to spoil the best king score Dad and I had ever experienced together, we called it a day.

After the traditional post-game ritual of delivering fish, refueling, giving the boat a good scrubbing, Dad and I wound up the evening at the pizza parlor. McCartney's "Silly Love Songs" wasn't playing in the background this time, but we knew this was a red-letter day. Watching Dad hit the road for his three-hour commute back to the valley, I couldn't shake the feelings I had for him. I knew all too well from my USCG days how it felt to leave Shangri-La and have to return to a more mundane routine. I hoped the euphoria of the day would eclipse those feelings of separation.

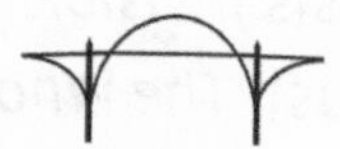

All good things come to pass, and that's what happened with the double-digit king scores for the season. The day after Dad left I scored nine fish. From there, it was a mix of just a couple small fish per day along with some wind and rain. It didn't take a lot of soul searching to know that the show was over. A few weeks later the boat was tucked away for a well-deserved rest in Salem.

With just a month left before I launched my college career, I needed to shift my priorities. The first order of business was to pack up and move to Corvallis, where I was able to find a tiny apartment earlier in the summer. From there it was all about getting into a new headspace. My rain gear turned into OP shorts, fishing gear was traded for textbooks, and shaggy hair transformed into a conservative mullet. Academic life and wedding planning became center stage, but my head continued to swim with reveries of the summer and of what might be in store for the 1987 season.

CHAPTER 11

SEASON 11

TAKIN' IT TO THE DEEPS

1987 Setlist

Boston *Third Stage*

Bruce Hornsby and the Range *The Way It Is*

Genesis *Invisible Touch*

Kate Bush *The Whole Story*

Kenny G *Duotones*

Tom Grant *Take Me to Your Dream*

There was no rest for the weary after the 1986 fishing season ended. My challenges shifted to settling in a good flow with the demands of college-level coursework. New albums from Boston, Kate Bush, Genesis, and Bruce Hornsby and the Range helped smooth the transition and fueled my commutes to and from class on Highway 34. As the year progressed, it became clear that I made the right decision for a career change. It was one of those gut feelings where you know you're in the right place at the right time. This set my new dream scenario in motion—teach from fall through spring and fish during the summer.

By the time spring break rolled around, wedding bells

were ringing for D'Ann and me. After a beautiful evening ceremony on a rare clear and sunny March Oregon day, we hit the road with our sights set on Northern and Central California's scenic wonders. The smooth jazz sounds of Kenny G and Portland's Tom Grant keeping us company as we wound through the Redwoods and wine country. Our adventure took us further south to the Bay Area, with stops in Carmel, Monterey, and Santa Cruz. It was refreshing to take in the sea and sand from the tourist point-of-view rather than experiencing it as work. When we cruised by some of NorCal's ports and salmon fleets though, I couldn't help but to take an extra glance or two.

It was back to business at the end of Spring Break. D'Ann began her new position at a credit union while I leaped back into spring term. The *Carolyn Kay* was in Salem, and in April Dad and I brought it out of its slumber. This began my weekend migrations an hour north to work with Dad on the annual ritual of boat preparation. D'Ann and I were enjoying our new life together, but even though she knew it was about dory time, the reality of the fishing commitments hit home. Fortunately, those feelings were short-lived and she embraced the routine.

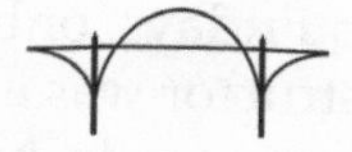

By mid-May, the boat was parked back in its slip at the Port Dock. Following the pattern of the past several years, there were a whole new set of rules and regulations to follow. A Master's degree in Seasonology was needed to interpret the complexity of the rule book. From May through June, it was chinook only. The first half of July added a 2:1 coho to chinook ratio in an area south of Cape Perpetua (between Newport and Florence), and then it was wide open for all species along most of the coast until the coho quota was met. If that wasn't crazy enough, it went back to 2:1, north of Perpetua, after the wide-open season. Adding to the complexity, some places had restrictions on the number of spreads of gear, gear type, and most everywhere required barbless hooks.

With our steadfast craft all suited up, we embarked on the ceremonial shakedown trip to work the bugs out. We puttered beyond the whistle buoy and a tad north for about an hour, stumbling all over the deck as we reawakened our sea legs. Much to our surprise, we put a medium king in the box to pay for the gas. The next Saturday, Dad and I scratched up eight hefty kings on an unseasonably warm coastal day where it would've been comfortable wearing shorts. This was a good sign and made us hopeful that our deep line springs would be hammering with big ones all season long.

Growing up, I never skipped school, partly because it would inflict a guilty conscience, and because I despised getting behind in the coursework. That mindset continued in college, despite realizing that some instructors didn't count attendance in your grade. This precedent of mine was put to the test during that spring term though. I was taking an intro poetry class, and each Friday we would gather in circles to delve deep into the likes of Robert Frost, Emily Dickinson, or the lyrics of Simon and Garfunkel. Not surprisingly, when it was warm and sunny on Fridays, only about eight students would show up. The instructor was a poet herself and the discussions weren't tied to a grade, just to the love of poetry itself. On the Thursday before Dead Week, Denny called to inform me that there was a school of kings just south of Newport off Seal Rock in about 25 fathoms of water. There was a low-pressure system approaching that would arrive late on Saturday, but before then the ocean was expected to be fishable. The wheels instantly began turning in my mind.

One voice said, *"Young married guy in college. Money is tight. Fish are biting. I could make a few hundred bucks!"*

The other voice said, *"You will be breaking a precedent. Missing classes could become a habit. Next thing you know, your grades will take a nosedive! You'll also miss Dr. Dave's science class, too."*

The first voice countered, *"Go fishing! You'll easily be able to recover the missed academics."*

Fishing won out on that conundrum. The next morning, I made the dark trek on the curvy path of the Coast Range on Highway 20, hoping and praying all along that my little scheme would pay off. I met up with Denny and we headed south to go chase the rumors. We nearly had the entire area to ourselves. While our endeavors didn't live up to the hype, we each ended up with a handful of kings. Even though I was feeling just a pinch of guilt for bailing out on my poetic and scientific learning, making a few bucks for the first time in a long time sure felt good.

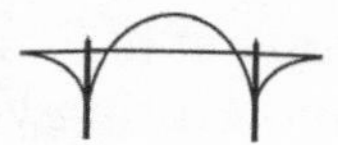

The day after I finished my last final exam, I hit the road for Newport. The next month of fishing was spent chasing kings anywhere from Newport to 24 miles south in the waters offshore of Yachats. The price was better than in 1986, and the daily catches were modest but profitable. The weather was typical of June with a week-long intermission where the northwest wind blew like a jet engine. Fortunately, Dad dodged the month's breezy spell and joined me a few times in between keeping the town of Salem outfitted in AC units.

In early July, the moorings of the larger trollers were noticeably vacant. News spread that those boats were down south off Coos Bay chasing a giant mass of kings. Off the south coast, there was a 2:1 coho to king ratio season happening, which was gravy on top of the riches. After a five-fish day where the ocean was like a country pond, I happened to see fellow doryman, Jake, in the parking lot. He asked how I was doing, and I replied somewhat proudly, "I've caught 11 in the last couple of days. I'm scratching a decent catch each day."

Jake didn't hold back. The previous year he had given me some great intel that led to our record-setting king score, so I was all ears. He emphatically stated, "You need to get your boat down south. Guys are putting in huge scores of kings every day."

Intrigued, I said, "Wow, that's amazing. That would be one long ride down there. I'm not sure where I would stay other than on the boat."

Jake surprised me with his next bit of advice, "Coos Bay is an absolute zoo with so many boats fishing there. The moorages are overflowing and the fish docks are a circus. I've been fishing just north out of Reedsport and doing well. I just came up here to get a few things and am headed down tomorrow." Then he added, "You should motor your boat down that way. When you get to Florence, put your gear in and troll down to Reedsport. Bring your sleeping bag and you can crash in my camper."

Jake's suggestion sent my head spinning. Knowing I had made the trek to Florence a few times in the past instilled confidence to pull off such a quest. Crashing at Jake's pad was a bit of a concern as I was pretty sure our after-work pastimes didn't mesh well. Instead of overthinking like I was prone to do, I decided to go for it. I told Jake, "Thanks for that offer. As long as the weather holds, I see you down there."

The rest of that evening was devoted to preparing for a new odyssey with some grocery shopping, packing clothing and extra supplies, as well as filling in D'Ann and my dad about my latest pilgrimage. Dad was surprised, but supportive.

"Wow, Ter, that's quite a journey. I think you should go for it though. I'll be thinking of you all the way. Give me a call tomorrow night with an update," he said.

"Thanks. I'm guessing this will be a brief trip. The fish will probably move, and I am hoping they'll make their way north," I replied.

Even though I had some experience with this sort of

thing, it was a sleepless night filled with things I forgot to do and "what if" scenarios that I hoped wouldn't psyche me out when the sun came up.

The sun rose over Coast Range in style, and the stars must have aligned during the night because I was greeted by a greasy-slick ocean. The skies were crystal clear as I crossed a flat Yaquina Bay bar. After an hour and a half of rocking to the sound of the outboard motor at full throttle with mile after mile of scenic shoreline to my east, I slowed to troll speed parallel to the Florence jetties. It had become a second homeport, and on that day, it was littered with a small city of local boats.

I tuned in to the CB channel where the Florence dory guys often resided and soon heard the familiar banter of Terry on the *Blue Angel,* Bill on the *Jireh,* Mark on the *Lady Scarlett,* and several others. Those familiar sounds eased some of the anxiety of the day, and I hailed Terry to announce my arrival.

"*Blue Angel,* Terry, *Carolyn Kay*. How are things going here?" I inquired.

"Hey, Terry. Good to hear you are joining the fun. Are you staying in Florence? You can stay in the camper if you would like until you get your rig," he enthusiastically answered back.

It was tempting to take him up on his offer, but instead of gravitating as usual to a comfortable route, I decided to carry on with the original game plan.

"I am going to keep going to Reedsport and see if I can get in on the bonanza supposedly going on there. I have an invitation to crash in someone's camper there," I explained. "Thanks, though. If I head back up this way, I may take you up on your offer."

"We're getting a few here. Probably not what they are getting down south, but the fish are headed this way. Good luck and let us know how it goes."

"Will do! Take care and good luck today!" I replied.

Continuing my migration, I arrived at another cluster of

boats, offshore of Lake Tahkenitch. It is a large inland fresh-water lake just on the east side of Highway 101 and served as a reference point for the southern fleet. In addition to Tahkenitch, there is a chain of beautiful lakes that are a hop, skip, and a jump from the dunes that can be found as you work your way south. As far as the ocean topography goes, the further down the south coast you go, the ocean depth drops off quickly from the shoreline. Thus, boats rarely troll very far offshore. When fishing off Newport, the typical drill was to sink your gear to the bottom, no matter the depth since it was a gradual decline. Finding myself close to shore and in 70 fathoms, I set my gear down to about 30 fathoms. I learned from the radio conversations that below that depth, it was littered with sharp-toothed, gear mangling hake.

Once the gear was set, I waited for the onslaught that had garnered so much dock hype. It didn't exactly happen, but a few silvers started hitting the gear, then some kings. Adding to all the newness was the radio banter. The familiar chatter of the Florence fleet north of me continued to fade into scratchy oblivion. The conversations in the new zip code were about the same as usual, but the cast of characters changed and so did their points of reference. There was no mention of the Rockpile, Beaver Creek, Heceta Head, or Sea Lion caves. These landmarks were replaced with Tahkenitch Creek, the Siltcoos River, and Ten Mile Creek. To quickly acclimate myself to the south coast real estate, I used any idle minutes to make sure I was familiar with where each was on the map.

Aside from a few back tacks north when I caught fish, I kept the boat's nose trolling for Reedsport's Winchester Bay. This port is formed by the confluence of the scenic and often-photographed Umpqua River and the Pacific Ocean. Most of the locals call it Windy Bay, as it is a magnet for screaming northwest winds.

Throughout the spring I had been struggling on and off with carpal tunnel syndrome. It had bothered me since the season began, but it really hit hard that day when I had a nice large king up to the boat. I gaffed the wriggling eighteen-pounder and hoisted it over the side. In mid-flight, a searing pain rocketed from my wrist to my elbow, and upon impulse, my arm flinched enough to allow the fish to slide off the gaff. The hefty struggling salmonid landed on the gear tray and thrashed chaotically, enough to tangle up the neatly coiled monofilament leaders in the gear tray into an unimaginable mess. I lunged and attempted to bear hug the big slug that had realized its predicament and its sudden opportunity for escape. It was too late to get a grip on it, though. The money fish made a nice splash and disappeared back in its emerald-green ecosystem, sadly as expensive crab bait.

In utter frustration, I flung my gaff toward the deck in a dark but impressive manner and yelled a few expletives to the fish gods. I usually kept my cool on the water, but I tended to unravel when big kings swam away or sunk in this instance. I happened to glance down and noticed the shiny sharp steel point of the gaff was implanted in the deck board and was standing erect, right next to my foot. An inch or so closer and I would have sunk it clear through my metatarsals prompting a rather inauspicious introduction to the Reedsport medical community. Quite humbled, I finished the day in a much more subdued manner and was thankful I didn't end up in the ER.

With a painful wrist, fatigue, and plenty of logistical questions on my mind, I decided to make a one-way tack to the whistle buoy. Fog was moving in, and I certainly didn't have the steam to navigate a new harbor bar in pea soup. *"Been there, done that, last year in Florence,"* I thought to myself. Once the buoy was close by, I pulled the gear. Of course, with half of it in the boat, I pulled another large king. I was so tempted to put the gear back down to catch its friends, but a voice inside my head reminded me all that I still had a lot of things to sew up once I stepped on the dock.

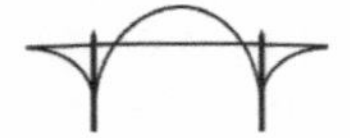

When I finally got the boat tucked away on the transient dock, I made my way to a payphone to let D'Ann know that I survived the ordeal and caught 10 kings and 17 coho. Not knowing how long I would be down there, I asked her if she would drive down to help me get my rig to Reedsport. Fortunately, we were basking in newly married bliss and she happened to love spontaneous road trips. She planned to meet me at the docks the next evening. This was a big relief since I knew that one night bunking at Jake's would be sufficient.

I finally caught up with Jake. We made our way a short walk across the road to an RV park to his camper. "Thanks for letting me crash at your pad, Jake! I really appreciate your intel about this place, too. It sounds much better than all the craziness in Coos Bay," I said.

"No problem. Glad you had a good start. There's fish here," he replied. "Oh, and by the way, a buddy of mine will probably be dropping by and will crash here, too, tonight," he added.

That got me wondering how the next eight or so hours were going to go down. To make a long story short, while lodging there that night, I am sure I accumulated enough THC in my bloodstream through osmosis to fail a drug test in style. While it was an unlikely scenario, I was certain being part of an illegal substance bust wouldn't help my aspirations to become an elementary teacher. When I woke up early the next morning, Jake and his pal were still immersed in their stupors. Craving some fresh air, breakfast, and a desire to plop some kings in my fish box, I gathered my wares and made my way to the marina. I'd reiterate my appreciation to Jake for his hospitality via CB later.

The dockside life at Reedsport was much like Florence. Fishermen were in small clusters here and there talking about current weather and water conditions. The tide was ebbing and there was enough of a swell for the bar to break all the way across. Everyone was in stasis until the tide changed. A few hours later, a migration began and boats started trickling out of the basin. Ready for another adventure, I crawled over two other dories and fired up the *Carolyn Kay*.

The drill for crossing the bar of Windy Bay was to stay well south as the north side was clustered with breakers. As I cruised alongside the south jetty, I happened to glance down at the deck momentarily and observed a hairline crack in one of the frames that was directly under the helm and fishbox. When the boat slapped on any sizable wave, it would flex just enough to be noticeable. It was like dealing with back pain where you become hyper-sensitive about any major movement or jolt. I found myself constantly analyzing it with every morsel of chop and swell the ocean delivered. After thorough examination, I didn't get the sense that it was getting any worse. It was something that would need addressing soon though.

Fish production fell well short of my expectations. I figured getting an early start would result in a 20-king day, but when all was said and done, only five kings and ten coho were in the box upon delivery. Even though I was disappointed, the upside was that D'Ann was there to meet me and we journeyed to Newport to get my truck. It was so nice to see her, and it took my mind off the lackluster start. After dinner, we said our farewells again. She was doing a great job acclimating to the whole fishing scene. Seeing some decent size paychecks on good days certainly didn't hurt the cause. That night I rested well in my Hotel Toyota and had high hopes for a rebound.

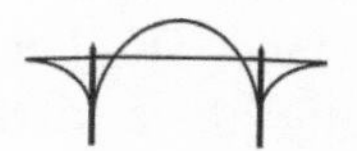

There was some talk from the previous day that high pressure was soon about to invade the tranquil seas everyone had been enjoying. When I awoke and made my way to the docks, I knew I needed to make this day count. To my delight, the ocean was like glass and it was t-shirt fishing weather. Even better, the final score for the day resulted in nine kings and twice as many silvers. Again, not off the charts, but certainly better than what I would have caught in Newport. I was keeping a keen ear for how the Florence guys were doing. I could hear Terry and the gang's CB conversations fading in and out, and it sounded like they were doing about the same as the Reedsport fleet. With the weather soon to be going to worms, it made sense to scamper north to Florence to fish where I would be surrounded by familiar faces. While the Windy Bay experiment had been mildly profitable, it wasn't firing my rockets enough to hang around long term.

The trip across the bar the next morning was a piece of cake, and with another ocean like a sheet of glass, I pointed the bow north with the throttle wide open. Looking east as I ran parallel to the beach, I was treated to mind-boggling scenery with the sun rising over the Coast Range mountains. The dunes were illuminated and speckled with coastal pines and the sprouting green beach grass. Standing, steering, and thinking. There was always a lot of time for pondering. I was mentally inhaling the awe, beauty, and the privilege of such a heavenly commute and thanking God for every moment. *"How many people get to go to work where you see spectacular sunrises, spouting whales, and majestic waters?"* I thought to myself as a reminder of how lucky I was to be part of such an extraordinary adventure.

As I drew nearer to the Siuslaw River bar, I was treated to some amazing marine wildlife phenomena. Huge schools of baitfish, about the area of a hotel swimming pool, repeatedly exploded to the surface. The Pacific water would go from dead calm to looking like a torrential rainstorm, and back to its tranquil self in a matter of ten seconds or less. After a few moments of standing with my mouth agape in total awe, I was struck with an a-ha moment to send the gear down amongst the chaos. My thoughts went something like this, "*Surely, big king salmon are terrorizing the candlefish, herring, and whatever else and causing the bait to boil, and when I drive my gear through the melee, I'll have kings hanging on every spread of gear!*" It was the scenario all troll fishermen dreamed of.

With the gear set, I waited for the onslaught. I had the area all to myself, and I was convinced that this would be one of those epic moments I would vividly remember years later. As it turned out, part of that was true. I still remember it quite well. The only parts missing were the fish. I trolled through each baitfish storm, bracing for impact on my gear...and nothing. This happened time after time. Talk about torment. Feeling completely and utterly flabbergasted, I resorted to the next level of dory scratch fishing tactics. I started making erratic maneuvers with the helm, with sharp rights, sharp lefts, and punching the throttle in short bursts. This generated a rising and falling action of the gear in hopes that it would be enough to entice a few of the reluctant to sample the cuisine I had to offer. After blazing a wake that looked like a drunken rattlesnake, I had nothing to show for my efforts. A bit dumbfounded, I kept trolling north.

By early afternoon, I was trolling north of the bar amid a brotherly fleet again. The ocean's pond-like conditions developed ripples, courtesy of the puffs of air movement from the northwest. This got me thinking back to the forecasted wind I had heard others talk about. Whenever the wind cranked up from the northwest, no matter which harbor you were fishing out of, you always wanted to keep north of the buoys. As we learned many times over, the penalty for going south is the repeated, sciatic pinching, teeth-jarring pounding with every single white-capping wave spewing salty spray with precision right in your face. It's an experience you don't forget and work to avoid at all costs.

Two things happened in the next half hour when I was about halfway between the bar and the picturesque Heceta Head lighthouse. Fish started pounding the springs, and the forecasted winds arrived, with gusto. As the wind speed accelerated, the drift became horrendous. Big kings hammered the gear, sometimes on both sides at once. When I pulled the gear on one side, the boat stubbornly turned to the opposite side with all the forces at play. To counter the pull, I adjusted the positioning of the gear on the floats creatively to try to balance things out a bit. This helped some, but the wind did its best to counter the advantage.

By late afternoon it was blowing a solid 20 to 25 knots and it was a big struggle to keep the boat pointing north when pulling gear. Big frothy whitecaps hissed everywhere. When a fish hit, I let it soak a bit so I could make as much headway north as possible. This was a good thing to let them tire out some days, but all of the jarring and slapping was shaking loose as many as I caught. Others were having the same problem.

"*Carolyn Kay*, Terry, how are you holding up in this slop?" *Blue Angel* Terry inquired.

"I'm getting a lot of pumpers and putting some in the box, but I've come up empty several times, too. It's crazy trying to keep the boat straight and the fish on the hooks."

"It is a wild one. There are some big fish here that are really active. Luckily I have my autopilot and Chris aboard to help keep the boat pointed right."

"Yeah, I really wish Dad was aboard right now. It would be a heck of a lot easier."

"No kidding. I'm not sure how you're doing it out here tonight solo."

Despite the thrashing I was enduring, my adrenaline was flowing and I was deep into the intensity of the situation. The wind ratcheted up yet to another level, which sent the sloppy sea into a fit of rage. I considered calling it quits despite the hot bite going on when the very official-sounding announcement from Coast Guard Station Siuslaw River boomed over the CB airwaves,

"...the Siuslaw River bar is closed to all traffic until the tide changes due to hazardous bar conditions with breaking waves. Please do not attempt to cross the bar until the tide changes. This is Coast Guard Station Siuslaw River, out!"

That put an interesting spin on an already entertaining evening. It meant at least an hour or more of a butt-kicking until there would be a chance to head back to port. I thought to myself, *"What else is there to do but attempt to head north and keep fishing?"*

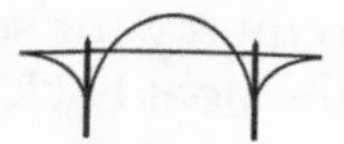

Kings kept giving the deep lines a workout and I did my best to put some more in the box. After the flood tide kicked into gear, some boats reported crossing with no problems. Those encouraging words motivated me to chuck the gear in the boat and head toward the hole as the wind was screaming. It was definitely one of those "what if?" scenarios though. If the ocean was calm, there was no telling how many kings I would have put in the box. I was sure it would be close to a boat record. With all boats barreling in at the same time, the bar resembled rush-hour traffic. The wait at the fish dock was equally as congested. It was like a parking lot at a big box store on Black Friday as I idled on the breezy river for what seemed like forever to offload my well-earned catch. Then there was another waiting game to get gas, and lastly the ritual of buttoning up the boat at the transit dock.

Since the Toyota was in Reedsport, *Blue Angel* Terry suggested that I crash in their camper. He and his son Chris also invited me to go with them to Abby's Pizza. In the euphoria of the day's events, I made one huge mistake—I failed to make a trip to the payphone and call D'Ann.

Later that evening I finally made that call as well as to my dad. I could tell by their voices right away that I really screwed up not calling earlier. They knew I had made the trip from Reedsport to Florence and had heard on the news about blustery winds. With no word from me, they feared something was wrong and were waiting with bated breath for the phone to ring. They both let me know how they felt, which was quite humbling. Dad had the knack of shifting into a mode that would make your hair stand up. I puckered upon hearing the directiveness of his voice and knew the look I would have received if he was in person. "You need to make sure when you get into port, you always call your wife. D'Ann was quite worried, as we all were." That's all it took. Hearing that, I didn't miss a call after that.

The wind showed no mercy for several days, and Dad and I decided to trailer the boat back to Newport with his Jeep Wagoneer for the start of the all-species season. It was going to be the first wide-open coho season since 1983. For safety and peace-of-mind, we installed a brace to deal with the cracked frame right below where you stood to steer. A few test-runs in the chop proved that it would hold up well for the rest of the season, but a long term solution was tops on the list for the offseason. Riding high from an adventurous start, we were ready to lay the hammer down for the season's next phase.

The opening scene of the all-species season greeted us with long and lazy swells up to ten feet, and an occasional larger one that would make us pucker.

"I'm glad we were at high water while crossing the bar, Ter. There are some monster swells today," Dad said.

"Luckily they are not very sharp and no wind is forecasted today. Another system is moving in tonight though. We need to keep a close eye on it all," I added.

Reports from sport fishermen, who were allowed to fish for coho earlier than the commercial fleet, were spotty. The barrage of northwest wind cooled the water and scattered the fish. It turned out to be a classic scratch-fishing day as everyone was struggling to find a school of silvers. Even though we boated six kings, we only found five coho and a halibut for a full-day's effort. The bottom line on our fish ticket read $237.12.

"That's a nice consolation for just scratching up a dozen fish, Ter. If the silvers show up en masse like last year, this season is going to be a money maker," Dad remarked.

"It's crazy to think that this would have been one of our most profitable days in 1977," I added.

Later, the forecasted wet and blustery system decided to come ashore and squashed the next day's fishing. The next morning, Dad headed back to the Valley for a few days while I decided to hang around. Life in a small trailer on rainy days could get quite boring. Fortunately, after calling D'Ann, she said she wanted to come over and see me. She wasn't about to stay in the dank confines of the trailer, so we agreed to get a room at one of the more reputable budget motels in town.

Even though it poured buckets all night long, I set my alarm early for the next day, just in case. Rising from my slumber, there were still pitter pats of rain hitting the motel room roof and window. I wanted to just roll over, sleep in, and then go out for a leisurely breakfast with D'Ann. A little voice in my head reminded me of past blunders where I assumed that the day would be a wash, only later to find out I had missed out on a nice paycheck. I told D'Ann, "I seriously doubt I'll go fishing, but I'd feel better to at least go make sure. Plus, I need to make sure the bilge pump is doing its job with all the rain. I highly doubt anyone is heading out. If I don't come back soon though, use the car CB and give me a call."

Surprisingly, there were signs of life when I pulled up to the docks. Fishermen were doing more than just BS'ing. I heard boat engines rumbling. CB and VHF radios blared with abundant chatter. *Blue Angel* Terry was docked near the ramp along with a few other of the dory guys, so I swung by to get the scoop. He said, "There are some guys who went out and said it's still a bit sloppy, but fishable. The wind came down overnight and it's been gradually improving. Sounds like there's some fish near the North End of the Pile."

For a few moments, there was a mental tug-o-war raging in my head—hang out with D'Ann and be a tourist for a day or pound out to the Pile in thick drizzle and maybe make several hundred dollars. Since I had mentioned there was a possibility of going out, I chose the latter option. It sure would have been handy to have a cell phone and send D'Ann a simple text or give her a quick call. Luckily, she did have the portable CB to contact me once she realized I wasn't coming back to the motel.

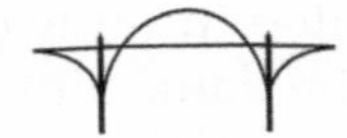

It was a sloppy, wet haul out to the inside edge of the Rockpile, but it was fishable. By the time I dropped gear, it had transformed to classic coastal rain with drops that found ways past the firewalls of my rain gear and traveled down my neck. The North End of the Pile was always a challenging, yet interesting place to fish. Just east of this underwater wonderland was "The Canyon" where the depth reaches near 50 fathoms. One of my favorite tactical maneuvers was to fish the edge, right where the canyon and the Pile meet. I would raise the gear and fish the edge as it became slightly shallower. I'd work that lane up to nearly the tip and then work my way back down. If things weren't working out, you had options where you could troll a half-mile and sink the gear to the sand of the deep water, or troll atop of the Pile in yet even shallower water. When fishing atop the Pile, you had to keep a keen eye on your location and the fathometer. Taking your eye off the ball meant likely hanging your gear up in the rocks in the blink of an eye.

Soon after I started my first tack north, D'Ann hailed me on the CB.

"Wow, I'm surprised you went out. It's raining hard here," she said.

"It is here, too, but the wind is coming down. Some guys roughed it out here yesterday and did quite well. Hopefully the fish are still here," I replied.

"I'm going to stick around today and I'll see you when you get in. Be careful!"

"Sounds good. Will do! Hey, you talked me on a fish. Gotta go."

The washing machine action of the ocean was just prime for trolling and the whirlings and pirouettes of the gear must have been downright tantalizing. There were few boats, so I had all the maneuvering room I needed. I loved days like this. I would just get in this zone of running gear, pulling fish consistently, steering, strategizing, cleaning a few fish, and then continuing in that cycle continuously through the day.

By late afternoon, the bite tapered off. With a long, wet run ahead of me, I put the gear in the boat and radioed D'Ann..

"*Carolyn Kay* Base, D'Ann, are you on here?" I transmitted.

"Hi Terry! How are you doing? It's been pouring rain all day. You must be soaked," D'Ann replied.

"Yeah, same here, but luckily my rain gear has kept me mostly dry. I caught some fish though! It was worth the trip. I should be in within an hour. Let's go have dinner at the Embarcadero," I said.

"That sounds good to me! See you soon."

At the fish dock, I delivered 23 silvers, 7 kings, and a halibut. A couple hours later, D'Ann and I enjoyed a warm bayfront restaurant view and enjoyed an amazing seafood buffet with some soft piano jazz filling the background. The forecast called for clearing skies and abating winds, so the next morning, we went our separate ways with her to Corvallis and me back to the Rockpile.

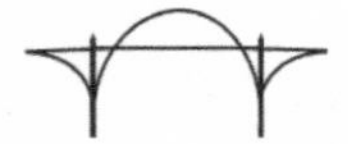

The northwest-fresh overnight rain worked like magic to wash away the salty residue and salmon blood and made for a squeaky-clean trek offshore. I set the gear a mile short of the previous day's coordinates, and it was a good thing I did. The fish had moved in toward shore and by day's end I had 12 kings and 34 silvers for my efforts. Each day the fish kept biting and moved toward the beach with the warming water, making for a shorter commute. One of the days included a torrid 64-coho day mixed with some kings that yielded a very nice paycheck.

The beach show abruptly ended, but another mass of kings invaded the Pile. On the treks to the fishing grounds, there were many boats traveling the same path. It resembled a train of prairie schooners on the Oregon Trail. The North End became a small nation every time there was a hot bite there. Boats of all sizes crammed into 10 square miles of liquid earth and trolled north and south like a busy interstate. Fortunately, Dad was able to join me for several days, and what a blessing that was. We had a four-day spell where our catches ranged from 10 to 18 kings and 20 to 30 silvers per day. As an added bonus, the average size of the kings we pulled were 15 pounds.

"A few years ago, I didn't think we'd ever see anything like this, Ter. This is special. It sure happened at a good time with you going to school. Boy, those kings on the Pile were sure slamming the gear," Dad stated before heading back home.

Like clockwork, the northwesterlies came back with a roar for ten days. The word from hard-charging large trollers who braved the elements was that the kings had moved on from Newport for the most part. Drawing from experience, I pointed the bow on August 13th to be part of the Florence scene once again. While Newport had become a chinook-only fishery for the remainder of the season, the south coast offered a 2:1 coho to chinook ratio. The coho would help pay for expenses on the slow days so it made sense to make the migration. Just like in 1986, several of the dory guys headed that direction and it was two-weeks that were well spent. While there were no lights-out catches, there were always at least a few kings around and the accompanying ratio of silvers. The price per pound was still strong and it was always worth the while as one could at least expect to earn a minimum of $100 a day.

The Florence escapade lasted a few weeks before the fishing withered and gigantic swells moved in and slammed the bar shut for a spell. Seizing a window of opportunity on a clear September morning, I sneaked across the bar at max high tide, hung a right, and made a beeline north. Three subsequent days of meager catches near Newport signaled it was time to wrap up another season. I couldn't help but to reflect that in two years, the state of the small-boat salmon fishery had gone from near extinction to a renaissance. With early prognostications pointing to a strong 1988 season, Dad and I were full of high hopes and had a lot to talk about over the winter.

CHAPTER 12

SEASON 12

WHEN THE STARS ALIGN

1988 Setlist

John Mellencamp *The Lonesome Jubilee*
Pink Floyd *A Momentary Lapse of Reason*
Sade *Stronger than Pride*

While it was always hard to bid farewell to a fishing season, I had plenty on my plate to extinguish my lamentation. Fall term was just around the corner and I was laser-focused on another successful school year. Much like the challenges of fishing, higher-level learning required a considerable amount of grit. When my nose wasn't buried in the books, I was basking in the bliss of being newly married, enjoying the college-town vibe of Corvallis, and reliving my hoop dreams on a city-league basketball team. I immersed myself in running, and throughout the year, D'Ann and I were having a blast dashing off to 5k and 10k races in Portland.

Squeezed into the controlled chaos, I kept in touch with Dad to plot out strategies for the 1988 season. The predictions were still zeroed in on another strong chinook season and there was a buzz on the grapevine that there would be a 100-fish per day coho quota. Full of anticipation, we designed a new fish box that would double up as an indestructible brace for the cracked frame that concerned us the previous summer. Adding to the excitement, the topic of hydraulics entered the picture again.

"Terry, I've been reading some literature I sent away for. I think we can put hydraulics on the boat again, but this time it would be much better. We can run them with a Honda five-horsepower engine that is way quieter than that old Briggs and Stratton we used last time. There are these couplings called Lovejoy connections that connect to the hydraulic pump. They're solid and there would be no more slipped belts. I did the math, too. I'm confident it'll work and pay for itself. We'll be able to place the gear deeper with heavier leads and that should help us put more kings in the box. I'll flip for the bill and we can work the details out later with the big paydays that we'll have. I even have a lead on some good used hydraulics for a good price. What do you think?" Dad explained and proposed.

"Sounds good to me," I replied. "You've really done your homework on this. Is this what you work on when you wake up at 3 AM?" Dad was notorious for waking up in the witching hours and filling out crossword puzzles, doodling, and undoubtedly penciling out calculations involving flow rates and RPM's.

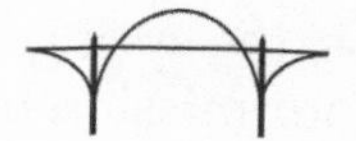

As the Willamette Valley warmed up and the stratus clouds started to give way to sunny skies, I began my weekend spring migrations northward to Salem to put all the pieces together. There were a few weekends with the boat on its trailer parked on the driveway devoted to installing and testing the hydraulic system. One of us would pull down as hard as we could on the cannonballs to test the relief valve while the other kept an eye out for leaky fittings. Our efforts paid off as it worked like magic after a few bugs were worked out.

By May 20th, the *Carolyn Kay* was resting happily once again at its berth on Port Dock 7B. We performed the ritual of righting the trolling poles, securing all the stays, and making sure the rigging was all in the right places. Often getting the boat ship-shape was an all-day affair, but everything fell in place faster than we anticipated.

"Wow, that went together fast. What do you want to do now?" I asked.

"The ocean is really nice. How about we go out just past the buoys for a few hours and test the hydraulic system and shake down the gear? Maybe we'll catch a king, too!" Dad suggested.

"I'm game. We've already got some snacks and water on board. Let's fire up the engine and go for it," I replied.

After our short run out of the harbor, we casually started setting the gear with the gentlest of swells welcoming us back to the fold. Just that sensation alone would have been enough to satisfy months of yearning to be back on the water.

"The hydraulics seem like they're working well so far," Dad said.

"Yeah, they run the gear real smooth. The Honda isn't too horribly loud either. Whoa! Hey, you have a king bouncing on your deep, Dad. Nice one, too. Go get it!"

Much to our surprise, the springs continued bouncing and before we knew it, our mission had morphed from a carefree boat ride to a full-fledged tactical plan of attack back through waypoints marked on the LORAN where fish were caught. By late afternoon, we strolled up to the fish dock with eight kings.

Coming off an afternoon like that, it was no easy task having to put the boat to bed and drive back to the Valley. Reluctantly, we said our farewells and he headed back to reality.

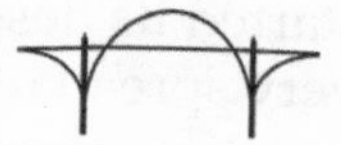

The next weekend I was flying solo, and it started with a mind-numbing one-fish effort on Saturday. My fish box was an empty cavern three hours in on Sunday morning. The current was running like a freight train, which caused my trolling wires to pull back sharply, almost amidships. I was doing my usual scanning back and forth of all four springs when suddenly a big pumper king slammed the port deep. My mindset went from being nearly comatose as I stood in the steady drizzle to an adrenalized state in an instant. Since we had the new hydraulic system in place, a new part of the process was to give a yank of the pull cord of the Honda engine when it was time to pull gear. It could be shut down for spells during scratch fishing to save gas and give the ears a bit of reprieve from dueling engine noises.

When I gave a pull on the cord, the spring inside the pull cord mechanism made a zinging sound, unwound, and became unresponsive. Realizing I was suddenly in a bit of a pickle in the dismal weather, my prefrontal cortex jumped into action to figure out a fix. I set a course so as not to run into any boats, tied off the wheel to keep running straight, and crawled up into the bow section to perform surgery. Aside from not being able to pull gear, I was a bit pissed since it was a brand-new engine. Looking at the glass half full, I was able to give the big king some time to soak and calm down. Fortunately, my surgical skills were adept enough to tediously wind the spring to its correct tightness, reinstall it, and low and behold, still put the fish in the boat. I was rewarded for my persistence, but it wouldn't be the only time that season that the pull cord and I butted heads.

Unfortunately, it wasn't the last MacGyver fix I had to employ that morning. While spying the springs, I spotted a huge wad of kelp just off the port bow. With it being so close, I didn't have enough time to veer away from it.

Seconds later, the tentacled kelp monster wrapped around the port deep line and started its descent down the wire, poised to dismember every spread of gear. The resistance it created caused the wire to drag several feet further aft than normal, which in turn made the boat want to veer to the left due to all the leverage applied to the port trolling pole. As I wound in the line next to the boat to better balance the steering and get closer to the intruder, I began using my gaff to pull the kelp limbs off as fast as possible. As I was doing that, the Lamanarian was working its way down the wire in sinister fashion, snapping off monofilament gear spreads like you would pull threads off a sweater. While it inflicted some damage, I was able to put an end to its destruction before it wiped out every gear spread. Between the constant drizzle, snotty ocean, lousy fishing, mechanical issues, and the kelp monster incident, I called it a day and headed for the barn.

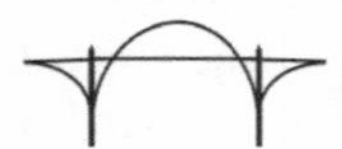

When spring term concluded, I had my sights set on trading books for hooks as soon as possible. After a day of celebrating a successful year of academia with D'Ann, I hit the road and blasted the sounds of some fresh Pink Floyd and John Mellencamp enroute to Newport.

The first sea of my summer was agitated and sported a persistent ten-knot southwest breeze and some five-foot swells generated by an approaching low-pressure system. It was still fishable, and I resigned to the reality that it would be like trolling inside a top-load washing machine. Rumor had it that there were some kings along the 25 to 30 fathom zone between Seal Rock and the Alsea River, so the boat and I persistently pounded southbound. Upon arrival there were two dozen boats including Denny and Terry on the prime patch of real estate.

Even though the boat bobbed around in helter-skelter fashion, the sea state wasn't dangerous. Often, a confused sea generated gear movement that was irresistible to fish. It didn't take long after settling into the first troll south to prove that theory true. A couple of kings hammered the deep lines on the first tack and took the skunk off the boat in short order.

"Hey, Denny, how did your first tack go over there? It looked like you were busy," I asked.

"Oh, hey Terry! We just put two nice ones in the boat! I think there's some fish here. The guy next to me pulled one aboard, too. It's sporty out here, but not too bad," Denny reported. "How about you?"

"Same as you! Two nice ones on my first pass." I'm going to crank it around and head back to that spot I marked. It'll be a quick troll though going with this wind. I'll check in with you a bit."

"I'll do the same. Talk to you later."

Sure enough, each pass yielded another fish or two. The pell-mell conditions amped up the school of kings into a feeding frenzy as many spat out our gorgings of candlefish when the fish landed in the kill box. Adrenaline kicked in, and it was one of those days where I felt as one with the sea. The waves inched a little higher and the wind cranked up a notch or two. I knew I was still within common sense boundaries though to shift into high gear while the window of opportunity was open. Kings kept pounding the springs on each pass.

As forecasted, the low arrived in style with driving rain and frothy whitecaps. A few fish-less tacks sounded the alarm that it was time to quit while I was ahead. The other guys were feeling the same.

"Hey, *Carolyn Kay* Terry, I'm going to put 'em in the boat and head in. The fish quit and it's getting gnarly out here," Denny announced.

"Same here, Denny. They quit for me, too, and I'm getting my butt kicked!"

"Hey, Terry, I'm doing the same as well!" *Blue Angel* Terry chimed in.

I was all smiles at the fish dock as I unloaded my 18-king catch, five of which averaged 14.4 pounds. The price-per-pound for kings was looking good and the $507.20 on the fish ticket made the day even better.

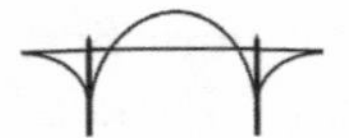

For the remainder of June, daily catches ranged from 2 to 10 kings a day. Dad also was able to join in on several occasions, and he was so thrilled to see his hydraulic gurdy master plan working so well. His beaming face reminded me of scenes in Willy Wonka's Chocolate Factory where Gene Wilder and his saucer-sized eyes stood transfixed in amazement at his chocolate wonderland. When July 1st rolled around, the Florence fishery commenced with a 2:1 coho to chinook season. Our gut feeling was that Florence was the place to be, so Dad and I loaded the boat on the trailer and towed it an hour south for a new adventure.

The move south proved to be a win. The first day started out with a bang. The local dory armada was out in force and we were stretched from the Siuslaw Bar north to the Sea Lion Caves in 24 to 28 fathoms of water. Occasional spells of fog would shroud us, only then to recede and return again. Winds were in the range of five to ten knots and were accompanied by five-foot swells.

Fishing solo, I had a few kings in the box early. It was apparent by noon that I was fishing in a sublime realm where the boat, the gear, the sea, the fish, and I were in perfect harmony. It was an awesome feeling being in highliner mode. The kings kept smacking the hardware I placed before them. *Blue Angel* Terry noticed my lack of participation on the CB airwaves.

"Hey, *Carolyn Kay,* Terry, you are very quiet today. What's going on, bud?" I was in the process of pulling aboard a couple of kings when he called and could not reply.

"I see him working the gear. I bet he's into 'em over

there," replied another doryman.

"Alright, Ter, give us a report when you're not busy," Terry concluded.

About five minutes later after sending the gear back down and establishing a northbound troll, I replied, "Hey, Terry, I'm here now."

"You must be plugging the boat. How many you got there?" Terry asked.

"I think those last two make 13 kings along with the 26 silvers. Most are mediums and they are nailing the hotspot-hoochie combos on every pass. Not red-hot, but pretty consistent," I explained.

"Highliner! We need to pay you a visit at the dock tonight."

"Yeah, sure. I think I am just in the right groove somehow. It's the same junk you all are using. My troll speed is really rippin' if that helps. Well, thanks for the call. You talked me on another fish. Gotta go!"

"Wow. Alright, go get it!"

The action continued steadily until late afternoon. The bar reports weren't great from those who had crossed and the pea soup fog was on its way to swallow those of us still fishing. When the fish finally took a siesta, I decided to pull gear and head for the river, but not before the boat was enveloped in a misty gray blanket.

As I approached the bar, waves were stacking up sharply and it was incredibly hard to decipher whether any were breaking in the foggy conditions. Making the crossing all the more difficult was the number of boats converging at the same time, and I ended up right behind a very slow small troller. With so many boats and so little safe space to maneuver, I wasn't able to punch the throttle to zip by the crawling craft. I just had to poke along at the same slow pace. This made the boat want to broach, or want to turn broadside when going down the backside of a steep swell. While fighting the forces, I heard a few waves hiss behind me and I prayed that they would not decide to break over my stern. Adding to my white-knuckled grip on the helm, I was inching closer to the sluggish vessel. I was essentially locked into this 30 to 40 foot chunk of water, and I started to have horrendous visions of having the following sea jettison my boat right up on the stern of the waddling craft. Fortunately, I was able to keep enough distance. When the waves lessened their grip and there was enough maneuvering room on the port side, I was able to punch the throttle to escape that foggy predicament.

When I was back at the dock and giving the boat a good scrub-down, Terry and another couple of guys dropped by for a visit. They were eager to gain some intel on what my secret weapons were that day. I was more than happy to share, and I certainly honored to have a few superstar dorymen pay a little homage that evening.

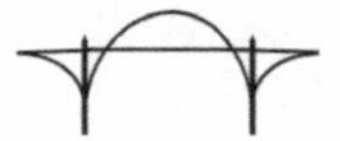

The following days were a mixed bag of results. However, patience and persistence pulled through again with another $700 payday before more wind put the kibosh on the 2:1 ratio season. It was blatantly obvious that every day was worth getting up and plunking the gear in the water. Even if it turned out to be a crappy day, you'd likely wind up with another $100 or more in your pocket. With the ratio fishery in the books, I took a five-day respite to unwind back home in the Corvallis before diving into the 100-a-day coho derby opener on July 15.

The sandblasting northwest winds preempted the opening of the coho season, but fortunately, they abated enough for the Florence fleet to venture out the following morning. For the first half of the summer, Florence's chinook production did not disappoint. The fleet was banking on adding good catches of silvers to the mix. Dad made the long trek from Salem to Florence, and I was more than happy to have him aboard. Fishing together with him on opening day was gospel on our boat. The added perk was that he made reservations for a motel room, so not only did I get to have him on deck, but it also meant two fewer nights in Hotel Toyota.

Much like the late 1970s and early 1980s, boats were littered all over the stretch between the jetties and Heceta Head. When we poked our noses across the bar, the residual northwest breeze from the previous blowout was a meager five miles per hour. The sea was still staggering in a confused state with lingering four to five-foot swells powering from the northwest. On the fishing front, Dad and I sprang back into our groove once again assuming our roles of pulling the gear and running the boat. It was as if those routines had become infused in our DNA over the years, never to be undone.

The silvers stepped up to the plate as 58 ended up in our fish box. It wasn't a king convention, but we managed to pick up four for the day. Aside from the fishing, a humongous log the size of a telephone pole in the water caught our attention. It was surging with the swells in a north-to-south trajectory. Acting like Nemo's Nautilus, it was poised to take out anything in its path.

"Holy crap, Dad. Check out that huge log off our starboard side!" I shouted while pulling gear. "Let's make sure to steer well away from it. Listen to the hissing sounds it makes when it's pushed by a swell. That thing is creepy."

"The swells are propelling it like a battering ram. That would sink a dory in an instant," Dad added. "I'm going to radio the guys around us to watch out for it."

The seven Benjamins on our fish ticket was the bigger story that day though. With indications that fish were going to be plentiful that summer, it didn't take a mathematician to figure out that there would be many more fish tickets to smile about in the coming weeks.

The second day just plain sucked. The weather was a carbon copy of the day before, but the fish disappeared. There wasn't a king to be found, and the silvers were few and far between. It was always the weirdest phenomenon when the fish would disappear overnight. We had a good idea that day where they went. The guys up in Newport were slaying them. We radioed Denny a few times for Newport updates and it just added to our misery.

"*High and Dry*, Denny, this is Bruce, you copy?" Dad hailed.

After a pause, Denny replied, sounding distant and immersed in static, "Hey Bruce, how is it going down there?"

"Oh, it's really slow down here, Denny. We're wondering how you're doing? We've overhead some guys up there on the Pile with good scores."

"It's really good here, Bruce. I've got silvers bouncing on the springs constantly and I've already put several kings aboard. Actually, I have to go. I have a big one pumping now."

"That's great! Go get 'em!'

It was maddening to hear the Newport guys constantly talking about how busy they were. In the past, it seemed the grass was always greener in Florence than Newport. It was not the case this time. To add insult to injury, the wind started to scream.

The wind blew for days on end. Since the fishing was red hot in Newport and the wind gusts didn't feel like punches from a heavyweight, we trailered the boat back there. Some boats there were voluntarily taking a beating in the slop and were being rewarded with some good paydays.

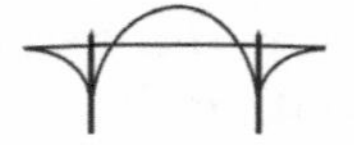

In the midst of our regrouping plan, we were met with more frustration. An electrical issue in our outboard engine bound us to the dock until we could sort it out. Unsuccessful, we finally sought help from a mechanic, and it even took him a few days to isolate the problem and to locate a part. It was maddening being affixed to the docks while you listened to your peers on the marine radio having epic days. We wanted to keep up with where the fish were, but knowing how much money we were losing made us want to tear our hair out. Finally, ten days after our last Florence trip, we were ready to make hay.

The first day back on the water was nothing short of epic. The silvers were rattling the springs all day long, but what had our attention were the heavy-pumping kings that were inhaling our gear. It was one of those hallmark days where fishing dreams came true. Our whole operation was firing on all cylinders as Dad and I were in a zone of synchronization that only father and son could understand. As if it couldn't get any better, the hot fishing was taking place on a pillowy sea that sparkled under sunny skies.

"This is incredible fishing, Ter. It might not ever be like this again, so take it all in and seize these moments. There's a lot of money to be made, too," Dad advised.

Sixty silvers and 18 kings later, we were basking in a record-setting performance. The frustrations from the prior few weeks had quickly faded into oblivion.

"So...what's the final dollar tally?" Dad asked with anticipation after I climbed back aboard with the fish ticket after our delivery.

"How's $1,200 sound for a day's work?" I responded.

"Twelve hundred dollars! Incredible!" Dad stated in amazement.

Much like an athlete who arrives at his or her peak performance, we were sailing into a two-week stretch where a myriad of *Carolyn Kay* records would be shattered and would be in the highlight reel of all future reminiscing. It was a Rockpile show. It was as if the salmon shot out a fire hose from the south coast to the North End, Day after day there was a well-worn path of boats migrating to the fishing grounds from the Newport jetties. Fortunately, Dad was able to stick around a couple more days. This was a huge relief. Fishing solo while dodging boats in heavy traffic, nasty currents, and hungry fish was like performing as a one-man circus act.

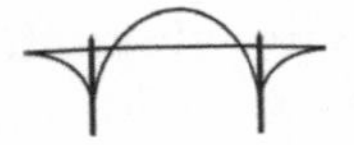

The North End continued to deliver even though the weather wasn't very forgiving. There was big money to be made though, and each day boats would head out borderline fishable conditions. There was always a stiff northwest breeze and some days included some thick, clinging fog. On several wet, jarring trips to the fishing grounds, I muttered to myself, *I can't believe I'm heading out to the Pile in this crap!* In leaner times, those snotty oceans would have been a definite no-go.

One morning after plowing through sloughing whitecaps for over an hour, I deployed my gear on a northbound course at the edge of the Pile. It was like merging onto a busy interstate where you just have to pick your spot and stay in your lane. The swell caught my attention as it had already risen a foot or two with a wicked extra measure of wind ripple. I thought to myself though, *"You're out here, so let's make this count while there is still time. It's going to be a short stay."*

It didn't take long before the deep springs started doing the king dance. I had to figure out though how to pull the gear, get the fish, and to not be the guy on the news who rammed another boat. Strategically, I pulled the deep line with the pounding fish and let out the opposing-side float line to generate a quick 180-degree turn so the boat would troll with the wind and waves. This made for a steadier course and led to plopping four kings aboard including a 23-pounder. The downside was that the boat was heading downhill, or south, at a rapid rate. The thought of having to take a beating on the trip home wasn't very palatable.

Pointing the bow north for another pass, I remarked to myself, "Oh boy! It's really getting mean out here now." I gained some more northerly ground before finally cranking the helm eastward for the slow, albeit turbulent, troll toward home. The gear produced a few more fish before I pulled gear and was in the snug waters of the harbor by 10 AM. It was another head shaker at the dock with the realization that I only had the gear down for about an hour and a half and earned over $300. Not only that, I had the boat all tidied up well before lunch time.

Like a slow drip, the solo treks out to the Pile wore me down. I gave Dad a call to beg him to adjust his work schedule to jump in on the action. It wasn't hard to convince him, and he weaved his magic to arrive by nightfall. Back at the trailer, I shared the latest fishing intel with him, most notably how the fish had adjusted their feeding schedule to mid-morning. It was important to front-load this information because I feared he would want to move on to some new fishing grounds if we weren't tossing fish aboard during the first hour.

As prophesied, the next morning got off to a very slow start. "Looks like the fish moved on, Ter. Maybe we should start exploring some new ground. No one else is getting 'em either," Dad announced.

I reminded him, "You gotta be patient with this bite. It's been happening at the tide change, which is around 10 AM this morning. I'm confident it will happen today."

Fortunately, like clockwork, the king show began...and boy did it deliver! We were boating a couple of kings with some silvers mixed in on each tack. Dad was having a ball, and it was fun to just take the wheel and watch him go at it. He was having such a blast tinkering with his side's gear arrangement and rearrangements as fish hit several different models of plugs.

"Wow. You're right about that tide change, Ter. It was like a flick of a switch and the bite turned on. Our Tomic plugs are sure working today and it was fun to get one on the good old Little Joe plug," Dad said with his eyes lit up with enthusiasm.

It turned out to be another one of the most profitable days we ever had with over $1,100 earned for the 28 silvers and 18 kings we put in the box. Much like NBA stars who sometimes describe a hot streak by "being in the zone," it is much the same with dory fishing. When we were on the water consistently, we developed a mental map of fish movement. Mixed in was prior experience and a special intuition that set us in a groove. It was an awesome feeling to be in it, and we definitely knew when we slipped out of it. During the 1988 Rockpile sessions, we were definitely in the dory-fishing zone.

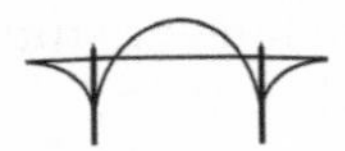

The mass of kings on the Pile faded out a few days later. Some of those fish moved toward shore and many boats followed. The first day in shallower waters yielded ten chinooks. For the next week fishing wasn't lights out, but scores of 20 to 30 silvers and a handful of kings were the norm. Upon hearing the season quota was nearly full, I fired up the afterburners up to the finish line. I was a staunch believer in what I called the "no regrets" philosophy. I didn't ever want to look back at the season in mid-winter on some rainy day and wonder why I didn't give it my all.

Often in late August, the silvers sense that it is time to get positioned for their river journeys and they tend to become fewer in number in the troll catches. This wasn't the case during the final few days of the all-species season. Fishing only a few miles from shore, most of the small boats were scoring 50 to 60 silvers and a handful of kings each day.

The second to last day turned out to be my season finale as I had some business to take care of the next day. In the late afternoon as the wind picked up and the fish finally went off the bite, I pulled the gear for the last time. As I was tucking the last spread into the gear tray, I took a few moments to reflectively gaze westward. Half the spread just dangled in the water. I just didn't want to put it away and leave. It had been an epic four months, and I knew the chances of having another season like it was slim. After a few more salty inhalations, I reluctantly finished putting all the gear in place, took one last glance, and then punched the throttle for the final run to port.

For an encore to the 1988 bonanza, Dad drove over that night to fish until the final curtain fell. My parents' anniversary was coming up and Dad wanted to do something special for my mother with cash earned from a day's fishing. I met up with him when he came to town, gave him the head's up on where to fish and what to expect, and then I handed the season's playbook to him. The next day did not disappoint as he hauled in about the same score as I did the day before. Quite happily, Dad went home with a nice chunk of change to do a little jewelry shopping for Mom.

With a perfect finale for an epic summer, we didn't bother participating in a late-summer chinook-only season. Dad was up to his earlobes in AC sales and I needed a break before school started. D'Ann and I shifted into vacation mode and broke in our new mountain bikes in Sunriver, Oregon, and then went all touristy in Victoria, British Columbia.

My junior year at Western Oregon University immediately served up a full plate of studies as I dived deep into the teacher education program. Everything seemed to be heading in the path that I laid out. Fishing had returned in earnest and it was clear that education was a career I wanted to pursue. The ideal pairing of my two occupations was becoming closer to reality.

CHAPTER 13

SEASON 13

WHEN THE WHEELS FELL OFF

1989 Setlist

Doobie Brothers *Cycles*

Huey Lewis and the News *Picture This*

Steve Winwood *Back in the High Life*

The afterglow of the 1988 season shone brightly throughout the fall, winter, and spring. Dad and I waxed poetic about the adventures of our best season ever that was still coursing through our veins. Looking forward, our hopes were filled with enthusiasm about the purchase of a new LORAN. It not only provided the comfort of pinpointing coordinates on the Big Blue, but it also had a course plotter and waypoint storing capabilities. Those features seem routine now to those who frequent the sea using GPS, but in 1988 we were feeling like we were on the cutting edge of marine technology. We plotted and schemed on how our new tool would pay for itself many times over.

My winter and spring school schedules were on steroids as I was juggling 16 to 18 credit hours and teaching practicums to boot. Still flying high from the previous summer, it seemed like it was a no-brainer that there would be another banner year in store for us. I hadn't fully learned how assumptions can really make an ass out of you. The summer of 1989 had some life lessons in store, and there would be some big questions going forward.

Consumed with busy spring schedules, there was barely enough time for Dad and me to prep the boat, let alone start fishing in May. By the time finals were done in early June though, we had the *Carolyn Kay* back in action. There weren't a lot of new tunes flowing from my tape deck for the new season. Many of my favorites started hitting burnout from their 1980s stardom and were either broken up or hiatus. Fortunately the Doobie Brothers regrouped and released an album sporting their classic early sound. I also started diving back into some material from a few years back that I rediscovered. The second album by Huey Lewis and News and Steve Winwood's *Back in the High Life* became new again and got heavy airplay on my valley-coastal commutes.

Launch day was very pleasant with light wind and a clear-blue sky. Upon pulling the boat into our moorage slip, we casually started to get all the gear rigging set up. It was a drill we knew how to do in our sleep. Just like the year before, the set up fell quickly in place. With the ocean in decent condition, it made sense to shake out the bugs and maybe run into a few launch-day kings like we did in 1988.

The ocean was very welcoming with 1-to-3-foot swells and just a whisper of northwest wind. We dropped our gear about 15 minutes out front of the buoys and it didn't take long for the springs to start hammering.

"Oh look," I said. "The first pumper of the year on your deep, Dad. Go get 'em!" Ten minutes later we had our first fish.

"I got a heavy pumper going on my side, Dad!" I shouted. After a couple more pumps, the spring was dormant. "Damn! It's gone."

"That must have been a big one, Ter. Reminds me of when we shook down the gear last year. There's some fish here so we might as well stick it out for a bit," Dad said excitedly.

"Yeah, it's a great sign, and it seems like the kings might be in big numbers like last year," I added.

Five kings were boated for our efforts, and we must have lost twice that many. We had tied some gear with the previous year's fishing line that seemed to be in good shape, but several snapped off leaders proved otherwise. Monofilament takes a beating ten months after being subjected to briny air, dirty hands, and random splatters of fish blood. It was a lesson learned to not cut corners.

"One thing is for sure, we need to toss that spool of line and buy some new stuff. At least we found that out right away," I said as we both nodded in agreement.

Following a spell of whitecaps that kept us off the water, it was time to try to lay into the fish that broke our leaders. Substituting for the wind was a thick blanket of fog, but at least the ocean was like a sheet of glass. Dad and I headed straight out the jetties and hung a left at the whistle buoy. We then headed downhill to that well-traveled 25 to 30 fathom path. After a slow morning, kings started coming aboard in small clatters.

"Here we go again, Ter. We'll get them to stick today with the re-tied gear. Go get those two fish on your side. I'm going to drive back through that same patch and see if we can drum up some more interest. Boy, this plotter sure is slick. This is going to pay for itself in no time, " Dad said encouragingly.

The plotter and waypoint storage features on the LORAN were a kick. Amid the chaos that often ensues upon running into small schools of fish, the LORAN screen was littered with dark gray waypoint dots and all sorts of squiggles marking our travels at troll speed. It was like a dot-to-dot drawing book, as we trolled back along our erratic paths through the previous hotspots that we marked. While using our plotter to navigate back to port through the soupy visibility with ease, we were all smiles about our final score of 13 kings.

"Here we go again!" I proclaimed. "Looks like the king fishing is picking up where it left off from last year."

"It sure does, Ter," Dad agreed. "This plotter is slick. It's going to make you a lot of money, and looking at the screen, we're zeroed in on the buoy!"

The following morning yielded a respectable eight kings, but our good fortune soon took a punch to the gut. Daily catches declined to about two kings per day. What was more unnerving though was the radio banter about the coho price for the upcoming opener.

"Yeah…I was talking to a guy at the fish dock. Sounds like silvers may be 90 cents a pound, maybe a buck," One fisherman announced.

"Oh wow! Ha! Well…that hardly makes it worth even putting the gear in the water for that. I guess those good prices from last year were too good to be true." replied his buddy.

Dad and I listened with our mouths agape. In a nutshell, that meant that every fish was only going to be worth about forty percent of the prior year. You didn't have to be a mathematician to figure out that the 1989 season was not going to hold a candle to 1988, no matter how many fish we caught.

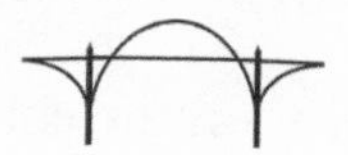

The opening day of the coho season started with a bang. Many of the usual fleet of small boats were eager to fill their fish boxes, despite the dismal fish prices. Springs were rattling all day long, which kept Dad and me constantly running the gear. There was a regional quota for silvers, and boats were allowed to retain 50 silvers with a 3:1 ratio of coho to kings thereafter. We tallied 59 coho and three kings for our efforts, and while the bottom line in the dollar column was a bit disheartening, we still held our heads high as $300 still paid the bills and then some. The next ten days that followed were nearly carbon copies. Coho schools were definitely in session, but kings were few and far between. Noticeably, the number of boats started to dwindle. With few kings to offset the low coho earnings, many of the guys just lost interest and went back to their "real jobs" or just took the summer off. Dad's participation became sporadic with such a busy work schedule.

There was no rest for the *Carolyn Kay* though. With the craziness of fishing solo for days on end, the dirty laundry kept piling higher. Eventually it became a morning ritual to perform a form of triage that involved culling the least vile smelling clothing out of the laundry bag. Nothing quite beats the feeling of being dead tired and slipping on damp smelly socks at 5 AM.

On July 13th, the word spread like wildfire that the coho season would end the following day. Fortunately, Dad was on hand for the finale.

"Damn, that came from nowhere," I complained. "I thought we would have a few more weeks of coho fishing. What a bummer. I'm not sure what to do after tomorrow."

"Well, let's put in a solid day. Maybe you'll get a better idea in the next day or so," Dad said to ease my anxiety. I had hoped to earn enough to pay for my final year of school and to avoid student loans entirely. Suddenly, I wasn't so sure.

Production was slower on the coho season's final day. In the late afternoon when all signs of life seemed to disappear, we finally agreed to pull up stakes.

"Well, Ter, we haven't had a fish hit in a couple hours. No one else is having any action, either," Dad said. "What do you think we should do?"

"We have 30 slips and a king. I was hoping we could nab another 20 in the afternoon, but all we have been doing is boat riding. Dang it. I didn't see this closure coming so soon. Yeah… let's pull and head home."

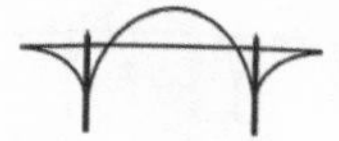

On July 19th I was back at it solo for the 2:1 ratio coho to king season. There was a little chatter on the docks of some kings at the North End, so I motivated myself to make the hour run out there to check it out. The action supposedly was in the deeper water, sometimes known as the Daisy Patch, in the range of 55 to 70 fathoms. At those depths, the amount of drag combined with the current and wind created dory hell when fishing solo. This was especially true while attempting to keep a course and fishing amongst larger boats. When a deep line was brought up from 50 fathoms or more, it was like the bottom of the boat was slathered with grease. The boat would abruptly make a sharp turn, despite every effort to balance things out. I was so thankful for the hydraulics. In the early years when we cranked the gear by hand in deep water, it was a nightmare, especially when a fish that was on a bottom spread dropped off sometime during the ascent.

Fishing at the Daisy Patch was a dumpster fire. The sparse population of kings was congregating close to the bottom, and so were the thousands of "shaker" or small halibut that would hit most anything you threw down there. As soon as the gear was set, the springs started to vibrate, which signaled an undersized halibut. Even the legal-sized ones could not be retained during that stretch. Seeing a spring quiver made my blood pressure soar as I had to bring the gear up all that way just to clear the line. This happened over and over again. When all was said and done, the day's catch was two medium kings and one coho. This barely paid for the gas, let alone anything else. I brooded during the entire hour-long run back to port about whether it was worth running back out the next day for another round of punishment.

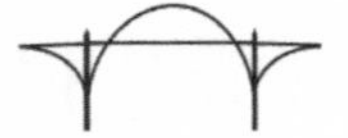

I took a few more days off to try to gather more intel for a better game plan. Mark on the *Lady Scarlett* clued me in on a small fleet of boats in Florence who were catching some monster kings by using whole-herring rigs on long leaders close to shore. They weren't filling their fish boxes, but two or three of those behemoths in a day would certainly make it worth the while and would inject some much-needed adrenaline in the season. About the same time, I talked to another doryman about a short wide-open coho season further north out of Tillamook Bay. It was an intriguing possibility, but Dad's Jeep Wagoneer was rear-ended, thus eliminating the possibility of trailering there. I wasn't keen on motoring north that far. Since I knew the area down south well, I decided to go that route. Later, I questioned my judgment on that move.

Early the next morning, I made the southbound trek like I had done several times before to lay into some big slabs. A northwest breeze had already kicked up by the time I set gear mid-morning off of the Heceta Head lighthouse, but it was an ocean that was still quite fishable. I re-rigged the gear with several spreads of whole herring as the main entree for the big ones, but I still kept a few spreads of hoochie-flasher rigs in action. Bait fishing was a work of art and it seemed everyone had a different twist on how to rig and present it for the fish. Ironically, I caught three decent-sized kings, but they all came on the token hardware spreads I was dragging. Regardless of how they were caught, I was riding with my head up high feeling that I had made the right decision. It was a good thing that I savored that day.

The wind revved up and blew everyone off the water until the last week of July. The first morning that the wind laid down enough to get back to business, I was very amped up to pick up where I left off. Right away I landed a

13-pound king and a couple of silvers, and then the fishing died off for everyone for several hours. There was a cold, penetrating breeze that severely tested my persistence. It felt like it was delivering something more though—like a foreshadowing of what was in store. Cold, bored, and without hope for another bouncing spring, I packed up the gear and headed into port by early afternoon.

Within a matter of days, a bitter taste spread over the whole scene. Scores among the fleet were ranging from zero to two fish, and I had a couple of days that I didn't get the skunk off the boat. I started to doubt my decision to go south and wished I had chosen the Tillamook Bay option. I was missing Dad's presence, too. My early season visions had Dad and me slinging chinooks in late July. With fishing so slow, Dad didn't bother making the long drive just to go boat riding. Adding insult to injury, the ocean flattened out like a pancake. For the first time in over three years, doubts about the viability of the industry started creeping back in my mind. I had to remind myself that a crash was bound to happen after banner years from 1986 to 1988.

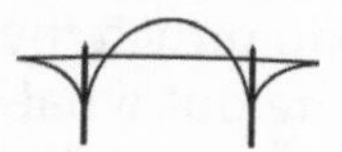

The Good Lord painted a beautiful masterpiece on His canvas on a morning near the end of July. I made my way downriver full of optimism for yet another valiant attempt to turn things around. Swinging north, my eyes met the breathtaking view of the Heceta Head lighthouse standing proudly to the north in its protective cove. In the background was a dazzling orange corona bleeding over the silhouetted Coast Range. The morning couldn't have kicked off any better. Setting my gear, I was poised and ready for the springs to start dancing. An hour passed with not so much as a quiver from the springs though, and those negative thoughts started their sinister crawl back into my hippocampus. In an effort to get creative, I ventured further north and into shallower waters in hopes that those rumored big ones were hiding there.

When all hope seemed to be lost, the port spring came alive and I sprung into action to haul in a big prize. My excitement lasted a few more seconds and then abruptly crashed and burned. Instead of a big king, I was hung up in a crab pot and the boat took a hard pivot to the port. Despite all my attempts to break free, the boat was welded to the ocean floor. The hydraulic relief valve screamed for mercy. It seemed if I kept trying to work free, something would have to give. I feared that might be my 2-inch diameter davit bending toward the waterline, or perhaps worse, a stress crack on the side of the boat. When I ran out of options to break loose, I made the dreaded snip with the cable cutters. With it came the sickening "zip!" as I watched the 120 feet of stainless cable race through the pulleys into the depths with a forty-pound lead and four spreads of line. Not only did I watch more than $100 of gear slip away, but in that fleeting moment, I also watched a very promising season slip away as well.

I was pissed and disappointed beyond measure. Upon impulse, with the ocean in such prime condition, I decided to put the gear in the boat, punch the throttle, and head north to Newport to figure out what on Earth to do. I'd worry about how to get my truck later. I just needed a change of scenery. The wake from the outboard motor left many concerns etched on the water as I powered on my northward course: *"What am I going to do with the rest of the summer if no fish are around? Do I need to get another job somewhere? Am I going to have to get a student loan this year?"* All of these deep ponderings made my stomach churn. I also ruminated on the bigger picture for the first time in a long time. *"Is this the start of a big decline in the fishery? How many more years do we have left on the water?"* At least the next few hours of running north provided a very scenic view. I had no way of knowing at the time that I had fished out of Florence for the final time ever on our dory.

The fishing never perked up that summer. I ended up

heading back to Corvallis to plot my next move. I checked in at the eerily quiet docks a few times and discovered that fishing effort was nearly non-existent. My game plan was not an easy one to swallow, but I started searching for summer employment in Corvallis and ended up scoring a job with a local painting contractor. The culture shock from being dialed in on fishing all summer to a sudden switch to painting was hard to swallow. At least I had a lot of brush and roller experience, so I felt confident that I could jump into the job quickly.

Using the work ethic I had gleaned from fishing and the military, I worked my butt off on the painting gig. I earned a few coins and a good reputation. It didn't hold a candle to the fishing life, but made me realize how fragile our fishing experience was. Like anything, you don't truly know how much you value something until it is gone. There was already talk of the 1990 coho season being a shell of what it had been over the past four seasons. This left Dad and I wondering if the well was finally running dry.

CHAPTER 14

SEASON 14

TROLLING ON A PRAYER

1990 Setlist

Fleetwood Mac *Behind the Mask*

Robert Cray Band *Strong Persuader & Don't Be Afraid of the Dark*

Even though the 1989 season ended with a dismal thud, Dad and I tried to remain optimistic. In news articles, publications, and some talk with some coastal locals over the winter, the scuttlebutt was that the Pacific Fisheries Management Council was leaning toward additional restrictions for 1990. That wasn't what we wanted to hear, and by spring, it was carved in stone that there would only be a 1:1 ratio of chinook to coho beginning on July 4th until a small quota of coho was met. Before and after that stretch would be chinook-only fishing. To make it worthwhile, we'd need to pour our hearts and souls into every chinook catching strategy we ever learned. We would also need a little luck with the weather and for some kings to hang in close to shore. Unlike in 1984, our king-catching confidence and skill level had improved dramatically. Some fishermen and the Oregon Department of Fish and Wildlife hinted that there would be a decent population of big ones around. Still, it was a big gamble.

Life was hectic during the final term of student teaching. My assignment was a third-grade class in a school with a high population of at-risk students where behavior issues were abundant, primarily due to the hardships they faced daily. Many of those students lived in poverty and more than a few lived in cars and homes where drugs and trauma were prevalent. Despite these challenges, it was heartening to see that these children deeply appreciated things that most kids take for granted. They would beam whenever they received small incentives or when given positive attention.

From March to June of that year, I was up to my earlobes in all the quagmire of paperwork that is required by the Teacher Standards and Practices Commission. There were units of study to develop and mounds of data that needed to be collected and analyzed. On top of that, as the term wore on, I started applying for teaching jobs as they came about painstakingly using an old typewriter and my neatest handwriting. This left very little time for boat prep and no time to fish for kings on the weekends. I worked my butt off and was able to get a few weeks ahead of schedule with my coursework. To maintain some sort of sanity, I ran a lot in the mornings, and was in the best physical condition in my life. I entered some local races and clocked at just under seven minutes per mile in one race, which for me, was off the charts as I was never much of a fast runner in my younger years.

In mid-May, I had just completed an 8K bridge run in Portland. It was a great course that culminated with the crossing of the majestic, arched Freemont Bridge into the heart of Portland's west side. I set a PR for that distance, and I was feeling on top of my game.

A few days after the bridge run, I was teaching a reading lesson and happened to scratch an itch on my head and felt a couple of bumps. While outwardly keeping my composure during the lesson, my heart raced as I felt a sinking feeling from my head down to my toes. There had been an outbreak of chickenpox at the school where I was student teaching. At the first opportunity, I dashed into a restroom to do a head check in the mirror. Frantically parting my hair follicles, two red spots glared back at me, justifying my horror. *"This couldn't be happening. It's the worst possible timing!"* I thought as I double-checked and tried to rationalize it was just a couple random pimples. I didn't say anything to anyone, including my wife. I had noticed a couple of other bumps that appeared on my head later on, but I had decided to shift into denial mode.

Late that evening in bed, D'Ann said, "Do you have a fever? You are radiating heat."

"I'm fine," I mumbled. "It's just me burrowing in the pillows and that's making me warm."

That feeble reply was about the best I could drum up at the moment to maintain my brush-off with the inevitable. In my fever-induced dreams that night, I had visions of being covered in pox. Upon waking up, I headed straight to the bathroom mirror, lifted my shirt to find out that sometimes dreams do come true. They were everywhere. About that time, D'Ann happened to pass by the open bathroom entry and stopped short to see what on Earth I was up to. It took a mere few seconds for her to officially proclaim my worst nightmare as she said, "Oh my, Terry, you have chickenpox. Your back is covered!" As I absorbed that dose of reality, I promptly passed out.

The next two weeks were mostly an exercise in frustration as I had to put my final student teaching practicum on pause. The advanced preparation in my coursework helped ease the trauma of being out of action. When I emerged from my quarantine, I managed to salvage my student teaching experience and subsequently earned my degree, albeit a bit scabbed up.

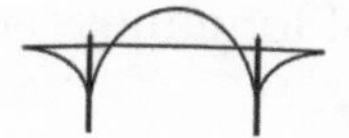

With my diploma in hand, I promptly shifted my focus to hook and line, all the while applying for teaching positions up and down the Willamette Valley. Since the outlook for silvers was dim, I looked for ways to reduce operating costs. It didn't make much sense to haul the trailer to the coast for potentially just a few weeks, so my game plan was to just crash in the back of my pickup. I knew it was going to be a challenge to find a place to park my rig since Newport was really cracking down on that sort of thing. As luck would have it though, Denny on the *High and Dry* wasn't too enthused about fishing commercially with the underwhelming season outlook. He had his boat moored at the South Beach Marina to do some occasional sport fishing, and he generously offered to let me bunk on his boat free of charge. This was like staying in the Hilton compared to the Toyota.

By late June, Dad and I had managed to get our very impatient boat prepped in the few weeks before the season and into the water. It was a weird feeling getting such a late start on many aspects of the process, but we had the *Carolyn Kay* ready for yet another rodeo. While everything boat-wise was in shipshape, the pounding and jostling that a dory inflicts on a person over the years was starting to take a physical toll on my dad who was 49 years old at the time. He was dealing with some sciatic pain as well as some other health issues that made the daily hard charging that dory fishing requires very difficult. Without a trailer to call home base that year, his plan was to get a motel room when he was in town.

By the time July 3rd rolled around, the small-boat fleet was a shell of what it had been just a few years earlier. Many just weren't interested in the 1:1 ratio season and never bothered to launch their boats. This generated mixed feelings on the eve of the opener that bore similarities to the vibes of the

1983 season. There was the excitement of getting back on the water, but a real sense of loneliness set in with the fleet's lack of participation.

Adding to the weirdness, I was full of anxiety. Start-up funds for the season were meager—a residual effect from the disappointing finish in 1989. A surge of thoughts rushed through my head. *"Maybe this is a bad idea to fish this season. I wonder where I should drop gear in the morning? I wonder if there will be any fish around at all? I hope I won't have to scrap fishing altogether and find a painting job like last season. Where are all the boats?"* I committed that evening before the opener to reading scripture and some very deep prayer for a John 21:6 experience to lead me to where there would be a bounty of kings. In all the years that I had fished, there was never such a cloud of uncertainty before a season as there was that evening.

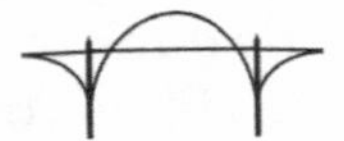

Fleetwood Mac's new album flowed in my truck cab on my first morning trek to the Port Dock. Their music was a fixture from the beginning so I figured the new tunes would be a good omen. The Good Lord provided His first blessings with a clear blue sky and flat seas. Dad and I had always subscribed to running south whenever we were in doubt of where to go for kings. I felt a strong sense to follow that notion, so I cruised on a southerly course along the 25-fathom line. The *Carolyn Kay* glided and kissed the smooth gentle morning swells for a few miles to a spot offshore of where Beaver Creek meets sand and sea off to the east.

To keep the incidental silver catch to a minimum, I didn't set any traditional silver gear. I ran some long leader flasher-hoochie rigs near the basement and had some of our hall-of-fame plugs arranged at different depths on each of the four wires. In stunned amazement, I started getting a few pumpers on the wires, and even more surprising, a few of the kings I boated were on plugs toward the surface. This was a rarity as the chinooks that took interest usually inhaled them in the depths. A sense of hope surfaced in my heart. If kings were swimming around at all depths, it would ratchet up the probability of putting more in the fish box. While it wasn't a banner day by any stretch, the kings kept climbing on the gear one by one along with the match of silvers. After each fish came aboard, I was giving thanks for the answered prayers.

When I finally hung it up in the early evening, I had nine decent-sized kings and nine silvers. With being so focused on putting fish in the box, I had completely forgotten it was the Fourth of July. Later that evening, the skies overhead the bay were stunningly illuminated and I had a front-row seat to all the fanfare. Between keeping in constant motion running gear all day, and some of the mental stress of the days leading up to the season, I was utterly exhausted. In the past, we usually eased into the season and got our sea legs with a few slow chinook-only days. By sundown, my legs were on fire and felt like they do when you have a bad case of the flu. Unaware at the time, I had been leaning up against the gear trays on the insides of the boat to keep my balance for most of the day. My lower extremities rocketed pangs and spasms that amplified whenever I laid down. I was in good shape, so feeling that incapacitated was quite foreign. Ibuprofen had not become part of my life yet, but it would have eased a lot of discomfort. Adding to my sleeplessness that night were the post-fireworks marina parties that lasted into the wee hours. This left me wondering how in the world I would be able to physically pull off the same amount of effort the next day.

With my mind locked on finding success on the first day, I hadn't paid much attention to the forecast. I awoke from my painful short night's rest with thick drizzle, a southwest breeze, and some fog for extra mental anguish. Poking my nose out on the back deck, I thought to myself, *"Really? How in the world am I going to pull this off? I'll bet it's too sloppy to fish today."* After painfully stepping aboard our drizzle-covered dory, I flicked on the CB. Those who had already ventured out reported the ocean was miserable, but fishable. Needing every penny I could earn, I sucked it up, donned my bright orange oilskins, and disappeared past the bridge into the soupy mist. I was hoping by tossing enough fish aboard, my legs would forget how they truly felt and that I could stay awake.

Since Beaver Creek had treated me well on the 4th, I pointed the *Carolyn Kay's* bow southbound as it slapped, pounded, and banged its way to its destination. Once the gear was in the water, I was poised and ready for a carbon copy of the prior day's good fortune. Sadly, other than just stretching with the jostling of the waves, there were no signs of life on the springs. Fortunately, a few medium kings and a couple of silvers fell victim to my gear and broke the monotony and misery by noon. By that time though, the ocean had kicked up like a frothy beverage, and it was clear that any further abuse wasn't worth the effort to catch another king. The next day felt like a kick in the shins with just one fish and then Mother Nature served up a strong ridge of high pressure, complete with a caravan of northwesterly winds.

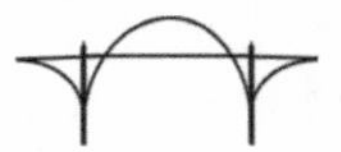

The wind blew relentlessly for two weeks before it decided to have mercy. The unexpected layoff had left me more than a little concerned that the season was going to become a financial disaster. I had been listening to a lot of tunes by blues/rock artist Robert Cray. While not very uplifting, his catalog was quite fitting with the mood I was in.

The pressure was on to make the next few trips count. The water temperature had dipped below the fifties, which meant a trip to the Pile to find a warmer salmon habitat. There were few boats, which was both a blessing and a curse. It was much easier to maneuver, but there was an ever-present feeling of emptiness. Very few of my main small-boat comrades had chosen to make an appearance. I didn't realize how much I relied on having a network of boats for community, intel, and safety. The day ended up delivering some hope though as I put four kings and the matching four silvers in the box. Nothing earthshaking, but there were signs of life and it was worth the boat ride. Even more promising, the kings came higher up on the gear again, engulfing plugs.

It was a foggy commute back out the North End the next morning, but at least I was blessed with a calm ride. Picking up where I left off, I worked the edge of the Pile hard, targeting the big ones down deep and running plugs and hardware in the upper half of the water column. My gear selection and placement worked marvelously and by the end of that foggy day, 10 kings and 10 silvers were sloshing around in the cool seawater of the flow-through fish box. Following that two-week blowout, I could have easily thrown in the towel. Patience and persistence prevailed and paid off for a chance to salvage the season.

Like many times before, the king congregation at the Pile scattered and soon the fleet was looking for greener pastures. Word leaked out late over the airwaves that a few boats trolling near the beach down south off Seal Rock found a few fish. It was a common scenario that had played out several times where fish disappeared offshore and reappeared inshore as the water warmed up and the baitfish moved with it. Once again, during a season that had so much going against it, another shot of optimism surfaced.

High pressure had enjoyed its hiatus, and it was ready to generate a new dosage of northwest wind. It was forecasted to be uncomfortable in the mornings and to get its mojo on in the afternoons. Typically, if it was a wide-open silver season, many of the day boats would fish straight out in front of the harbor or north, so as to avoid the trauma of the punishing northerly slog home. Since south was where the action was, those who were still fishing planned to just scurry down there early before the wind started screaming and take it in the shorts on the trip home.

Upon arrival off of Seal Rock, there was a small, congregated fleet of boats aggressively working the shallows. Despite all the pounding into the slop and the struggle to keep the boat straight while pulling gear, it was much easier than dragging twice as much wire around offshore. While far from an epic score, the day's catch yielded five and five. It was an encouraging sign to see a few kings in close and again, they were coming up high on the wire on plugs. As prophesied, the trip home lived up to expectations with sharp wind chop on top of four-foot swells. A generous serving of spray sneaked about repeatedly on the port side and left half of my body looking like a wet seal.

Just when I was starting to wear down, Dad arrived in town, I filled him in on all the details and laid out the game plan for the next morning. At daybreak, we had the boat warming up like old times with each of us dividing up the preparation duties without any discussion of who needed to do what. Included in our ritual was Dad's tap-tap-tapping the barometer and setting it before we departed. Leaving the moorage, l was more than happy to have him take the helm as I knew it was a banquet for his soul.

"What do you think about dropping in the gear off of Beaver Creek, Ter?" Dad suggested.

"I think that's a good idea. We don't want to overrun the fish," I agreed.

Just as the day before, fish started banging the deep lines and float lines. Even more delightful, the kings were hitting the plugs up high again. Dad's unbridled enthusiasm above the ongoing puttering of the outboard motor and the five-horsepower hydraulic engine was like music to my ears.

"Oh, another one took a plug, Ter, on the fourth spread down. It's a lively one! That's two so far near the surface. There it goes, veering away from the boat like big kings do on the long leaders," Dad announced.

"They've been coming up high all month. The baitfish must be spread out on the water column," I replied. "Go get 'em!"

When the wind kicked up and the fishing switch flipped to "off," we made the wet exit again back to port with eight and eight. At least this time we were much closer to port as the kings had indeed edged northward three or four miles. The following day was much the same with the fish continuing their northward migration and being stationed straight out in front of the jetties. This made for an even more tolerable jaunt home with nine kings and seven silvers for our efforts.

"Boy, there are enough kings this summer to make ends meet. They really have saved your bacon. The Tomic plugs near the surface sure have produced. I hope it can last a few more weeks for you, Ter," Dad commented.

"Me, too. Yeah, to be honest, a few weeks ago I thought it was a lost cause when the wind was screaming 24/7," I replied. "Hopefully we can get out tomorrow. The ocean has a nasty look to it."

The stubborn wind was in a mood and chose to ramp up that afternoon to a new level.

Dad went with a glass-half-full outlook and stuck around in hopes of getting out the next morning. When we awoke though, we could hear the whistle buoy's distinctive hoot from town, which was always a bad sign. Foaming whitecaps had already formed and were forecasted to intensify for the next several days. We both made our way back to the Valley to take care of business and soak up some spectacular Pacific Northwest summer weather.

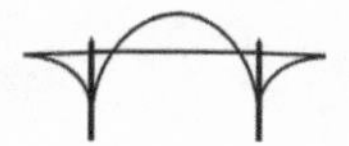

Little did we know though that the season was nearly over, and that we wouldn't fish together again for nearly another year. The 1:1 ratio season ended on July 31st, so days fished thereafter were chinook only. I made a few more trips resulting in meager catches of smaller fish. I took this as a sign that it was time to move on to more pressing matters.

I needed to find a teaching job. I had missed some fishing days for a few promising interviews but hadn't nailed my first position yet. A week later after hitting a real low with no prospects, I got a call from the Newberg School District. One thing led to another, which led to another, and soon I was readying a classroom for my first fleet of fourth graders.

Using the same preparation skills as I had done countless times in the fishing industry, I rigged up the classroom for the new school year. Doing this, I felt the rush that I always got prior to a fishing season. The learning curve was steep and time was a precious commodity that first year. I had found a new passion that helped fill the void of being off the water in the dark, cold, and rainy days in the winter. Even better though, I had finally put together what I thought could be the perfect combination of occupations with teaching for ten months and then salmon trolling during the summer break. It was simple. All that was needed were the stars to perfectly align for a real coho season that would keep our dory dream alive.

CHAPTER 15

SEASON 15

ALL GOOD THINGS MUST COME TO PASS

1991 Setlist

Seal *Seal*

Styx "Come Sail Away"

Rush *Roll the Bones*

I never imagined that teaching could be like operating a fishing boat, but after a great first year in the classroom teaching fourth graders, there were a few parallels. The most prominent was that running the classroom was like being the skipper of a boat. With a large crew of young learners, it was a huge responsibility in keeping the whole operation flowing smoothly and staying afloat. As the skipper of the learning environment, it's essential that morale is high and that everyone carries out their duties. Much like a dory, you have to have systems in place and organization for materials and daily routines. It struck me several times throughout that maiden voyage on how I fell back on many of those skills to get my first classroom underway.

Science was always one of my favorite subjects, and I was fortunate to land in a place where I could cultivate that passion and share it with my young learners. I also connected with a fabulous veteran teaching partner, Dwight, and we found we had similar visions in keeping kids engaged and excited about learning. Our students mixed solutions that fizzed and changed colors. They created series and parallel circuits. Our students became engineers and designed and constructed toys, cars, and bridges. A few years later, we began to raise and study salmon. Being that the subject matter was so close to my heart, I couldn't resist sharing many captivating stories of my adventures on the water.

When the 1990 season concluded, Dad and I both were keeping a wary eye on the future of the industry. The great resurgence of the allowable harvest and larger runs of silvers and chinooks between 1986 and 1988 made it seem that the good times would last for many years. The downturn of 1989 and 1990 had cast a cloud of concern again. We didn't talk about it much then, but both of us mused when and how our great adventure would ultimately come to an end. Fortunately around spring time, the stars aligned, or at least gave it a good try. Word on the street was that there would be a short, but wide-open, no daily-quota salmon season commencing on June 24th. Dad and I certainly didn't see that coming, but it perked up our enthusiasm to get the boat ready. There hadn't been a wide open coho season for many years. My dream of weaving together both of my chosen professions still had a chance to coalesce.

There was one catch to the whole scenario. The season's quota was small and would be reached quickly. With the season looking like it would resemble the brief one in 1982, we decided to leave the travel trailer in the Valley. Once again, Dad planned to seek shelter in a motel room on days he would be in town. When solo, I would just find a place to crash in my truck. I wasn't sure where I'd park my rig in Newport, but I planned to figure out something.

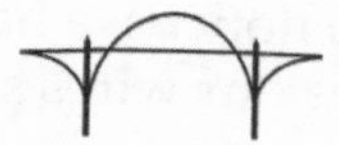

With Dad in town the night before opening day, our ambition levels were maxed out as we made last moment adjustments with our gear. In classic Oregon Coast summer fashion, a thick drizzle greeted us as we made our way toward his rig from the motel room. The wispy mist shrouding the city lights created an eerie glow in the darkness. It clung to the windshield before his Jeep Wagoneer's wipers could clear the view. On drizzly mornings, I always dreaded stepping aboard the boat with dry clothes as any contact with a wet surface instantly adhered and then permeated anything not named wool. The first boat task of the day was to don the rain gear as soon as humanly possible.

The rising sun revealed the moody gray fog and ghostly apparitions began to emerge out of their moorings. The famed Yaquina Bay arch bridge and its lights faded in and out of view as well. The game plan was like many openers before—head south, find some 52-degree water, drop the gear, and let the fish lead the way. The gear boxes were loaded with the traditional arsenal of pink tear-drop spoons with black polka dots and hoochie-flasher combos on shorter leaders. They fluttered and zig-zagged through the water in crazy gyrations that drove the early-season silvers bonkers. In the basement, or near the bottom, the longer-leadered king gear was poised and ready for the big ones.

The drizzle was still thick as butter as we set our gear on our southward troll offshore of Beaver Creek in about 40 fathoms. Just like hundreds of times before, deploying the gear felt so fresh. I loved the anticipation that came before dropping the first spread.

"Oh, I am pumped, Ter. I have a feeling we're going to load the boat. The conditions are perfect. It's great to be back out here again!" Dad proclaimed.

"Same here. The water temp is good and the water color

just looks fishy," I replied.

It didn't take long to notice we had plopped down on some prime real estate as our wires started to exhibit coho-like pulsations.

"Holy cow, Ter. Just like the old days. Look at my wire load up. I'll send my side down and then let's get your gear down. Then it's going to be a circus with a lot of slips coming aboard!" Dad exclaimed.

"No daily quota this time either. We can load the boat!" I emphasized.

With two of us in the boat, weaving through the opening day armada of boats was a snap. One of us would steer while the other pulled several fish off a wire. While there wasn't a salmon on every spread, fish were chomping on the gear consistently throughout the day quite often in doubles, triples, and quadruples. By early evening, the large ambushes on our gear had subsided and settled into sporadic singles. This signaled that it was time to throw the gear in the boat to offload, refuel, and refresh. Sometimes it was hard to decide which was of more value, trolling for a few more hours for a few more fish, or prepping for the next day.

At the fish dock, we pitched 73 coho into the bin that registered 302 pounds that evening. It was one of our highest coho totals ever, and it got us thinking that this could be the year to hit a hump, or 100 fish. We could have easily hit that mark several times in 1986, but the quotas prevented that highly desired milestone from coming to fruition. Oddly, we didn't catch a single king all day. Perhaps there were a few around, but the silvers were biting so heavily that the kings didn't have a chance.

Day Two was a carbon copy of the opener, and we managed to toss aboard a couple of kings.

"That was a blast, Ter. The boat sure is a catching machine. Keep me posted and I'll get back over as soon as I can." Dad said as he headed back to the Valley to dive back into the HVAC world.

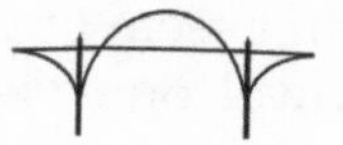

With the hotel room option off the table for a while, I needed to figure out where I could park my truck for a night's rest. Already knowing that the South Jetty area was off limits to overnight camping, I searched for other possibilities. Newport was becoming enough of a tourist destination that finding nooks and crannies to crash for the night were becoming few and far between each year. It was certainly no Florence. I opted for the Port Dock parking lot, which shared similar restrictions, but I knew that it was still loosely monitored by security.

I covertly parked my rig between some trucks of fishermen who likely worked on larger boats and were at sea. Then I slid into the truck-bed cavern of my little home on wheels, which luckily had a canopy with tinted windows. I was amazed by how much activity there was in the wee hours there. Most of the passersby were likely making their way back to their boats after a night at one of the bayfront watering holes. It was probably the worst night's sleep I had in the Hotel Toyota since it first opened in 1986.

Needless to say, I dragged my weary self to the dock on the third day. Those who staggered to their boats in the witching hours probably slept better. The fish-konking fest continued in thick drizzle and flat seas with 68 coho and a complimentary king. There was always such a stark contrast from fishing with two onboard instead of one. Every task took just a little bit longer. I had to work a lot harder to catch 68 than the 73 the day before.

Fresh tunes from Seal's first album oozed through my tape deck's speakers as the sun tried to hide behind the bridge's arches. They fused with the barks and groans of real seals and sea lions on the bayfront. Amidst all the beauty, I settled in for another night at the Port Dock lot that was much like the first. Judging from some of the obnoxious banter I heard the night before, I was wary of how it was all going to go down. It didn't seem out of the realm of possibility that I'd have some unwelcome visitors in the wee hours. Fortunately, D'Ann was coming over in a day. Lodging in a motel room would buy me some time to find another hideaway.

The second night at the Port Dock was no better than the first, but at least no ne'er do wells paid a visit. The big win was the ocean; it was as flat as a flounder again. This was a rare phenomenon. There always seemed to be a northwesterly that would intentionally show up to throw a wrench into any comfort and good fortune. The boat zipped at full speed and I plopped the gear right where I left off the previous evening. It wasn't more than a few moments when my first wire started loading up on fish on the way down. The derby kicked off in full gear and instantly I became immersed in a chaotic cycle of pulling fish and cleaning fish. Amongst all the commotion, there was something absent—radio banter. People were so busy loading up their fish boxes that there wasn't time to chat. Everyone knew everyone else was knee-deep in blood, sweat, and scales.

There were a few lapses in the day where I could catch my breath, but I had to use that time for the fish cleaning operation. Unlike the previous days where the drizzle kept the fish cool, the fourth day of the season was clearer and warmer. This prompted the need to dress out the fish right away. Other than taking a few swigs of water now and then, munching on a granola bar, or a quick pee, I was in constant motion all day long.

Later in the day, the tallies on my notepad revealed I was in the 90-fish range. Of course, seeing those stats, I went all out for the century mark. With a little energy surge, I kept plugging away even though the coho feed fair had slowed to a scratch. By late afternoon I finally reached the prestigious 1-0-0. It was a new *Carolyn Kay* record of 99 coho and 1 king.

Later that night from the luxury of a motel room, I gave Terry of the *Blue Angel* a call for a fish report. From an earlier conversation, he had asked if I would give him an update. He was planning on joining in once his vacation started.

"Hey, Terry, good to hear from you. How's the fishing, bud?" *Blue Angel* Terry asked.

"I hit the hump mark today, Terry. You need to be here. Word has it that about half of the quota has already been reached. There are fish all over the place," I reported.

"Hey, way to go! Thanks for the report. The boat's rigged and ready. Chris and I will be haulin' the boat over there in a couple of days. I'll give you a shout when I am rolling into town."

"Alright! It will be great to have you out here!"

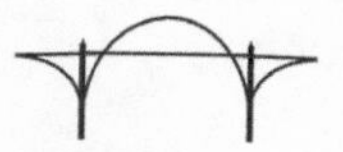

Stiff, sore, and tired, I overcame inertia and crawled out of the comfort of our motel bed. D'Ann slept for several more hours before driving east to Corvallis. My destination lay west back to where the Cohopalooza took place the day before. Braced for another 12-hour frenzy, the sea offered a tamer version of what I envisioned the day would be like. It wasn't a desert by any means, but when your previous low fish total was 69, a score of 38 coho suddenly was humbling. To help bring things back to perspective though, I would think of all the dismal days in the early years where Dad and I would have done anything to catch 38 fish. Looking at it through that lens, it was a fine day.

Still fired up from his last visit, Dad made the drive to get another fix of all-out coho fishing. Since fish weren't congregated in any particular area, boats were spread out in all directions. Fishing was spotty at best, so Dad shifted into strategizing mode.

He announced, "Well, time to make some changes, I'm going to switch up the gear and try..."

"I'll do the same, and we'll see who emerges victorious," I replied.

We proceeded to dip into the gear archives and put some oldies but goodies back into service. By early evening, it was Dad who was crowned champion in our friendly competition, and we delivered another score of 38 hard-earned silvers plus a couple kings.

Earlier in the day, Terry was trailering the *Blue Angel* down Highway 101 and announcing, "*Carolyn Kay, Carolyn Kay, Blue Angel,* Terry, you busy?" It was good to hear that familiar voice on the CB. While there were several familiar dory fishing faces around, it was nice to have Terry back in the fold. He was one of the few links left when we entered the whole crazy scene back in the 1970s. It was going to be great to have him on the water to strategize with the fish smacking the gear so much.

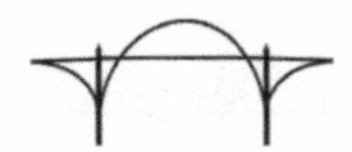

The next morning greeted us with a light, but determined early-morning breeze, which was never a good sign. Reports offshore were that the sea was already looking like a sheep pasture. A few boats that had ventured out were already heading back in, so we resigned to it being a day on the beach. While Dad would have loved to get back out on the water, tinkering around on the boat was a nice consolation prize. He loved the dockside chats with many of the dory guys and other small boat fishermen. Since he had been tapering off his fishing over the years, being able to catch up with some of the old acquaintances such as Al was equally satisfying.

Another little stiff breeze greeted us the next morning, but there was a small window before it would develop into a blow out.

"What do you think, Ter? We could get in a few hours before the northwest blows us off the water? Want to give it a go?" Dad asked.

"We might as well get in as much fishing as we can. The

quota is filling up fast," I added.

After a bumpy and chilling ride straight out to the 35-fathom line, we dropped our gear. With a sharp wind chop developing, the springs danced wildly with bouncy gyrations. The bow would come off a crest and slap down on a trough, and the deep springs would stretch out in the same psychotic rhythm. The float springs would signal abrupt lurches as the float bags astern would plow into the oncoming seas.

"Hold on to your bootstraps. It's going to be a gnarly ride," I proclaimed.

Spring reading on sloppy days was a challenge, but we loved spying them. It was more like we examined and interrogated them. Both of us eyeballed them with great accuracy. We were able to distinguish the pump of a king, the bouncing action of a silver, the single pull of a rockfish, the pump-quiver combo of a halibut, the more prominent oscillation of a blue shark, and the dreaded lazy stretches and spasms along with excessive drag on the wires when several lines loaded up with hake.

On that short morning, we were able to decipher the twelve crazy bouncing episodes of silvers in between all the other maniacal wave-induced spring extensions.

"How much more teeth jarring do you want to endure today, Ter?" Dad asked.

"It's really getting after it out here now. I'm ready to toss the gear in the boat. If we were tossing fish left and right, I'd be willing to get pasted, but not just for the boat ride and an occasional silver." I replied.

As predicted, a strong ridge of high pressure set in hard and strong, which blew the fleet off the water for several days. Assuming that Dad and I would pick up where we left off after the blow, we said our farewells and each headed our separate ways back to the Valley. I never would have guessed that we had just completed our last day ever fishing together on the *Carolyn Kay*.

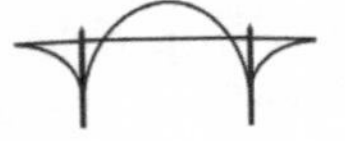

Eight days of windy, yet ecosystem-healthy upwelling later, I was ready to finish out the season. The warmer 52-degree water was well offshore, and there was some uplifting scuttlebutt about some silvers and kings on the Pile. It always amazed me how even in crappy weather conditions, there always was at least one daring soul who braved the elements and found some fish. While the silvers had been in good numbers, it had been a rather bleak king year. The thought of putting some big ones in the box made the one-hour jaunt to the North End much more appealing.

A month earlier, I had purchased some concert tickets for D'Ann and I to see the band, Styx, play in Salem. I figured the season would have already concluded when it was showtime. I was torn as I wanted to see one of my favorite bands who had a new album out, but the thought of fishing a partial day didn't sit well either. What if it turned out to be a banner day? Wanting to make the best of both worlds, the game plan was to fish up to about 2 PM, and marathon it into port. Then I'd drive two hours to Salem in time for the show. I would rise during the witching hours of the following morning and arrive at the docks by sunrise. It sounded crazy, but I had done all sorts of commutes like that between the coast and the valley more times than I could count.

The marine air was crisp, clean, and calm as I headed west on a pillowy ocean. There was something else, too—a feeling of something big, something to write home about. I couldn't pin down what or why, but there was a good vibe around the boat. A destiny to fulfill perhaps?

Upon arriving at the Pile, *Blue Angel* Terry was out there with his son, Chris, as well as some of the dory workforce. It was a steady scratch fishing day. By noon, I had just one king and about 20 coho, but I had lost a couple other hefty pumpers. Near the north tip of the Pile, I was making an east tack off the ledge into deeper water when my starboard deep line started pumping aggressively. Dad and I called the really big ones gorilla pumpers as it was like there was a big gorilla down in the depths just yanking on the wire with all its might. The springs were stretching hard enough to tip the boat slightly to the starboard. The fish had an impressive mechanical advantage on the end of the 22-foot wooden trolling pole extended at about a 45-degree angle away from the boat. My astonishment turned to anxiety as I wondered which spread it was on. I hoped and prayed it was on a long stretchy leader instead of the short "lead spread" that I always clipped just about the 40-pound lead at the end of the wire. This was a flasher-hoochie rig that sported a lot of drag and had poor elasticity.

Trolling wire wound around the rotating hydraulic spool as the gear emerged from the depths. The wire pulsated, and the fish moved the 40-pound lead around like a toy. Looking down into the translucent emerald-green water, I eventually spied the spread's flasher shimmying in the sunlight. Behind it on the shorter leader was a ginormous king, definitely in the 35 to 40-pound range, maybe larger.

It seemed like an eternity before the lead spread crept to the surface and that big old king did what big old kings do. It immediately veered 90 degrees off the starboard side and just suspended there, eyeing me, seemingly saying, "You don't have a prayer in the world to get me!"

The monofilament was tight as a piano string, and as much as I wanted to think that I could get it in the boat, I knew my chances were slim. The amount of drag created with the flasher was significant enough to place extra stress on the line. That flasher's shimmying rate ramped up tenfold. I began to wonder if there were any nicks in that monofilament and shuddered to think that if there were, it would break off any second. Seeing that the lunker was too fresh, I sent it down a fathom or two to chill out. I brought it back up five minutes later as I knew too much soak time was not good either. Finally, when I grabbed the line to bring in the fish, that big king jerked its immense head to the right and I heard a sickening snap. In an instant, all I saw was a caudal fin waving goodbye to me as it swam out of sight.

I never handled losing big fish well. It was usually accompanied by some of my finest colorful language and shouting at the fish gods for allowing something so traumatic and disappointing to occur. I always made sure to torment myself to another level by calculating the earnings that had swam away. It was without a doubt the largest fish in all our years that we had up to the boat. There likely were larger ones that we hooked, but those were all momentary and usually resulted in a snapped leader or a mangled hook.

What annoyed me the most though was the likelihood of never having the opportunity again to bring aboard a fish of that size. Since trolling spreads were much shorter than the amount of line on a fishing rod, it was rare to see many kings above 30 pounds dressed at the fish dock. As a pale consolation prize, I did manage to cajole another king in the boat though to go with 28 silvers. By early afternoon the fish had scattered and according to plan, I hailed a few of the dory guys on the radio announcing my early departure. I cruised back to port, hit the highway, and shifted into rock-n-roll mode.

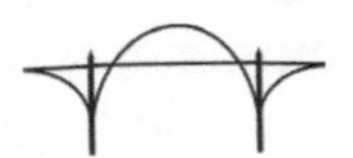

After our evening with Styx, I motored back out to the Pile the next morning with "Come Sail Away" still ringing in my ears. The flat-calm ocean and sunrise provided some much-needed warmth and reprieve as I emerged from my post-concert stupor. There was further talk that the coho season would be coming to a close soon, perhaps in a couple days. Hearing that, I vowed to make the most of what remained.

Overnight, a train load of silvers must have arrived as it didn't take long for the springs to start dancing and the bells to start clanging. A few kings smacked the gear, too, and by early afternoon I had a decent day's catch going on. Running through the gear constantly and using the wickedness of the North End currents, I was determined to make my offerings irresistible to any passing salmonids.

Trolling eastward, the starboard deep spring started hammering away. After letting it chill out for a few minutes, I went over to engage the gurdy to bring it up. At that moment I felt the boat lunge and heard the spring bells on the port side make a big clang, followed by more intermittent heavy pumps. The port float spring was being stretched taut perpendicular to the trolling pole, complete with pumps and vibrations. Looking at the float itself, it bounced noticeably as it was being trolled along 15 yards behind the boat. The spring vibrations appeared to be more characteristic of a blue shark than anything else. I didn't have that wire's gear sunk to the bottom, so the chance of it being a halibut was slim. Whatever it was though, I knew it was huge. My thoughts flashed back to the big one that got away the day before. I had heard a few other guys on the radio putting aboard some big kings, so I held out hope that I would soon be having a second chance at a big hog.

Not wanting to mess anything up, I let the starboard wire soak. Pulling the floats alongside the boat just inside the deep lines was always dicey, and sometimes ended up in a tangle. To avoid a mess with a possible record-breaking fish on, I pulled my port deep up completely, and hastily put the gear in the boat. The downside was that I had all my gear out on the starboard side. This created a huge amount of drag. Thus, the boat began trolling in a series of wide-arching circles. I didn't care though. I just wanted to get the fish without getting in anyone's way or snagging the jagged ocean floor.

As I brought in the float gear, the davit pulsed heavily. My heart was beating wildly, and I was coaching myself for being prepared for whatever was ascending from the depths. The davit continued to rattle and the wire lunged away. Would I be staring soon at a big blue shark? Maybe something even more exotic? As I pulled the spread to the surface, the leader made that very familiar veering motion perpendicular to the side of the boat and I knew exactly what it was. On the other end was a huge king on a Tomic 232 plug, a top producer. The great news was that it was on a six-fathom leader with lots of stretch, but would it still be strong enough to hold a behemoth specimen that scientists sometimes refer to as Oncorhynchus tshawytscha?

When I grabbed the leader, the battle was on. Facing the stern, the monster first greeted me at the four o'clock position and then made a run back to the propwash. I knew the big king's instinctual strategy—head for the prop to sever the leader. I scrambled to the stern to lift the leader away from the engine well. The gargantuan king kept traveling counterclockwise to ten o'clock position. This heightened my tension as it ran the risk of becoming tangled in the starboard side deep wire. Keeping it out of that hazard, it then zipped back clockwise to the port side and proceeded to try to kick my butt and break free. It was a delicate balance of handlining as I had to keep tension on the line while trying to make headway in getting it closer to the boat. The 60-pound-test monofilament squeezed the blood from my gloved hand and fingers each time it made a run. Without the layer of puller's glove material to intervene between the line and my flesh, it would have been like receiving repeated deep paper cuts. All the while I needed to make sure I didn't force it in too quickly in fear that the line would become too tight. I had to become one with the line and the fish to know just when to pull it in and when to back off. Even though my heart was beating like a jackhammer, I was much more confident about getting it in the boat than the previous day's monster. The boat continued to make its clockwise troll. From a distance it must have looked very peculiar to see a silhouetted dory making large gradual repeated circles.

After 15 minutes, the monster showed a little wear and I was able to bring it closer to the boat. I had to be conscious of my safety as I tried to gaff the fish. I had the presence of mind to do some mental safety checks to avoid falling overboard and not getting stabbed by the gaff. I wanted the fish, but it wasn't worth dying for. It finally gave up some ground and I was able to get the fish to the boat. I swung the gaff, made a direct hit in the head, and dragged it over the edge of the boat and on the floor. It flopped wildly with its muscular caudal fin until I gave it a ceremonial bop on the head. Adrenaline coursed through my veins. "Whooo-Hooo! Yesss!" I screamed across the endless sea. The disappointment of losing the big one the day before immediately dissipated. Destiny was fulfilled, just a day later. Oh, I wished in that instant that Dad was aboard to share in the euphoria. I had to tell someone, so I hailed Terry. "*Blue Angel, Carolyn Kay*, you busy?"

"Ya, Terry, what's up?" *Blue Angel* Terry inquired.

"I just pulled a huge king, Terry. It's huge!" I emphatically explained while hyperventilating.

"Alright! Way to go! I was wondering where you motored off to. We're getting a few kings, too, so there are more here!" Terry enthusiastically replied.

"I just have been doing circles for the last 20 minutes while battling that fish. I'm still… catching my breath. Wow… I'd better get the gear back in the water. I still have another large soaking on the other side. I'll catch up with you in a bit," I concluded.

What do you do after you just land the largest fish you've ever caught? You get your gear back down as quickly as possible. I had veered about a half mile off where I hooked the big one. Once I got the port-side gear back in the water, it was time to go check what was going on with the starboard wires. With all the drama, I needed to attend to the king on the other side. I vaguely recalled hearing a few other spring jingles during the epic battle. Sure enough, there were several silvers along with the king hanging on, probably wondering what took me so long to check on them. I finally trolled back through the waypoint where the big one bit.

Almost like it was rehearsed, two more kings came aboard. The largest of the two turned out to be 18 pounds. I laughed out loud because it looked rather puny in comparison to the prize fish. One more pass through the hotspot yielded yet a few more medium kings.

Fishing tapered off in the early evening, so I put the gear in the boat and punched the throttle for an epic ride back to port. The ocean offered just enough swell for our dory to act like a bitchin' 22-foot surfboard. With a sunset preparing a breathtaking backdrop that Claude Monet would admire, I took in the moment for all that it was worth. With nary a puff of wind, mother nature revealed surfacing porpoises, finning salmon, zigzagging blue sharks, and birds feeding on small baitfish in exquisite detail. The experience was like being totally immersed in a long, deep album track. With it came an unexplainable sense of peace that enveloped me as the boat perfectly surfed wave after wave to make for a quicker trip home. As I neared the bar, I followed an internal cue to break protocol. Instead of zipping between the north and south jetties, I hung a right and took a detour outside of the surfline for a little joy ride parallel to the beach. The little excursion just added to the grandeur of one of the most serene moments of my fishing career.

Although thoroughly mesmerized, I snapped to and refocused on delivering the big king and the rest of the catch at the fish dock. I couldn't wait to see the astonished faces of the dock workers when they set eyes on the record-setter. When it was thumped onto the scale, the red needle dialed clockwise, bounced indecisively for a few moments, before settling on 33 pounds. In 1991, that fish was nearly a hundred-dollar bill. Just like I anticipated, my catch was met with bulging eyes and it was the talk of the dock.

It was dark by the time the boat was tucked away. I

made my way to the Port Dock phone booth and shared the day's news with D'Ann and then Dad. The only thing better would have been to have him aboard the boat to share in such a grand experience. *Blue Angel* Terry, and a few other dory guys, had found a quiet little nook in South Beach to park our rigs a few nights earlier, so I was back to bunking it in the Toyota. It was hard to get to sleep at first, but finally physical and emotional exhaustion took over and made way for some much-needed rest. I wanted to be fresh and ready for the coho season's final act.

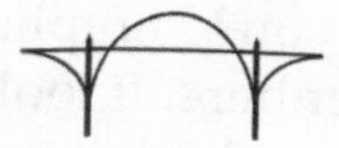

Traversing back out to the Pile, I inhaled the morning's sensational sunrise and stellar ocean conditions as the *Carolyn Kay* sped across the water like a puck on ice. Chatting with a few of the guys on the radio, the previous day's big catch came up in conversation as those who delivered after me expressed their awe and kudos.

"Yeah, I saw it on ice when I delivered there last night. That was one big hog," one fisherman remarked.

Their complimentary chatter amplified the morning glow. It was a moment that accentuated how blessed I was to be part of the whole dory fishing scene.

Once the gear was plunked down, it didn't take long for the wires and springs to commence their signature dances. Silvers were coming aboard with regularity as well as an occasional king. It was another blissful morning until the Coast Guard's blunt interruption at noon. Their no-nonsense announcement on the CB and marine radio stations stated the season would end at midnight. Pausing at midday after the hustle and bustle, reality sunk in that the party was almost over. It was like being at Disneyland on the final day of vacation and receiving the message that the park would be closing early.

Not wanting to waste another precious moment, I put

every ounce of effort I had into the remaining hours. The day was like the perfect meal. The portions were just right, flavor exquisite, and the ambience second to none. There wasn't a monster fish brought aboard, but 48 silvers and five kings made for a satisfying season exit. An intensifying band of orange-glowing haze crept upon us during the dinner hour, signaling to us that it was time to pull the gear and get out of Dodge.

"Hey, Ter. Do you have anything going on where you are?" *Blue Angel* Terry hailed on the CB.

"Aside from a couple silvers this past hour, I've just been boat riding. How about you?" I replied.

"About the same over here. It looks like the fog is starting to move in. Chris and I are thinking of heading in soon. We'll run in with you when you're ready to put the gear in the boat."

"I was just thinking the same thing. Running in with fog and darkness isn't how I wish to finish up the season. I'll start pulling the gear and meet up with you while we still have some visibility left."

"Sounds good. We'll do the same. Give me a holler and we'll meet up."

Every fiber of my being didn't want to pull away from the moment, but I knew it was the prudent thing to do. Lucky for us that we chose to pull and run when we did. London-thick fog moved in as soon as we got underway. It was all we could do to keep our boats within sight of each other on the homeward journey. Thanks to the accuracy of the LORAN plotter, an hour and change later, the whistle buoy unveiled itself majestically out of the viscous mist. The other buoys and bar followed suit and materialized out of the coastal vapor. We were set free from the fog's cloak just as the bridge lights greeted us brightly and brought a sense of warmth, security, and finality. By the time we were tied up at the docks, it was pitch dark except for the amber glow of the bayfront. Even though the whole show ended way too early, it was a perfect final performance.

Fishing for chinooks after the coho derby never happened. The northwest wind revved its engines, the fish scattered, and the necessity of gearing up for my second year of teaching took precedence. The boat was trailered and tucked away by early August. In September, the band Rush released a new album and I was already thinking how well tracks such as "Dreamline" and "Ghost of a Chance" would be fine additions to my expansive coastal playlist. Dad and I didn't know it at the time, but 1991 was a season of lasts for each of us. Our last voyage together on the *Carolyn Kay*. The last fish. The last interactions with a special group of people. Even the last lodging in the Hotel Toyota. Our fifteenth and final season had come to a close.

AFTERWORD

1992 Setlist

Neil Young *Harvest Moon*
Sade *Love Deluxe*
Toad the Wet Sprocket *LP's*

I hit the ground running with my second year of teaching in the fall and didn't have much time to dwell on the next salmon season's status. The best news was that D'Ann and I were expecting our first child sometime in late June of 1992. Thoughts about fishing definitely were placed on the backburner.

By January, the word on the street was that the wild coho population predictions for 1992 were dire. Hearing this, it was highly unlikely there would be a coho season. There was even some chatter about coho permanently becoming a sport fish, meaning that they could only be caught by sport fisherman with rod and reel. By spring, the rumors became reality and it was officially going to be coho-less summer. It sure was sounding like 1984 again.

In 1986, I never thought there would be a better June 24th than when I landed 24 kings. I was proven wrong in 1992, when our daughter Kelsey was born on June 24th. Her birth exceeded anything that fishing could ever offer. Like any parents of newborns, spare time was nonexistent and sleep was a rare commodity. Making the summer of 1992 even more chaotic, we purchased our first home in Salem, a fixer-upper with a DIY list a mile long. There was no room for fishing and it made little sense to give it much thought.

It turned out to be a very hot summer, so Dad was consumed with selling AC units like hotcakes. Fortunately, we were both so busy that we didn't have much time to pause and lament the absence of the sea, the salt, and the season. As it turned out, very few small boats even bothered to drag gear through the water. Those who did give it a go found inshore chinook fishing inconsistent at best. Having experienced the pause in our operation in 1984 and 1985, we still held out hope and had visions of us resuming those dreamy salmon voyages to Seal Rock, Beaver Creek, and the Rockpile in 1993.

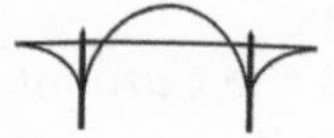

The next year brought more disappointment with no coho season again. With another year founded on bad news, many dory fishermen and other small boat fishermen went into deep hibernation. The 1993 and 1994 seasons came and went. The rationale to jump back in the fishery just didn't make sense as I was up to my earlobes with Master's degree courses, family life, and doing a lot of DIY projects. Despite the hustle and bustle, my heart and soul still yearned to be on the water. Much like the sirens in Greek mythology, it was as if the northwest winds, the changing tides, and the rolling swells would call my name during the landlocked summers. Unlike those destructive maidens, the elements meant no harm, but kept tugging at my heart and soul. When I would hear Neil Young's *Harvest Moon* LP or Sade's *Love Deluxe* album, my mind would go adrift as those sounds would have fit perfectly with the coastal vibe.

Dad shared the same lamentations as I. We talked about the uncertainty of it all, but we held out hope that some type of season would be resuscitated that would be worth the wear. Another cloud that hung over the situation though was Dad's health. He had a number of issues cropping up in the 1990s that would've undoubtedly hampered his participation.

Time rolled by at light speed. In 1996, we welcomed our youngest bright star into the family, our daughter McKenzie. She was born in May, so in addition to the three weeks I took for parental leave, I had a summer break to care for her. As for the *Carolyn Kay*? The situation clearly did not move the needle enough to spend the time, energy, and money to gear it up. It was waiting in outdoor storage nearby, but you could feel that it was losing hope. Every few months, Dad and I would check in on our wooden comrade to let it know we still cared. With each visit, I felt a greater sense of guilt as it sat dormant on the rusting steel trailer that was cold and wet in the winter months.

I had always viewed the *Carolyn Kay* in a personified sense. Along with my guilt, our dory radiated a great sense of sadness as it was eons away from its natural habitat. Dad and I never wanted our boat to become a dilapidated old craft, but it looked like that was the direction things were headed. With each visit we'd find some more rot in the steering console, peeling paint, and once there was evidence of some rodents that set up residence for a while. There came a point where Dad and I finally broke the ice and broached the unthinkable. It was time to find a new owner for the *Carolyn Kay*.

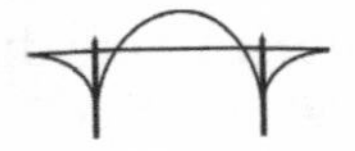

Even though the elephant in the room was finally acknowledged, we didn't have the nerve at the time to place the dreaded ad. The small-boat fishing industry was at a low point. Coho were officially deemed as a sport fish. The value of commercial dory, its gear, and the salmon troll permit, had declined significantly from what it was in 1988. It just so happened that the husband of a colleague who worked in my classroom in the late 1990s was part of the Pacific City dory fleet. He was looking to purchase another dory. Even though it was painful to come to that fork in the road, it felt like the humane thing to do was to breathe new life into our beloved craft. We knew it would be in good hands and wouldn't just sit and rot somewhere. With the industry in the cellar and commercial dory value in the dumpster, we sold it for far less than we ever imagined.

It was a gray overcast day when we made the official sale at the storage facility. I always wondered how it would go down, and to be honest, there wasn't too much to it. Dad had the wherewithal to remove the four-foot-long *Carolyn Kay* name plaque from the stern as a keepsake. The new owner hitched the boat up to his truck, we talked about how great the boat was, completed the transaction, shook hands, and then the truck pulled away as we watched fifteen seasons of memories disappear around the corner. It was a quiet trip back home. I mean, what can you say after you bid farewell to a big part of the fabric of your life? There would be much more time for conversation later.

As Dad always seemed to do, he opened the door to another adventure. In 1997, he was rocking AC and furnace sales to the point where he earned a trip of a lifetime to Hakai Pass, British Columbia for an epic salmon sports-fishing adventure. Not wanting to go solo, he invited me to be his wingman. By July of that year we were taking off in a seaplane from Lake Washington northbound to a floating lodge, and we spent five days fishing the pass, inlets, and ocean for salmon and halibut. On our assigned Boston Whaler boat, we had nearly free reign to fish anywhere and anytime during our stay. The trip reawakened our camaraderie, teamwork, as well as our love for the water and the briny air. Two years later, that same opportunity came our way again, and we also had my Uncle Steve along for the ride.

After those two rejuvenating adventures, the next dozen or more years were nearly waterless. D'Ann and I had a part-time home subcontracting business on the side that consumed our evenings, and this was in addition to my teaching job that kept me hopping as well. Our family was in the fast lane of life with our daughters involved with sports, other activities, and school. D'Ann and I embraced every moment of those years as Kelsey and McKenzie were growing up, and we put our heart and soul into every moment. Every now and then I would yearn for the opportunity for my daughters to step aboard our dory to get a taste of what it was all about. It wasn't meant to be though. To gain a reprieve from life's craziness, I immersed myself in running longer distances, which included three half marathons. The footsteps I left on the asphalt were an effective antidote for whenever the Pacific pulled on my heart.

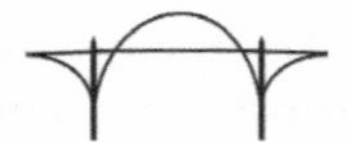

While life was traveling at light speed, Dad's health was declining due to ongoing congestive heart failure along with several other issues along the way that included several hospital stays. In 2008, though, his health was relatively stable, and we took a family vacation to Puerto Vallarta, Mexico. One of the perks there at the all-inclusive resort was unlimited kayak rentals. Seizing the opportunity to be reunited with the salt, I embarked on a few paddles on the Bay of Banderas from the beach and fell in love with the simplicity and connection that kayaking offered with the water at nearly eye level. The simple feeling of the tiny craft navigating the gentle swells sparked my salty synapses. This brought about an epiphany that for the price of a cheap plastic kayak, a paddle, and a life jacket, I could be back in the saddle again. A few more years passed before I finally took action and purchased a basic set up at a local sporting goods store.

In no time, I was exploring all sorts of local freshwater bodies of water, and I eventually began to migrate to the salt. I explored some Oregon bays and estuaries such as the Salmon River, Nestucca Bay, and Siletz Bay. Near dusk, on a New Year's Eve, I even made a short jaunt along the Newport Bayfront before the winter sun dipped below the horizon. It was a feast for the senses as I paddled past landmarks and structures that brought back flooding memories. By then I had realized that this was my new element and calling. More profoundly, I discovered that all along my connection with the sea, salt, and sand wasn't about the fishing as much as it was just being there—on the water taking in all of the glorious creation that God had to offer. Being so close to the waterline offered a whole new perspective. There was so much to see that I never noticed motoring along with my head six feet above the surface on a dory.

One October evening in 2014, I noticed an email from my father in our inbox that included the word Pygmy in the subject line. It seemed like a rather odd word for him to use. Upon opening and reading it, I learned that he had gifted me something that would bring about a connection to water that I hadn't experienced since that final dory trip in 1991. That word referred to wooden kayaks from Pygmy Boats from Port Angeles, Washington. He was emailing to let me know that he would be almost entirely funding the purchase of a Pygmy kayak kit and that my Uncle Steve would construct it over the winter in his Madras, Oregon shop. Steve had built three Pygmys and had the assembly down to a science. All I would need to do is kick in the funds for any accessories that I wanted to add. Pygmy kayaks are beautiful wooden crafts that often garner many oohs and ahhs from passers-by. They track incredibly well, come in many styles, and are quite seaworthy depending on the skill of the paddler.

Despite undergoing shoulder surgery, Steve amazingly worked on the new vessel over the winter. By March I was able to make a trip over his way to help out a bit, and then in May, it was ready for the maiden voyage on Lake Simtustus in Central Oregon. I fell in love with the kayak instantly as it glided across the water like a hot knife through butter.

Watching Steve take it for a spin, its displacement and appearance in the water was incredibly dory-like and gave me a few chills watching its forward motion. I had hoped that Dad could make the trip across the Cascades with me to be there for the christening, but his health just wasn't up to it. The first chance I had, I texted a few photos to his eagerly awaiting flip phone.

After that initial voyage, the floodgates opened in my exploration of a long list of salt and freshwater wonders that I wished to explore or revisit around Oregon. Suddenly I was making frequent trips to amazing water paradises nestled among the majestic Central Oregon mountains, spectacular sections of the Willamette River, and of course many salty sanctuaries along the Oregon Coast. With each trip, my thoughts turned to my great appreciation for my father who made this all possible. Just like the dory days of old, new tunes and old favorites started to become anthems on the drives to my favorite paddling destinations. Fleetwood Mac's *Dreams* and *Silly Love Songs* by Paul McCartney earned automatic spots on the starting lineup, especially on the coastal expeditions. Tunes from Toad the Wet Sprocket naturally primed the pumps for a good day on the water. Toad tunes would have fit in so well with the dory days.

While it was nearly impossible for Dad to give the new craft a test run for himself, I had hoped that he could at least see it in action. The best-case scenario was for him to see it glide in the bay at Newport, but lengthy car travel just wasn't in the cards. We finally arranged for him to see his grand plan in action near his home in West Salem on the Willamette River. While it wasn't a place chock full of great memories of the past, it did bring about a grin of satisfaction knowing he had made possible something incredibly special. I also spotted a yearning in his eyes—a touch of sadness, as I knew he would have given anything to somehow have been on the water himself.

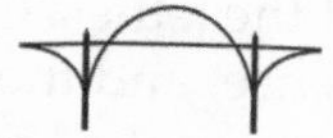

During the summer following Dad's passing, I made a trip along the Central Oregon Coast with plans to paddle Beaver Creek—the one we fished offshore from so many times. It is special as it is not tidally influenced. A paddler can experience a wonderful trip upstream among a plethora of wildlife and beauty and then venture downstream until the creek bleeds to just a few inches of depth across the sand to its salty destination. Driving southbound on Highway 101, the sky was a blend of blue and a smearing of thinly veiled cloud cover. The ocean was as smooth as a pane of glass. Old sensations never leave us, and I knew from so many prior journeys that the weather conditions had created a window of opportunity to retrace some old steps. Seizing the moment, I changed my game plan and detoured to the old port docks in Newport. Before I knew it, I was paddling the familiar currents in Yaquina Bay. As if a magnet was pulling me westward, I heeded the call and only planned to retreat if commonsense said otherwise.

It felt like time travel as I paddled by the breakwater, fishing vessels, and pilings. The briny atmosphere was accented with wafts of fish company processing, seafood eateries, and even a hint of diesel. The water traffic was incredibly light considering it was late June, so I kept paddling and soon had passed under the Yaquina Bay bridge. Ahead of me lay the north and south jetties that appeared to converge as they followed their lines of perspective toward the vanishing point. The water was like glass and it felt as if that familiar stretch was inviting me home. Feeling so inclined, I paddled my Pygmy Pinguino against the flooding tide westward as I hugged the north jetty. The view from just above the waterline provided a sense of newness to the well-traveled path. On the dory, the outboard motor and the grainy CB radio drowned the sound of the water's current that rushes by the aids to navigation in the channel and through the huge boulders that comprised the jetties. On the kayak, it was an entirely different experience, and the audibles of the flooding seawater seemed to be cranked on high volume.

As I approached the bar, I ceased paddling and assessed the situation. It was nearly flat with just a slight one to two-foot swell. The crossing would have been a piece of cake at full throttle without hesitation on the dory. My eyes and ears were keen to notice the swirling currents, which made intricate patterns on the water's surface along with some subtly sweet tricking noises. These observations came easy as I navigated with less than a half-inch of wood, epoxy, and varnish between my butt and the water. I eased forward with caution. With the coast clear, I paddled with vigor out just beyond the Number Three buoy and then veered north about a hundred yards to stay clear of buoy line traffic.

My heart had been filled with a yearning to seek closure of my father's passing. I wasn't sure what that meant or looked like, but I was driven to answer the call. With every paddle stroke, I was thinking about Dad and hoped that he was with me as my 13-foot 4-inch craft glided over the gentle swells. I paused and swung my craft 180 degrees and scanned the shoreline to the south. My heart pounded a little harder at the recognizable indentation that was Beaver Creek, and further south, the Seal Rocks seemed to wave hello and welcome me back to the neighborhood.

I embraced the moment as if it would be the last time I would be able to take in the view. If Dad happened to be along for the ride, he probably had a big grin and was beaming, knowing he had paved the way for me to return to our nautical home in a most unique way after a 25-year absence. Feeling a faint breath of northwest wind on my cheeks, I decided against reacquainting myself with it and made the wise decision to catch the flooding tide back into port. The trip home was almost equally as fulfilling, and within the hour I was paddling into the familiar matrix of the Port Dock.

While loading the kayak on the car rack in the parking lot, I scanned the path that I had just traveled. *"Wow, did I just do that?"* I thought to myself, shaking my head. It felt like everything had come full circle. Did the offshore trek bring about any closure? I wasn't sure at the time, but it certainly felt like it was a step in the right direction. There would be several more paddling trips that summer and beyond. Some were in the salt and others in Cascade Range lakes that Dad used to wax on and on about. I couldn't help but to think that I likely retraced a few of his courses from back in the day. We all navigate the grieving process differently, and I discovered that my healing involved connecting dots to his past and breathing new life into his dreams and adventures.

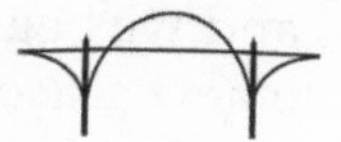

For several years I've had a vision that still pops in my head now and then. Perhaps it is more of a hope, but whatever you call it, it has been persistent. Aside from what I've read and learned on my spiritual journey, I don't even begin to pretend to comprehend the complexity and wonders of Heaven. Nevertheless, a Heavenly scene rests deep in my mind, heart, and soul of when Dad and I will meet again. I picture him on our dory moored at a dock on a beautiful morning warming up the boat and getting it ready for another day of fishing. The setting resembles Newport, but there is something in the background that is grander beyond description. The skies are a wash of the most unimaginable palette of colors and light that make the most beautiful of sunrises pale in comparison. I carefully step down the declining gangway and make my way on the dock just like old times, only this time with a little more skip in my step. There is a briny sensation of perfection enveloping me and the sounds of rumbling engines, squawking marine radio conversations, and the piercing "keow" sounds of seagulls fill in the white space. It feels so right to be there. As I arrive at the dew-covered boat, Dad turns toward me with a big smile as I sense that he has been patiently and eagerly waiting for my arrival.

"Hello, Ter! I've just about got everything ready here" as he taps on the barometer and gives the hand-controlled wiper blade a couple smearing swipes. "I packed a really good lunch that I think you'll like. What are your thoughts about where we should fish today? Maybe head south? I heard a few guys were getting them down that way," he'd say in his morning greeting, just like he always did.

I would step aboard as my weight would rock the boat slightly and jingle the spring bells to welcome my arrival. "That sounds like a good plan, Dad. It's good to be back aboard with you. I have a great feeling about today," I reply as he offers me the helm, and we begin motoring through the harbor to start a whole new season that this time around, never ends.

PHOTO GALLERY

Terry holding a big king caught at the Rockpile.

Dad looking like a true doryman gaffing a coho.

Dad running the hydaulics and checking his deep line gear.

Six kings in the landing box in the first couple hours of a hot king bite in 1986.

D'Ann smiling after a perfect couple of days as a deckhand.

The Carolyn Kay heading to the gas dock in Newport after a long day of finshing in 1983.

FISHING VOCABULARY AND PHRASES

basement—the bottom of the ocean
cannonball—a lead ball of 20 pounds or more used to weigh down a trolling wire
coho salmon—also known as silver salmon or slip
chinook salmon—also known as king salmon or smilie
clip—an implement used to attach a fishing spread to a trolling wire
commercial fishing—fishing for profit
day boat—a commercial fishing boat that returns to port each day
deep line or wire— one of two wires attached to a trolling pole and gurdy that supports spreads of fishing lines
dory—a flat—bottomed boat either pointed at both ends or with a square stern that is capable of launching off a beach through the surf.
dry dock—a place where boat maintenance is accomplished out of the water
fathom—a measure of six feet
flasher—metal or plastic blade up to the size of a legal envelope used with bait or hoochies to create action and attract fish
float bag—a rectangular styrofoam float used to float a trolling wire behind a boat
float line or wire—one of two wires attached to a trolling pole and gurdy that supports spreads of fishing lines and is floated off the stern of the boat
flopper—stopper— a metallic piece of gear shaped like a

fighter jet that when suspended in the water off each trolling pole helps to stabilize a fishing boat
gurdy—hand or hydraulic winches used to haul up deep and float wires
highliner—a top—producing salmon fisherman
hoochie—squid or cuttlefish—like plastic lure usually attached to larger metal or plastic flasher, with leaders anywhere from about 16 inches to 36 inches
LORAN—(LOng RAnge Navigation) a precursor to GPS that assists navigators on determining position
pink salmon— also known as humpback salmon
plug—a wobbling salmon lure that resembles a herring or large bait fish
scratch fishing—a term describing catching fish on a slow or sporadic day
shaker—an undersized fish, usually a salmon or halibut
spread—a length of monofilament line, typically between 6 and 36 feet, with a lure or bait at one end and attached to the trolling wire with a clip
skunked—returning to port with no fish caught
spoon—a slightly cupped metallic salmon lure that resembles a herring or baitfish
sport fishing— fishing for recreation
tagline—a braided length of cord used for attaching a trolling spring to a trolling wire
trolling pole— outriggers on the port and starboard sides of a fishing boat, that when lowered in a 45—degree position, spread fishing lines away from the boat
trolling wire—stainless steel cable used to attach salmon spreads or lines

ABOUT THE AUTHOR

Terry Evers has lived most of his life in Oregon's Willamette Valley and has spent the past 33 years in various roles in elementary education. His passion for spending time on the water has led him to the commercial fishing industry, the U.S. Coast Guard, and many miles navigating fresh and salt water by kayak. When he's not working with elementary-age children or on the water, he enjoys hiking, biking, cooking and grilling, reading, the Portland Trailblazers, and most recently, being a grandparent. Terry has been married to his wonderful wife, D'Ann, for 35 years, and has two daughters, Kelsey and McKenzie, who are amazing young women.

DANCING
MOON
PRESS

Made in United States
Troutdale, OR
03/08/2024